S0-AXT-570

The Liberal Papers

JAMES ROOSEVELT has represented the 26th California district in the United States House of Representatives since 1956. Since graduating from Harvard College, he has also pursued an active business career mainly in the insurance industry and in connection with firms he has helped to establish on the West Coast. During World War II he served in the U. S. Marine Corps. He is the author of *Affectionately, F.D.R.*

The Liberal Papers

EDITED BY JAMES ROOSEVELT

Anchor Books

DOUBLEDAY & COMPANY, INC., GARDEN CITY, NEW YORK, 1962

The Liberal Papers, an Anchor Original, is also available in a hardbound edition from Quadrangle Books, 119 West Lake Street, Chicago, Illinois.

Grateful acknowledgment is hereby made for permission to reprint the following articles:

"The American Crisis," by David Riesman and Michael Maccoby. Reprinted by permission of *Commentary* and *The New Left Review.*

"Communist China," by Allen S. Whiting. Copyright by The Yale University Press. Reprinted by permission of *The Yale Review.*

"Economic Adjustments to Disarmament: Research and Policy," by Emile Benoit. This article is one of a series, *Research for Peace,* prepared and published by The Institute for International Order. Reprinted by permission of the publisher.

Library of Congress Catalog Card Number 62–10458
Copyright © 1962 by James Roosevelt

All Rights Reserved
Printed in the United States of America

Design: N. Sylvester

Introduction

by James Roosevelt

This book of foreign policy essays[1] grew out of discussions and papers prepared for a group of fellow congressional colleagues during the 86th Congress, 1959–60. The discussions were initiated because of disillusionment with many of the seemingly mindless policies that we as a nation were following. We were apprehensive of policies which did not solve problems but rather created even greater difficulty—a kind of difficulty that would end in decline and catastrophe for the United States both as a free society and first-rate world power. One could assign many causes for the treacherous course. We felt one important reason for the decline in content to our public policy resulted from a breakdown in communication in politics between the intellectual and the politician. The transmission belt of ideas, a *sine qua non* for successful politics, and provocative, but substantively sound positions indeed had become quite threadbare. Personally I felt that many of the ideas both in foreign policy and in domestic policy

[1] Since the essays were completed by the beginning of 1960, I am sure that in certain particulars and various assumptions the authors of the essays might well have wanted to change their essays in the light of fast-changing events. I have felt, however, that in broad scope the relevance and importance of these essays still stand.

were ideas fashioned for another time and for other problems. A good number of those ideas were carried over from the New Deal. Ideas and political conceptions which were once exciting and relevant became cliché-ridden, formalistic, and sloganized. Because of this, political discussion among the citizenry became tangential and irrelevant. This ominously dangerous political climate caused us to call on intellectuals whose ideas were uncommon and provocative.

It goes without saying that I do not subscribe to or agree with everything that the contributors have said in this volume of *The Liberal Papers*. Indeed, although in general outline there is much agreement among the contributors themselves, there is disagreement and differences of emphasis between some of the contributors to this volume. Hence, the primary function of these essays is to reopen the political forum and reinstitute the dialogue of politics in our attempt to lead to new directions in public policy. I am hopeful that such controversy which might be attendant to the publication of these and other essays will not be *ad hominem*, but will be related directly to the arguments themselves.

This foreign policy volume of *The Liberal Papers* attempts in broad outline to formulate a program that is rational and responsive to our obligations as a great power and a free society. The essays are reflective, critical, and constructive attempts at an analysis of the constitutive parts of U.S. foreign policy: our defense system and its relationship to true power, international economic development, the American society as it relates to foreign policy, our relationship to international organization, and alternative-area foreign policies that now should be considered in the political arena.

It is not the purpose of these essays to denigrate or in any way play down the importance of domestic policy. Indeed, in a contemplated future volume of *The Liberal Papers* there will be discussion of the kinds of programs and policies that we need domestically. I have felt that in recent years we have forgotten the interrelationship of domestic and foreign policy. By so doing, we have allowed, over the past ten years, many problems to fester at home; problems which unless dealt with will leave us a much poorer nation intellectually, spiritually, and qualitatively. Indeed, unless we see what is happening to us internally, we will fulfill the Cassandra-like prophecy of President Eisenhower when he stated in his farewell address:

"This conjunction of an immense military establishment and a large arms industry is new in the American experience. The total influence—economic, political, even spiritual—is felt in every city, every statehouse, every office of the federal government. We recognize the imperative need for this development. Yet we must not fail to comprehend its grave implications. Our toil, resources, and livelihood are all involved; so is the very structure of our society.

"In the councils of government, we must guard against the acquisition of unwarranted influence, whether sought or unsought, by the military-industrial complex. The potential for the disastrous rise of misplaced power exists and will persist.

"We must never let the weight of this combination endanger our liberties or democratic processes. We should take nothing for granted. Only an alert and knowledgeable citizenry can compel the proper meshing of the huge industrial and military machinery of defense with our peaceful methods and goals, so that security and liberty may prosper together."

And externally we live now with the horror of nuclear destruction, with the threat of imperialist expansion by the Russians and Chinese, and with the hopeful but ever fragile revolution of men all over the world who wish for freedom and a better life in their time. These are problems which we face as citizens of the United States and as members of the community of man. We cannot close our eyes to these problems or shirk them. We must deal with them and attempt to solve them. In this task I am hopeful that the essays in this volume will give us the added insight to see ourselves and others in ways that will further the chance for the United States to get back on the road to peace and freedom, a road always difficult to find but one we must pursue if man is to survive the thermonuclear age.

Contents

The Liberal Papers

ONE

The American Crisis

BY DAVID RIESMAN AND MICHAEL
MACCOBY

David Riesman is Professor of Social Science at Harvard University and author of *The Lonely Crowd* and *Individualism Reconsidered*.
Michael Maccoby is a U. S. Public Health Research Fellow and is doing a social and psychological study of a Mexican village.

There has never been in American life anything comparable to the Fabian Society. Woodrow Wilson and Franklin Roosevelt gathered around them an *ad hoc* team of advisers who included a number of bright lawyers, economists, and political scientists, but neither these nor their journalistic and academic allies created anything like an ethos or a basis for interpreting the relation between specific pragmatic measures and over-all social and political change. Moreover, both the Wilson and Roosevelt administrations soon ran dry of ideas for domestic reform and were, so to speak, rescued by World Wars from the necessity of demonstrating their weakness. Although in part thanks to them Washington, D.C., has become somewhat less of a cultural and intellectual desert, it still remains a city dominated by middle-level civil servants, the military, the lobbyists, and the service trades dependent on all of these, and not a city tied in to *avant-garde* ideas in American life.

Several of the state governments have been in this respect somewhat less badly off in recent history. The Uni-

versity of Wisconsin has been a kind of unofficial Fabian
Society for the state government, or at least this was the
case during the Progressive Era; and the state government
and state university of Minnesota have had somewhat
analogous relations. But neither locally nor nationally has
there been a disinterested intellectual stratum tied in any
systematic way to government activity.

In the congressional elections of the fall of 1958, however, a group of Democrats were elected to the House of
Representatives who have banded together as the Liberal
Project in an effort to change the state of affairs. Some of
them had in fact attended the University of Wisconsin, or
fallen under the influence of men trained there. They were
frustrated to discover that the Democratic victory in the
elections was not to be translated into public policy; but
they also realized that, even if they were to have a larger
voice in affairs, there was no substantial seed bed of ideas
on which they could draw for measures that went beyond
what might be regarded as the mopping-up operation of
the New Deal: while these men were sensitive to the large
residual areas of deprivation in American life, they did not
believe that a policy could be based on this alone. For one
thing, they had a concern, unusual for members of the
House of Representatives who are supposed to leave foreign policy to senators, with foreign policy; they were, for
instance, among the small group of congressmen who opposed the sending of nuclear information to the Adenauer
government (in spite of the fact that some of them came
from districts with a heavy German population). Others
were concerned with the lack of preparation, either economic or psychological, for possible disarmament.

Such considerations, however, did not constitute a new
policy; and for this the congressmen turned to a group of
university professors and writers whose books and articles
they had read, and who they thought might furnish them
not only with specific proposals that would point in a new
direction but also with a philosophy of liberalism that

would locate the specific measures in an ideological context. In seeking such contact, the members of the Liberal Project had to overcome the characteristic attitude of American scholars and intellectuals toward congressmen—and toward politicians in general—whom they tend to regard either as cynical opportunists or as stupid windbags.

Since these exchanges have become more common, we have talked to a number of intellectuals who are astonished to discover how academic in the best sense is the intelligence of the group of congressmen and with what integrity and dedication they approach their work. Except for James Roosevelt of California (who is in his fourth term in the House), none of the members of the Liberal Project is well known outside his home state in the United States, let alone abroad; a scattering of people were familiar with Charles Porter of Oregon, who has been a notable critic of the Atomic Energy Commission and of American policy vis-à-vis Latin America, but who was defeated in 1960. A few congressmen, past and present, with wider reputations, of whom Chester Bowles is best known, have been close to the Liberal Project, although not active members. The majority of the dozen or so congressmen who have been members of the Liberal Project have held their seats by the barest majority; all of them have been told by sager heads that there is no political "mileage" in what they are doing. Certainly the intellectuals they have recruited to meet with them and to write papers on assigned topics for a volume to be modeled in some measure after *Conviction,* coming as they very largely do from New York, Boston, and Chicago, cannot help the election campaigns of men scattered over the congressional districts of the North. And it should be remembered that American congressmen are virtually on their own—a better example of "free enterprise" than is to be found in most businesses. They are dependent on local support rather than on any over-all party effort on their behalf, though to be sure they can be greatly helped or hurt by the way the national presidential campaign goes down in their home districts. Moreover, the inevitably bureaucratic management of 35 independent entrepreneurs in the House makes it very difficult for any one member to attract attention as a dynamic and colorful senator might. Hence, few Americans realize that the congressmen of the Liberal Project, as well as a number of others who are potential recruits, are on many specific issues and in general outlook far to the "left" of well-known Democratic senators such as Humphrey. Indeed, the congressmen would probably feel that the tag, "left," is one of those dated legacies they hope to surmount.

Since this paper was first published, five members of the Project lost their seats in the election of November 1960. Although personalities and local conditions were in part responsible for the defeats, all five seem to have been victims also of pressures generated by the presidential campaign, for in his district each ran ahead of President Kennedy (indeed, Congressman Kastenmeier, the chairman of the Liberal Project, who was re-elected, increased his lead over his opponent while Kennedy lost the district.

Although some observers feel that the reason for their defeats was the Catholic issue in their predominantly Protestant areas, it would seem that they were also hit by a crossfire which kept them from clarifying their complex views on the cold war. On the one hand, they had to fight the idea that the Democratic party is the war party and the spending party. On the other hand, the campaign stimulated a brash jingoism, through the confusion in the televised debates about Castro and Quemoy-Matsu, which, combined with the failure of the summit and Khrushchev's visit to the UN, aided those with simple positions. For the small voices of men like Porter and William Meyer of Vermont to be heard in the commotion was almost impossible, especially since their arguments about alternatives to reliance on massive retaliation could not be put in pat phrases. In fact, their opponents and the press further clouded the issue and kept them on the defensive by dubbing them "appeasers" and "soft on communism."

The essay that follows was prepared for the Liberal Project and reflects the concern of the congressmen with an American political climate that makes it difficult for them to develop a coherent program. It was discussed in June 1960 with the congressmen, their staff assistants (one of whom, Marcus Raskin, has taken a leading role in the development of the Project), and a few newspapermen.

I

Although America has been for much of its history a belligerent and expansionist country, it has not been a militaristic one, and up until the present it has resisted military control of political policy. While this encapsulation of the military might have been a protection for the peacetime life of the country, for only rarely did generals as such get involved in politics, one consequence has been that during wartime America has lacked a politically sagacious military elite. With a few famous exceptions, our generals have considered destruction of the enemy at the least immediate cost in American lives, or even the least budgetary cost, to be their sole concern. In the Second World War, this outlook gave a mindless justification for the mass bombings of German cities (also participated in by the British) and for the terrible and unnecessary destruction of Hiroshima and Nagasaki (when in fact the Japanese had given much evidence that they were prepared to surrender).

Only as the Second World War progressed did the American military begin to enlist advisers from civilian life, and a large number of intellectuals (a number of them ex-New Dealers) became involved in its planning and execution, while the physical scientists were of course heavily engaged. At the end of the war, in order to maintain this link, the Air Force set up the Rand (Research and Development) Corporation; the Army has a similar "brains trust" in the Operations Research Office of Johns Hopkins University; and the Central Intelligence Agency, while not outside the government, has a somewhat similar immunity from immediate supervision. Science and social science departments in a number of major universities have close personal and professional ties with these agencies. It would not be accurate to say that all these men have been mobilized on behalf of the policy of deterrence through the threat of mass destruction either of a counterforce or "balanced" deterrent force. Indeed, there are probably men working for Rand who have done as much to subject defense policy to rational scrutiny as have men who are known to be dedicated workers for peace.[1] Furthermore, men working for these agencies are involved in a great number of technical studies, not only of military but also political problems and of foreign policy, so that on the one hand the strategy of deterrence may be viewed in a wider ambit than within the AEC or SAC, while on the other hand many policy matters of a general sort are colored by a cold war filter, as if this were the only possible background for an extrapolation of the present.

Not only the exigencies of the cold war per se but the exigencies of interservice rivalry in the Pentagon have led to the recruitment of many exceptionally intelligent men whose full-time task it is to explore the justifications—and in some measure also the limitations—of the defense dogmas relevant to their arm of the service (including the Atomic Energy Commission). Thus, while some of the men at Rand and elsewhere have been intrigued by the possibilities of stabilizing the arms race by maintaining what Albert Wohlstetter has termed "The Delicate Balance of Terror," others have bent their scientific efforts to discovering holes in any possibility of a test ban which could be negotiated with the Russians.

Such holes are not so very difficult to find, for the Rus-

[1] See, for a sympathetic account, Joseph Kraft, "Rand: Arsenal for Ideas," *Harper's*, Vol. CCXXI (July 1960), pages 69–76.

sians—valuing secrecy for military, political, and cultural reasons—are very reluctant to permit inspections (which some of their own scientists regard as the first opportunity for a genuine window to the West), while American scientific polemicists are prepared to denounce any treaty which does not offer the impossible, that is, a hundred per cent security against any opportunity for Soviet evasion. Take, for example, the fantastic idea, developed in Edward Teller's Livermore Laboratory, that deep holes might be dug in salt mines and bombs exploded therein without anybody's noticing—a notion that is fantastic, not because the Russians couldn't do it, but because it would take a long time, require immense commotion of men and machines, and would therefore be very hard to keep secret, if not from us, then from the Russian people themselves. As more recent events have shown, when the Soviet decided to test both small and large bombs, they openly broke agreements, demonstrating their cynicism but not stealth.

Once upon a time, the Navy in its own interest opposed reliance on massive retaliation, and its experts were therefore free to explore the dangers of this doctrine. But then, faced with a declining strategic role, the Navy traded doctrine for budget—reaping a harvest in big carriers and atomic submarines—and joined the Air Force in alliance against the remaining Army men (such as Generals Ridgway, Gavin, and Taylor) whose recurrent protests have usually led to their leaving the intraservice battlefield altogether.[2] For reasons we hope to explore in this paper, there is no organization comparable to the Rand Corporation, dedicated to disarmament; in fact, only a few journalists (among whom Walter Lippmann is outstanding), some university professors, and in the government the members

[2] Our understanding of these matters owes much to Eric Larrabee's work on postwar military policy. We have also profited from the discussion of absolutist military thinking in Morris Janowitz, *The Professional Soldier*. Glencoe, Illinois: The Free Press, 1960.

of the Liberal Project and a few others are free fully to explore the risks of current military policy and the foreign and domestic policies to which it is tied.

The authors of this essay are neither experts on defense nor on foreign policy. At the same time, we have had some experience in seeing the experts make mistakes by virtue of their expertise. This does not mean that amateurs are necessarily better than professionals; but until a serious effort is mobilized for peace, amateurs will probably have to be relied upon for new ideas in the field of defense and foreign policy.

Among the most important and interesting problems of education is that of exploring the means by which people can learn to make a proper judgment of expert opinion. One way is to become expert in a particular field oneself. Another approach is to gain some sense of the kind of perspective or style of perception that the experts use, as a basis for seeing what might be the possible limitations of their view in a given instance. Thus one can find experts privy to discussions concerning deterrence who talk about the American ability to "accept," let us say, ten or thirty million casualties—experts who are familiar with the post-Second World War disaster studies but who fail to ask what sort of backwoods reactionaries would take over whatever would be left of America if our major urban centers were destroyed in a nuclear (or biological or other mass) war, nor in the same connection do they ask what the effect would be on the survivors of the sudden death of millions of their countrymen in a holocaust so extreme not to be justifiable by the rationalizations that have in the past sustained mass killing. Some who do concern themselves with this issue assume on the basis of the disasters of the Second World War that recuperation is possible at astonishing speed, but they are thinking at best of economic and not of cultural or moral recuperation, and at worst of the now ample possibilities of a military so-called second or third strike.

So, too, there are other men, intelligent enough to grasp some of the inherent weaknesses in the strategy of deterrence, who have speculated about an automatic deterrent, protected from the possibility of human frailty on our side. One mechanism that has been proposed for achieving this is a cobalt bomb, aimed at all countries having nuclear power themselves and primed to go off without reference to a human chain of command the moment any nuclear weapon is fired at us. The argument for such a scheme is that if a potential enemy thinks that we, as human beings, might decide for some reason or other not to hit back (despite the fact that we are equipped to do so), then our deterrent, though still terrifying, loses its absolute value; therefore we must try to set up a system over which none of us has any control. This reasoning, logical as far as it goes, typically leaves other variables out of account altogether—like the fact that becoming the prisoners of our own mechanisms would intensify the dangerous feelings of helplessness which the policy of deterrence has already succeeded in producing. It would mean surrendering the hope that the human race can get control of the arms race —even though it has been argued that once the automatic cobalt bomb was known to exist, no one would tempt fate.

One further point about experts: they have fended off outsiders, including many intelligent congressmen, by establishing as a condition of entering the debate on armaments a knowledge of highly technical matters (frequently "classified") and the possession of a polished rationality of the game-theory sort. We want to make it amply clear that we are of course not opposed to rationality, whether polished or unpolished: human reason, slender thread though it be, is the thread on which our hopes hang. Rather, the difficulty is that there are styles of rationality, based on eliminating certain variables from consideration and pursuing others as far as they will lead. These have become accepted by many strategists as the only available styles—one is said, in a boyish and overworked phrase, not to have "done one's homework" if one is not fully at home in this particular style. (The phrase about "doing one's homework" is one of the many by which the real terrors of the arms race and the human situation today are glossed over by cavalier phrases—quite "American" in their juvenile sports derivation.) To repeat: this sort of rationality can be very useful in dealing with problems, provided that its limits are well understood and that other sorts of rationality are also available. And there is the further difficulty that both we ourselves, that is the public at large and our allies and prospective enemies, listen in on our discussions; and if the tone of discussion seems inhuman because of its icily strategic style, then enemies may assume that they must develop analogous intellectual as well as military weapons. Thus our strategic approaches become eventually both self-confirming and self-defeating.

In criticizing the experts, furthermore, we are not supposing that the gentlemanly amateur is better at these things and that it is best to muddle through, without taking disciplined thought. Indeed, if we had to choose we would surely prefer to trust our fate to the experts of Rand than to some of the blustering generals (or senators) who have enjoyed talking tough (a great help, no doubt, to their opposite numbers in China and the U.S.S.R.). Our hope is that the practicality of ethical considerations may become more widely understood, and that discussion of deterrence and its alternatives can be enlarged, and more differentiated modes of thought encouraged.

II

The tone of the election campaign indicates the fringe position of the pacifist groups in American life. These groups have tried to state their case in a variety of ways: through mass meetings and leaflets, through the picketing of missile bases or the bases of nuclear-powered submarines, through lobbying and personal appeals. They must constantly combat the charge of being "un-American," while in more serious circles they often appear to be all heart and no head. They have had no pocketbook to tap (and of course the politically active groups have lacked even the fringe benefit of tax exemption). In spite of these handicaps, the Committee for a Sane Nuclear Policy has had some influence in keeping ideas afloat that would otherwise not get a hearing and especially in acquainting Americans—millions of whom have yet to learn the news— with the dangers of fallout and nuclear disaster. Understandably in this situation, Americans concerned not only with disarmament but with opening up the political climate to debate on the issue have looked at Britain as a country where issues confined to the margins of discourse in the United States are openly debated. For example, George Kennan's BBC lectures of a few years ago excited much greater response than any comparable talks he has given in this country.[3] While the British government in power has been somewhat less effective as a restraining force on the Americans and the Soviets than would have been salutary for both, and while the Suez adventure showed that the British blimps had enough air left for another flotation, the Americans can indeed envy the ease with which Englishmen discuss alternatives to nuclear war, ranging from unilateral disarmament to diplomatic maneuvers aimed at easing particular points of tension in the cold war, whether in China or in Germany. As against the tiny handful of American university students who feel anything can be done about the Bomb (a far larger number are concerned with the struggle for racial integration), Americans look on the Aldermaston marchers as something quite inconceivable at present in this country.

What accounts for this difference between Britain and America? The problem of dealing with experts is the same

[3] See Kennan, *Russia, the Atom and the West.* New York: Harper & Brothers, 1958.

in both countries, although in Britain—which is smaller and still partially aristocratic in nature—political leaders are less cut off than ours are from intellectuals, literary men, and scientists. It may be that people feel safer in this country because it is big and powerful and seemingly remote from the traditional areas of danger. This is an irrational feeling in the modern world of deterrence, since our fearful power and our weapons themselves become a lightning rod inviting attack; nevertheless, the feeling does seem to exist. A Gallup poll in January 1960 roughly mirrored the results of a poll taken by Samuel Stouffer a few years ago: when people in a national cross section are questioned about their worries a large proportion of them mention health and family troubles, and another fraction money troubles, but only one in fourteen allude to the international situation.[4] Yet half the Gallup sample also thought that there would be another war before too long—a war that, as the general texture of their answers indicates, has very little reality for them. Mothers, for instance, said that they didn't want their sons to serve overseas—evidently still unaware, despite the headlines, that in effect there is no "overseas" in modern war. The mothers, in fact, often quietly favor the Republicans as the "peace party," but they do not want to seem either unpatriotic or timid; and for many of them, of course, foreign affairs are really "foreign"—something to be left to the menfolk.

Furthermore, whereas war in other countries has left a legacy of fear or fatalism, there is little comparable popular anti-war feeling in America. The frightful catastrophe of the Civil War has left a romantic halo both in the North and in the South. The First World War was a shock for some; it led others into a rejection of Europe rather than of war itself. Whatever suffering the Second World War involved for a few was more than matched, for millions,

[4] Stouffer, *Communism, Conformity and Civil Liberties.* New York: Doubleday & Company, 1955. The Gallup poll is reported in *Look,* January 5, 1960.

by the fact that the war brought the great depression to an end. Besides, the war left a legacy of wild Keynesianism that continues in a new war economy to sustain prosperity: as Gerald Piel points out in the April 1960 issue of the *Bulletin of the Atomic Scientists,* it is the war economy which during the last fifteen years has brought a full third of the population into relative affluence. The Korean War was popular nowhere, but it had the paradoxical result of allowing the Republican party to appear as both the party of peace and the party of anti-communism, forcing the Truman-Acheson wing of the Democratic party to continue the effort to prove, over the dead body of Senator McCarthy, that it is even more ferociously and belligerently anti-Communist than any Republican.

Americans are famously generous. There is great and admirable concern for individual life, as when somebody falls down a well or into the sea, or is captured by the enemy. In recent decades, Americans have become less cruel, enjoying less barbaric sports and appreciating gentleness in personal relations. Still, the lack of suffering leads to a certain callous lack of sympathy for the suffering of others, particularly when this can be rationalized in terms of American ideals and explained as not the result of visible injustice.

There is still another difference which Edward Shils has noted in his book, *The Torment of Secrecy.* The British, protecting their privacy better, fear spies, secrets, and invaders less than we do and have never been as hysterical about communism. Even after the Klaus Fuchs case, they in effect decided that they would rather risk losing a few secrets to a few spies than turn the country upside down in the alleged hope of flushing all enemy agents out. One result is that the ex-Communists in Britain are not nearly so eager to prove their virtue as the ex-Communists in this country.

Though McCarthy is dead, the fear of invasion by spies and secret agents on which he played is endemic in American life and operates locally even when it is quiescent nationally. In the last decade, for example, a great many municipalities have been aroused against the chimerical and imaginary dangers of fluoridation in their water supplies (chlorination as a safeguard against the pollution of American streams and subsurface waters is already an accomplished fact); the doctors and dentists and local civil servants who have proposed fluoridation have met a barrage of suspiciousness and have been regarded as poisoners, alternately puppets of the aluminum companies (which manufacture fluorides) or the Communist party. Of course it is safe and even patriotic to attack these men, who have no great vested interests behind them, either contractual or ideological; and correspondingly it has been extraordinarily difficult to rally people in America against the real poisons of fallout or the dangers of chemical and biological warfare. For in the latter case, fear of realistic dangers, if openly expressed, might invite the accusation we ourselves have often met from student audiences when we have discussed these matters, as to whether we would rather live on our knees (as appeasers of world communism) than die on our feet. The trail-blazer attitude behind this rhetoric was well expressed a few months ago in a conversation with a nine-year-old and very bright little boy. We had been talking with his parents about the news that day in the paper that Khrushchev would come to America, and were expressing our hope that perhaps there would be a detente in the cold war. The boy piped up to say, "They're both chicken," meaning by this that both the United States and the U.S.S.R. were afraid. We asked him if it was chicken to fear the end of the world, and he said, "Well, we all have to die sometime"; and then after a moment he added, "Anyway, I'll go live on the moon."

It is along just this line that we see perhaps the deepest difference between ourselves and the British, namely that American men seem constantly pursued by the fear of unmanliness and therefore feel the need to present themselves as hard and realistic. This way of being realistic may have nothing to do with reality. Often "realism" becomes no more than the opposite of idealism, reasonableness, or morality. Many men of an older generation, having witnessed the excesses to which sentimentality and self-righteousness can take us, and completely sure of their own morality and dedication, are sometimes unwitting models for what is only a seemingly similar realism in others, a pseudo-realism that springs from fear about masculinity. The British seem less obsessed than we are on this score. Nor do they have a proponent of tragic realism so brilliant as Reinhold Niebuhr.[5] What produces the difference? What is the aim which in America has been distorted into a need to feel tough?

One possibility is that for those to whom being American means being a pioneer—a trail blazer and producer—the lack of new frontiers creates a fear (felt within and reinforced from outside) that the country is going soft. Perhaps, having escaped the bombing and much of the suffering of the Second World War, many Americans have never established their courage in their own eyes. To recog-

[5] Niebuhr's contention that man in this vale of folly cannot be wholly rational, just, or disinterested has led a number of his disciples merely to an intense distrust of the Soviet Union and hence a suspicious negativism toward any efforts at a *modus vivendi*. Paradoxically, the logic of the arms race means that such men put their trust in having both the United States and the Soviet Union behave rationally, as in a game with missiles and hardened bases as the pieces, even as the cold war and the arms race intensify the pressures toward irrationality. The realists today would seem to be those who know full well that the arms race cannot go on without something going amiss just because of the nature of man; it is widely recognized, for instance, that one psychotic commander could set off a catalytic war. For a further discussion of such game-theory logic, see Maccoby, "Social Psychology of Deterrence," *Bulletin of the Atomic Scientists* (September 1961). As to Dr. Niebuhr's own views, compare his preface to Harrison Brown and George James Real, *Community of Fear*, Fund for the Republic. Pasadena, 1960.

nize and admit the enormous dangers that grow every day the cold war continues would feel like weakness to these people; it would seem but another step leading to a retreat from the heroic stand against nature, a stand that makes sense when, in order to survive physically, man must fight, but which now becomes merely a "posture"—a term that is increasingly and symptomatically coming into use in describing American policy (along with the somewhat analogous word, "position"). This "posture" which so many people insist upon becomes self-destructive in a world of fantastically rapid change, where survival depends on flexibility and on willingness to accept some responsibility for what is happening in the world as a whole.[6]

Such people have been brought up to feel that worthwhile national action is to be defined mainly in terms of military or semi-military attacks on obstacles, either physical or human. They view with horror their countrymen who, captured by the ideology of consumption, have none of the Spartan virtues, and in fact seem drones heralding the collapse of the state. A number of these men are the American analogues of Tory patricians (or, in some cases, would-be patricians) who since Theodore Roosevelt's day have seen war and preparation for war as the condition of national health.[7] Having no goals for America in its

[6] Here again is a difference between the British and the American situations, because many Americans who feel responsibility for defending what they perhaps too glibly term the "free world" see no alternative to adding military strength to military strength (although the total may only, in fact, in the weird nuclear arithmetic, increase weakness), whereas a number of people in Great Britain believe that their country could restore itself to the status of an important power only outside the American alliance, becoming once more the "honest broker" between nations and leading the nations of Asia and Africa by taking a position on nuclear arms that appeals to the neutrals in all countries.

[7] President Kennedy was quite in the patrician tradition when he concluded a Senate speech, "An Investment for Peace," of February 29, 1960, by saying, "I urge that this Congress, before the President departs for the summit, demonstrate conclusively

own terms and (like most of us) more attuned to what they despise in their countrymen than to what they hope for, they cannot help being preoccupied with the Communists as a possible barbarian threat (often failing to realize how necessary we in turn are in the Soviet Union as a model for emulation, frequently for our worst Victorian excesses). So much, in fact, do these Americans depend on frightening their own countrymen with the not entirely fanciful bogy men of a Soviet take-over, and so much do they rely on generating and maintaining a mood of crisis, that we ourselves are troubled lest the title and themes of this paper, too hurriedly read, add to the image of menace, when our own spirit, though no less critical, looks further and more hopefully ahead. It is one of the many ironies of the current situation that people who fear the missile gap (a presently unrealistic fear, as the U-2 flights have helped to show) and those like ourselves who fear the arms race as the gravest danger have virtually cancelled each other out, thus creating a climate of complacency among the many and hysteria among the few.

These contradictory images of our hardness and of our softness cannot help but cloud the vision of those military men and political leaders who are charged with the defense. Because they fear softness, they seek to maintain a climate in which only hardness can thrive—so much so that perhaps a general is best able to move toward peace, since a general is less vulnerable to accusations of softness. Cor-

---

that we are removing those doubts [about the missile gap and like weaponry] and that we are prepared to pay the full cost necessary to insure peace. Let us remember what Gibbon said of the Romans: 'They kept the peace—by a constant preparation for war; and by making clear to their neighbours that they are as little disposed to offer as to endure injury.'" In fairness it should be added that President Kennedy in this and more explicitly in other speeches has called for active steps toward disarmament and for something comparable to a Rand Corporation for peace, and we hope the responsibility of the presidency will strengthen his promise to negotiate seriously for disarmament.

respondingly, many people who have different goals in mind seek to hitch them to the defense star, with the result that something so magnanimous in conception as the Marshall Plan very soon after its inception became a weapon in the cold war. By the time of the Mutual Security Act, economic aid took second place to military assistance, so that now we find ourselves propping up or even creating military regimes in countries, like Pakistan, whose officials can persuade us that they are real made-to-order anti-Communists.

III

Obviously it is not so hard to be anti-Communist if that is the way to build up one's military faction in a still emerging nation. But as the cold war continues, it becomes increasingly difficult for decent Americans, humane enough to prefer peace to an egocentric national honor, to be outspokenly and genuinely anti-Communist. For example, we had very mixed feelings about the idealistic and dedicated Americans, some of them our colleagues, who in the summer of 1959 went to Vienna and set up shop to oppose the propaganda of the Communist Youth Festival. We had misgivings because it was impossible to escape the fact that, whatever their personal motives, these students became, in effect, emissaries of our State Department and our national cold war line. While this is the last thing many of these students wanted, the Iron Curtain creates just such ironies.

And the problem is equally grave for the radical opposition. As Margaret Mead observed in a recent address, a student in this country a generation ago who had radical ideas had the advantage of being powerless, of being on the side of a future which did not yet exist. Today, however, such a student may find that his particular idea happens at the moment also to be part of the Communist party line, in which case he is not in alliance with a non-existent and therefore uncontaminated future, but with an extremely menacing and totally unwelcome power.[8] On the reverse side, someone like Pasternak, or many young Polish writers who are acclaimed in this country, may feel themselves betrayed by their very courage and virtue. Thus, as long as the cold war goes on, we lack an uncorrupted political debate.

Under such conditions, it is not surprising that so many people prefer to withdraw from the field altogether. Although they are willing to countenance arms spending, a large number of Americans cannot bring themselves to contemplate the true horror of war, and so they simply go to sleep when they are asked to "wake up" to the dangers that face them. They have learned that the thing to do with anxiety (whether based on real danger or not) is to rid oneself of it through drink, drugs, or canned fantasies.

There are other Americans, however, whose anxiety and escape take more productive forms. Like many of the Soviet intelligentsia who hate the system but feel powerless to change it, certain American elite groups have chosen the road of "inner emigration," retreating from social responsibilities into, at best, a concern with their immediate surroundings, family, and friends. Though such people are often aroused by issues like education, urban renewal, or mental health, they are estranged from the system because it seems to them run for political motives in the narrowest rather than in the best sense. Unlike the escapist security seekers, they are not alienated from themselves as human beings; yet the fact that they remain without

---

[8] Some politically inexperienced students may so resent being lumped with the Communists whenever they take an unpopular position as to conclude that the cry of "communism" is simply a reactionary myth; hence, they may be susceptible to the propaganda of Communists and fellow travelers, small and splintered as these latter groups are today in this country. Such students may prefer to accept "guilt by association" to what they regard as the cowardly course of vigilance against the Communists.

political purpose beyond their small civic circles limits their vision and hence their growth. It is for this reason that they may today be ready to give enthusiastic support to a far-reaching idealistic political movement that will provide them with a way of reasserting their faith in democracy.

Still others who are intelligent enough to be concerned with the world have escaped into cynicism, considering the system as corrupt and finding a sense of purpose in expertise, even if this means selling themselves to the highest bidder. Such people, amorally working for personal gain within the system, have in fact supported many of its worst elements. But perhaps "support" is too strong a word, for one often finds in talking to them that they have a streak of buried idealism hidden as much from themselves as from others by this mask of cynicism. Whereas the hypocrisy of the Victorians consisted of concealing mean motives under noble rhetoric, our own hypocrisy often conceals a cankered decency beneath a cloak of *Realpolitik*. Sometimes the decency manifests itself only in the family and in intimate relations, sometimes in the restlessness that underlies the purposive exterior, sometimes merely in the aggressive defense that is put up by these people against any suggestion that their public and private selves need not always remain so completely at odds.

Whether in foreign policy or in personal life, Americans appear today to suffer from an inadequate formulation of their alternatives. It has become extremely common among the well educated to denounce "blind conformity" and "mass society," often symbolized by such minor irritants as tail fins, TV, or gray-flannel suits. But the only alternatives many people see to the organization man is the nostalgic image of the cowboy or the rebellious artist; hard-shelled individualism and a rejection of human solidarity are mistaken as signs of strength and independence. Even the best students in our colleges tend to assume that they must eventually make their peace with "the system"—which they see as even more monolithic than in fact it is—and they will then often become vicarious fellow travelers of the Beats, whose passive and almost entirely non-progressive defiance serves to publicize a private helplessness.

Students in recent years have frequently said that helplessness is realistic: "What can you do about nuclear war?" Searching for a guarantee that life never provides, a guarantee not only that action will be effective but that all its consequences will be good, such young people never get started and therefore never gain the realistic political experience necessary to make them less helpless.[9] Again, there is a tendency to jump to extreme alternatives: either total control of the total weapons or total inaction.

The sit-in strikes in the South and their support in the North may be the first sign of a change in these attitudes, for they have shown how much can be done even by relatively powerless and unorganized students. We ourselves have a very vivid sense of the rapidity of this change, for a few years ago we visited briefly several of the southern Negro colleges that have been in the forefront of activity; and at that time they appeared to be quite somnolent institutions, run by despotic Negro patriarchs who were used to wheedling support from white leaders, at the same time dominating their own faculty and student bodies, while the students themselves appeared to hope for a safe passage into the world of the black bourgeoisie behind the wall of segregation. No doubt recent visitors to West Africa are equally struck with the speed with which things can change: at the very moment when the "system" appears impregnable to the realist, it often turns out to be vulnerable to the quixotic. Of course we are not saying that "where there's a will, there is always a way," but we are saying that many of the most gifted and sensitive American students have been oversold on cultural and historical determinism—in which, incidentally, there may be self-serv-

[9] For further discussion, see Riesman, "The College Student in an Age of Organization," *Chicago Review*, Vol. 12, No. 3 (Autumn 1958), pages 50–68.

ing elements, since determinism allows us publicly to accept the existing political structure while we privately deplore conformity, perhaps even showing by minor and irrelevant rebellions like sexual promiscuity or wearing a beard that we are rebels at heart.

IV

If we see only two choices in our personal behavior, such as conformity as against individualism, or adjustment as against neurotic loneliness, then it is likely that a similar dichotomizing tendency will capture our political life. Thus, the American is asked to choose between democracy and communism, when in fact neither system is monolithic, and both have many things—literally things—in common, in contrast with the less industrialized and bureaucratized parts of the world. As already implied, our relationship with Russia is similar to that of a big brother who is obsessed with the fear that his little brother will overtake him, and this overconcern keeps us, the older brother, from realizing our unique potentialities. In this case, the sibling rivalry runs both ways, for the Russians gear their system to show that they are as good or better than we in those areas we most prize—technology, sports, and education. The tragedy is not only that because of our obsession we are rejecting utopian possibilities and ignoring more pressing problems (at the lowest level the much greater threat of Red China) but also that we are missing a chance to provide a better goal for Soviet growth. We may hope that the Russians will get rich enough to be preoccupied by the problem of national purpose which currently plagues us; and in the American-like desires of the Soviet elite, we find signs of this development. Conceivably if we were to show that our system can be mobilized to produce a better life, drawing its meaning from activity rather than from consumption per se or from national might, we would eventually shift the emphasis of Soviet emulation.

In fairness it should be added that a surrender to apocalyptic alternatives is sometimes found on the more humane side of current American debates concerning deterrence. It would be surprising if this were not the case, for the dominant ways of perceiving in a culture generally turn up, sometimes in a disguised form, in the very models of opposing such ways. Thus, there are some pacifists, among the many different schools of pacifist thought, who see the present situation as demanding either preparation for total destruction or a complete cessation of all military measures through unilateral action. We believe that if the world survives these next critical years and becomes less uncivilized, we shall move away from the anarchy of nationalism, reducing arms to the level of police forces and handling as imaginatively as we can the problem of coping with despotic governments. Naturally, it is hard to see how the transition from the fully armed nation-state to the fully disarmed nation-state can be accomplished. It is easier to envisage a diplomatic give-and-take between ourselves and the Soviet Union that (without complete disarmament) would settle outstanding conflicts of interest in Europe and Asia—even though attempts at such a settlement would encounter the opposition of Adenauer and Ulbricht, Chiang and Mao, American cold warriors and their Stalinist opposite numbers in Russia. Efforts at disarmament not coupled with diplomatic moves to settle the cold war will make Americans as uneasy as high-flying spy planes must make the Russian people, and hence may boomerang. In our judgment, one must work simultaneously on both fronts, diplomacy and disarmament, keeping in mind the long-run pacifist goal of a world in which conflict is settled without weapons and war. Perhaps however we should not speak of this goal as "long run," analogous to some New Jerusalem that will never come; for we are faced with a situation in which the very preservation of life and social order requires political and technical measures that now seem "impossible," if they can be envisaged at all. We need as much inventiveness and confidence in what man can accomplish as were possessed by the framers of the American Constitution.

What we wish to emphasize here, however, is not the details of the various positions, but rather the way in which the American style of thinking has suffered from a tendency to oversimplify alternatives and to leap always to absolute positions. It is wrong to insist that one must choose between conformity and individualism, slavery or freedom, absolute toughness or unilateral disarmament. Our need to plan distant as well as short-run goals, to work out the full implications of alternative actions, is confused with simplistic self-definitions, and thus we militate against graduated approaches. Where the arms race is concerned, a graduated approach would start with a definition of the goal as disarmament and would continue with a step-by-step attempt to find ways of overcoming our fears on the one hand and Russia's distrust of inspectors on the other. An illustration of the kind of imaginative plan that is needed is Leo Szilard's idea of an inspection game.[10] Recognizing the reality both of our fear of secret Soviet operations (and of the unreliability of any government's promise, including our own) and theirs of foreigners poking around, Szilard would allow inspection in detail any time that either party suspected clandestine atomic activity or decided that a tremor might not merely be an earthquake. However, if we turned out to be wrong we would have to pay the Soviets a huge indemnity and vice versa. The goal of such a game is greater trust through experience rather than an idea of security through armaments which suggests either a statuesque posture or a swaddled, unrealistic existence, perhaps lived underground in concrete shelters.

To think in these terms requires something of a science fiction mentality, coupled with this sort of understanding

[10] *Bulletin of the Atomic Scientists*, (April 1960).

of political inspection that one finds in Ithiel Pool's contribution to the *Daedalus* symposium on arms control.[11]

v

How does one begin the effort to change current patterns of thinking about security through armament? Because different people in the United States are at different stages of alertness and health or flight and cynicism, answers will vary depending on which group in the population one addresses.

When a man is being overmanipulated to the point where his very existence has become unreal, he cannot be "made" human by more and better manipulation from the "right" direction, by mere bombardment with pressures and appeals. It is this very habit of ignoring the human qualities of men in order to get them to run smoothly that has caused much of our trouble.

Manipulation "downward," from the elites to the public, inevitably intensifies apathy and saps the strength of an alert public just when it is most needed. Thus—to return to an earlier point—by a propaganda campaign which persuaded people to view the Marshall Plan–Mutual Security Program as a semi-military stroke against communism rather than as an idealistic and ultimately practical acknowledgment of our new world responsibility, we increased the chances of a quick acceptance of the program at the expense of setting a pattern in which all economic development of underdeveloped countries would carry the imprimatur of our particular sort of idealism. By reinforcing the ideology of cageyness, we have been killing the very quality in ourselves which might save us from a moral disintegration that armaments can never arrest.

However, while manipulation downward or sideways leads to dysfunctional precedents which narrow future al-

[11] See Ithiel deSola Pool, "Public Opinion and the Control of Armaments," *Daedalus*, Vol. 89 (Fall 1960), pages 984–99.

ternatives, lobbying "upward" is necessary and in the best traditions of keeping our leaders responsible. Today, as free citizens, we need energetically to influence the military, industrial, political, and educational leaders into letting go of their investments in the cold war and into working not only for a safer but for a better world. These investments are very seldom "vested interests" about which we hear so much. There are of course vested interests in the armaments industries, but there are very few businessmen who would rather make weapons than make consumer goods for the civilian population. Many of these businessmen consider themselves "realistic idealists" and are men of good will whose economic advantage makes it easier for them to rationalize their work by putting full blame on the Russians and by parading the horrors of communism. Many of them know deep down that this is dangerous and that the economic advantage is precarious also, especially since their customers in the armed services are constantly changing their requirements, as contractors for another service may come up with a better or more saleable weapons system. Most of these industrialists would probably not object to studies such as Seymour Melmans has been making on the economics of disarmament—or to plans, for example, for deploying part of Raytheon into a government-supported project for the renewal of downtown Boston. One could argue that some of the scientists are more wedded to the arms race than their commercial employers, although even the scientists could certainly be retrained and much of what they now do could be applied to non-military developments. Or, to take another instance, programs might be developed for the retraining of officers of SAC and other agencies whose existence depends on the cold war. Fortunately, many men and much equipment can be deployed into inspection for disarmament; but in a less bellicose climate others may not find jobs with defense contractors. Still, such men often have unusual organizational ability and remarkable dedication and with retraining could be prepared for many governmental, corporate, and educational positions. There would seem to be less technical but graver political difficulties in the workers and their unions now involved in defense activities, for these cannot so readily afford as the businessmen and military leaders to take the "long view." Many are making more money than they ever did before and if their companies were to close down would be stranded in an economically depressed area. The situation is far more serious than in the period at the end of the Second World War when there was a great demand for civilian products; and it seems essential for the federal government to give assurances to the labor force now employed directly or indirectly in defense work that it will not suffer in a period of transition.[12]

It has been our experience that there are elements of idealism in even the most apparently cynical men who engage in defense activities for short-run gains while letting the future take care of itself. This cynicism often reflects a feeling of powerlessness to change anything important. The irony is that in an age when so many feel so powerless a single irate letter can often have a totally unanticipated impact. The men in positions of power are often both divided and confused, and a "grass roots" complaint about a TV show or a congressional measure can, as often for the worse as for the better, show the fallacy of those who believe that there are no channels left for effective political action. Even a freshman congressman who asks questions of the State Department or the Defense Department and persists at it is often able to exercise leverage that would astonish the defeatist.

[12] Despite the threat to the defense worker, Chester Bowles reported after his 1958 congressional campaign that many New London submarine makers supported his anti-cold war position although they recognized it threatened their jobs. They were, however, close enough to the actual weapons of destruction to feel a healthy fear.

VI

Yet, if we get out of the immediate crisis, we shall still be faced with the underlying disorder in a society in which —partly as the result of its great past achievements—people feel there is plenty for all, but little joy in using the things we have made.

For the Russians, a decrease in defense spending means the beginning of television and toasters for all, and perhaps a slight loosening of despotic controls. For us, much more is involved, and more difficult problems—those of "abundance for what?"[13] Indeed, no society has ever been in the American position before or anywhere near it (although the Scandinavians and West Germans are close, and the British not too far away), and thus the dream of plenty until our time has remained unsullied. We cannot look to the experience of other times and other countries for models for the American future. Neither can we discover much relevant wisdom in earlier prophets of abundance. Very few of these prophets foresaw the actual cornucopia of even so modestly efficient an industrial plant as ours (a plant which, if we were not so afraid of productivity or of controlling waste, would produce in a manner truly comparable to the myth of American efficiency).[14] For example, Edward Bellamy's *Looking Backward*, which had an enormous impact on the Gilded Age, envisaged an industrial utopia whose amiable and genteel standard of living has long since been attained throughout a large American middle-income belt—though the inner peace and spaciousness that were supposed to go along with this prosperity have scarcely been approached. Even

[13] We have drawn in what follows on Riesman, "Abundance for What?" *Bulletin of the Atomic Scientists*, Vol. XIV, No. 4 (1958), pages 135–39.

[14] This myth remains unpunctured because most other countries not only have fewer resources but are even less efficient.

the most devoted apostles of capitalism in previous generations seldom foresaw that it would outrun their grandest
hopes (though Schumpeter did grasp this)—while enemies
of capitalism like Karl Marx, who acknowledged its power
to surpass all earlier levels of production and consumption,
never predicted its chastened managerial form nor indeed
its bounteous exploitability. We are a generation who, prepared for Paradise Lost, are afraid that if we enter Paradise Regained, we shall deprive ourselves not merely of the
incentive to produce but even of the incentive to live. We
therefore resist such a predicament as a temptation of the
devil, and in the process fail even to take the necessary
steps, first toward peace, and then toward improved social
conditions and better education and medical care.

We have been trained for a world of scarcity and we
have developed an image of man under the psychology of
scarcity. The maturation of America and correspondingly
of world civilization requires that we begin a program for
abundance with a new view of man and his potentialities:
neither the inherently weak and sinful puritan nor the self-
indulgent consumer, but instead a being whose nature is
fulfilled through work that truly engages him, both because it draws upon his creative power and because it gives
him the responsibility for helping to decide the form and
use of what he makes. In this way we would be able to
consider human destructiveness as the manifestation of a
thwarted need to create and to initiate—a need thwarted
by inadequate education and opportunity (as Paul Good-
man declares in his book, *Growing Up Absurd*). In *Man
for Himself* and later writings, Erich Fromm argues that
man does not live merely for the release of tensions (as
Freud's writings often suggest), but that when this is all
society asks of him, his passive-receptive orientation to
life can fill him with a nagging self-doubt—which may in
turn be exploited in the fantasies of omnipotence that
virulent nationalism demands.

These conflicting ideas concerning man's nature are

dramatized in contemporary American arguments about the educational system. A belief in the spontaneous potentialities of human nature, and in the relevance of schooling to those potentialities, animated some of the original leaders of the progressive-education movement, notably, of course, John Dewey. In practice, however, many followers of this movement simply came to terms, as new social strata swamped the schools, with the latter's diluted demands for a laying on of educational hands. Now, in reaction against this laxity, many American leaders have found in the cold war an opportunity to "tighten up" education. Men like Admiral Rickover espouse a climate of rigor, based not on the intractable tasks set both by knowledge and by life, but by a need to keep up with the Russians. One of the most profound lessons a child learns in school is how he is to feel about his later lifework, and if he is taught to approach the idea of work only with a sense of duty, competitiveness, and fear of failure, he will never develop the capacity to impose meaning on whatever tasks he comes to undertake.[15]

[15] Of course many people today will say that while they may not be "mad" about their work, neither do they mind it. In *The Lonely Crowd* (1950), the senior author took a sanguine view of the attenuation of "meaning" in work, arguing that in an affluent society arduous and demanding work would become increasingly unnecessary, and that the productive impulse would have to be expressed in leisure and play. Further reflection has convinced us that here we are not necessarily the prisoners of our technological fate, of our given forms of mass production, and of the organization of work. We now believe that a rich, heavily automatized society is precisely one that can afford to reorganize work so that attention is focused no longer exclusively on the product, but on the worker himself as a product of his work. We have been greatly excited and impressed by a few pioneering examples, like Edwin Land's Polaroid factory. There, deep involvement in work and a concept of the factory that continues the process of education for the workers have significantly enlivened many workers (without any loss in productivity when measured by the traditional standards of the balance sheet, although this must not be the sole or even the crucial measure of

The problems, political and technical, of reorganizing work along lines we can now only dimly envisage are so enormous as to be almost inhibiting. If one ponders on these matters, one finds oneself facing into a new frontier that is neither physically nor politically simple, but that requires as much resourcefulness and tenacity as the older frontiers did. For example, one might consider the changes involved if every job in America were reanalyzed, not with an eye only to its efficiency in terms of traditional output, but in terms of its long-run effect on the worker, his family, his friends, and his political life. We now assume that production will go on as usual, and that humane progress demands only ancillary adjustments, fringe benefits, which repair some of the ravages of work, on the one hand by making the work place less physically exhausting and despotic, and on the other by trying to shore up the leisure life of the worker with a variety of welfare measures. It is difficult to change this pattern, even if management is willing to initiate the attempt. Edwin Land has found that workers in his Polaroid factory are not eager to leave the assembly line, to whose routines they have become accustomed, for an unspecified job in a laboratory. They doubt their ability to cope with a larger untried situation, just as some students prefer rigid routines, which give them the assurance they are learning something, to less predictable programs of self-directed study. In Dr. Land's experience, workers, like students, need support and encouragement to attempt new tasks.

Another example of inertia is provided by Professor Chris Argyris of the Yale Department of Industrial Administration. The president of a small corporation, Argyris reports, decided that all foremen should determine their own rates

---

success). To be creative in leisure while mindless and passive in work demands a schizoid attitude which even if psychologically possible would put too great a burden on leisure, just as the family bears too great a burden when it becomes the only reservoir of decency in a disordered civic and national life.

of reimbursement. One day he announced that there was a payroll of so many dollars to which he would add an annual increment, and that the workers should divide it among themselves as seemed equitable to them. At first they jumped at the chance, but not long after they asked to be relieved of the responsibility. The president, however, did not give up. It took him seven years to create a work milieu in which the foremen could develop respect for themselves and one another. In the course of making his innovations, the president discovered how deep were the feelings of alienation, of separateness, and how low was the sense of self-esteem among the foremen. He found also that these feelings could not be changed by propaganda, that such persuasion merely increased self-hate and alienation. The foremen preferred paternalism until they had developed a confidence in themselves based on an altered work situation in which they made decisions about style and methods of production. And the president was secure enough not to feel that he had to hang on to traditional prerogatives; as the workers took over more activities, he was freed for new ones.

VII

When in discussion we have stressed hopeful illustrations like these as models for social change, we have sometimes found them quickly dismissed by people brought up in the shadow of Marxism. Such people believe that the coming of abundance does not change the vested interests, and that political commitments will continue to reflect economic advantage. They look to what is left of the American disinherited as the potential cadre to displace the power elite, and they see hostility rather than hope as the principal lever of political change; therefore, they do not even try to move men by rational appeals. One might ask whether they are in fact good Marxists. However, one need not be entirely theoretical: recent student rallies for Negro

rights at leading universities; the interest of the number of
students in problems of disarmament; and perhaps above
all the enthusiastic response of students in many parts of
the country to the possibilities of a Peace Corps all illustrate what seems to us to have been generally the case in
historical development: that it is not the most underprivileged who are most concerned about justice and about the
future. Even the hangovers of scarcity psychology—for example, the prevalent notion that, even if there should be
enough of the good *things* of life for all, there would always
remain a short supply of status—do not alter the fact that
those who worry least about having enough (including
enough status) frequently show the clearest sense of responsibility. This is true not only for the Tory patricians re-
ferred to earlier but also for many of their opponents in
politics and in intellectual life. What is lacking today is an
audience of restless poor (save among Negroes) awaiting
the leadership of the better-off.

As higher education expands and as blue-collar work
gives way to white-collar work, the often denigrated bour-
geois idealist, the pilot fish of the Marxian theory of revolution, becomes a member of a class quite as large in number
as the factory workers. This group is only residually a
"class" in the traditional sense, for it lacks any sense of
identity of interest and any large reservoir of hatred or of
solidarity. Unlike the well-to-do of other times, it is not supported by servants—indeed, its lack of the habit of command is one of its present political weaknesses. On the
whole, its members, children of the industrial revolution,
have thought that any increase in productivity automatically spells progress; but today this has become a tarnished
belief, and little as yet exists to take its place. The answer
for which many radicals look is the highly unlikely prospect of another depression. In our judgment a depression
is unlikely at present, less because the Keynesian weapons
of fiscal and other governmental intervention are well understood and politically available than because, as we have

45

already argued, an increase in "defense" expenditures can again be used, as it was in the recession of 1957-58, to maintain the flow of income. But even if such measures should fail and another depression would threaten, the result at best would be another New Deal—if one could imagine such coasting on inherited ideals which were barely adequate in their own day, let alone in our era of potential abundance. Another formula, occasionally suggested by the engineering-minded, is to regard the race for outer space as a safety valve for the arms race, furnishing an outlet at once for imperialistic energies and cowboy imaginations. While it goes without saying that this latter "solution" is preferable to the arms race, it seems to us a fictional frontier, reflecting a nostalgia for a long-past day when the West had to be settled, the industries developed, the cities built, the immigrants "Americanized."

To summarize our argument: many Americans think that the only changes needed in our national life are minor ones, or choices between starkly stated alternatives. In this they are like patients who come to a psychiatrist and say, "There is nothing basically the matter with me except that I have this ulcer." So it is with the ulcer of the cold war which, as much as it is a reaction to a real conflict, also exposes the failure of a style of life. Though the immediate peril demands the beginning of disarmament as one first step toward ending the cold war, in doing this we only patch a symptom. Disarmament and eased international tensions are not the end of therapy, and true peace is not merely the absence of war but a state in which the quality of existence becomes humane and generous rather than destructive.

The analogy goes further. Just as no therapist can cure anyone but merely provides the support for another's steps toward health, so our leadership cannot manipulate us into utopia. In order for us to live with our abundance, there must be greater participation in the political life of the

United States and of the world. The traditional American ideology which is concerned only with equality of economic and political opportunity and freedom from control—in other words with the major problems of scarcity alone—must readjust to face the problems that have suddenly become visible because of abundance: lack of participation in life and lack of opportunity and education for self-expression. Once these problems can be faced, a people of plenty may be able to use its power for helping other people toward economic prosperity (as an essential step toward further difficult alternatives).

As has been suggested, if really promising steps could be taken, the release of fear and anxiety that people would feel—the ability to breathe freely again and to make long-term plans—will have at once a productive and an unsettling effect: old agendas and ways of regarding the world will have to be scrapped and new ones discovered. Our imagination must focus on other frontiers, work at bringing more people into participation by forming many small groups, by decentralizing industry, by creating better means for continued education not merely for children but for adults throughout life. To be sure, none of the problems of scarcity has been dealt with in a wholly satisfactory way: not all Americans are affluent, many are destitute, and many of the traditional issues of welfare and social justice—markedly, of course, the race issue—remain exigent. But a movement of renewal dedicated only to these issues is not conceivable. We shall move faster on these older fronts if they do not usurp all our attention and if we can invent an American future which is exciting, active, and responsible, but neither murderous nor imperialistic. It is for this that political programs are needed which transcend the details of the present.

TWO

A Re-Examination of American Foreign Policy

BY JAMES WARBURG

Expert in Foreign Policy; author of *United States in a Changing World, The West in Crisis*, and other works

I

A. Introduction and Background

It is not unusual for most nations to go through alternating periods of adventurous progress animated by hope and periods of retrenchment animated by fear. These pendulum swings are reflected in a nation's foreign policy.

For the past seven years, the United States has been in a period of retrenchment dominated by complacency and a desire to preserve and enjoy the fruits of past progress. As a consequence of this pseudo-conservatism at home, United States foreign policy has consisted for the most part of a series of negative reactions to external forces deemed to present a threat to the *status quo*.

In addition, these external forces have been mistakenly identified as arising solely out of the existence of aggressive Communist dictatorships.

The fact is, however, that since the Second World War, the challenge to the United States and to all of Western civilization has been posed not merely by these dictator-ships but by a world in revolution—a many-faceted revolu-tion caused largely by the West itself. The Communists have ruthlessly and skillfully exploited revolutionary change and have thereby magnified the danger, but communism did not initiate the mid-twentieth-century revolutions; nor would these revolutions cease if the Communist dictatorships were to be overthrown.

The Asian and African revolt against colonialism was the product of a dying European imperialism. It burst into flame once the European powers had sufficiently weakened themselves by fratricidal conflict.

So also Western progress toward ever higher living standards, Western failure to share that progress to a sufficient degree, and Western dissemination of ideas, of knowledge, and of techniques through Western-invented means of communication set off the revolt of the underprivileged in what has aptly been called "the revolution of rising expectations." Communism has exploited the revolt against poverty, hunger, and backwardness by offering an open sesame into the twentieth century more relevant to the aspirations of the peoples on the march than anything offered by the West. Where communism has succeeded it has done so by demonstrating that it could catch up to centuries of slow Western progress and lift an entire people out of feudal conditions and into the twentieth century in the span of a single generation. The fact that it did so at the expense of individual freedom has meant little to peoples who have never had a taste of such freedom.

Finally, it was the West which opened the door into the atomic age and initiated the revolution in weaponry which has rendered war useless as an instrument of foreign policy.

Thus communism has become a serious threat to Western civilization chiefly because the West lost control of the great processes of political, economic, and technological change which—partly through its virtues and partly through its shortcomings—the West itself had initiated.

B.

At the end of the Second World War, the United States stood at the apogee of world-wide respect and power. For a short time the United States appeared ready to fulfill the world's hopes and aspirations. It had had no part in kindling the flames of war. It had made a decisive contribution to victory. Having done so, it initiated world-wide relief (UNRRA), took the lead in forming the United Nations, offered voluntarily to surrender to the new world organization its monopoly of atomic power, came to a ravaged Europe's rescue with the Marshall Plan, sponsored the International Bank for Reconstruction and Rehabilitation, and, finally, launched a program of aid to the development of the so-called underdeveloped countries.

During these early postwar years the United States seemed dedicated to an affirmative purpose—the purpose of binding up the wounds of war, of building the machinery for the preservation of peace, of aiding and guiding the revolution of the underprivileged, and of directing the great newly discovered forces of atomic energy exclusively toward peaceful human betterment.

This was the short era of magnificently good intentions, many of which were realized. Unfortunately, it was also the era of dangerous delusion.

One such delusion had been expressed in the wartime slogan of "unconditional surrender," implying that the United States was fighting the war for the sole purpose of achieving military victory as quickly as possible, and implying also the belief that peace would be assured once the Axis powers had been brought to their knees, had been disarmed and rendered incapable of renewed aggression.

The second delusion was that the Soviet Union, having (thanks to Hitler) been an ally in the war, could henceforth be counted upon to co-operate in restoring the world to something like its *ante-bellum status*. This belief assumed that past Western hostility to the Russian Revolution had been forgotten; that Lend-Lease, El Alamein, and the Normandy invasion would be equated in Russian eyes with the turning of the tide at Stalingrad; and that Stalin himself, by some osmosis of association with Roosevelt and Churchill, had acquired the manners, morals, and value standards of an Anglo-Saxon gentleman.

This dangerous delusion led to the belief (or hope) that, without any major *quid pro quo*, such as the promise of massive postwar aid toward Soviet relief and reconstruction, a ruthless dictator would actually allow free Western-style democratic governments to come into existence in countries over which, through enormous sacrifice, the Soviet Union had gained absolute physical control. In other words, that, by a single stroke of genial diplomacy, it would be possible to undo not only the results of "appeasement" and the prewar betrayal of Central Europe to Hitler but also the clear consequences of the subsequent Russian "liberation" of Warsaw, Vienna, Budapest, Prague, and Berlin.

Upon the belief that this diplomatic miracle had actually been accomplished was erected the structure of the United Nations; and, largely because of this fantasy, the Western powers dismantled their great military power in Europe before anything like a European peace settlement had been achieved.

The shattering of this delusion by Stalin's aggressive assertion of domination over Eastern Europe ushered in the past decade of the cold war, which diverted the United States from its originally affirmative and largely altruistic purposes.

C.

Soviet satellization of Eastern Europe, Communist conspiracy in France, Italy, and Greece, and the failure of the four-power experiment in Germany caused the American government to adopt the oversimplified theory that "one country and one country alone" was responsible for the failure to establish a just and honorable peace. This myopic view served to focus American attention upon Moscow as the fountainhead of all evil and caused the United States to adopt the purely defensive policy of "containment."

Furthermore, a fatal misreading of Soviet intentions caused the United States to concentrate its attention upon Europe and to adopt a Europe-oriented policy in Asia and the Middle East—a policy which utterly failed to take into account the indigenous forces at work in these areas.

The disorientation of American foreign policy was accompanied by the belief that the threat of Soviet communism—like the earlier threat of Nazi Germany and Japan—was essentially military and could, therefore, best be contained by military means. (This misreading of the essentially political nature of the Communist threat was no doubt inspired in part by Soviet probing actions and by failure to understand that the "military" victory of the Chinese Communists was achieved more by political than military means.)

D.

The attempt to contain communism by surrounding the Sino-Soviet periphery with military bases and alliances entailed a number of undesirable consequences.

1. It deepened the distrust and hostility of the Communist dictatorships and stimulated their own military efforts. (Power inevitably attracts countervailing power.)

2. It left the initiative to the Sino-Soviet bloc, enabling it to start or threaten to start brush fires anywhere along its giant periphery, thus forcing the United States to adopt a fire-brigade function of rushing from one point to another to extinguish incipient conflagrations.

3. Since containment was beyond the power of the United States alone, it necessitated a multiplicity of alli-

ances, some of which were merely useless while others actually harmed rather than strengthened the anti-Communist coalition.

The core of this system of containment was the NATO alliance, formed for the defense of Western Europe; yet this alliance never succeeded in raising even the minimum forces required for its mission. The recruitment of German forces and the attempt to make up for the lack of defensive manpower by equipping its meager conventional forces with so-called tactical nuclear weapons diminished NATO's credibility as a purely defensive force, without making it any more capable of holding off invasion by vastly superior and similarly equipped Soviet forces. In spite of this, NATO remained the strongest link in a lamentably weak chain—the strongest deterrent ground force ironically placed *at the point least likely to be attacked.* (There is no evidence that the Soviet Union has ever intended to attack Western Europe. There is ample evidence that Soviet intention has been to outflank Western Europe in Asia, the Middle East, and Africa.)

Outside of Europe, the ring of military containment has existed largely on paper, except for the American forces stationed in Japan, the Seventh Fleet in Far Eastern waters, and the Sixth Fleet in the Mediterranean.

Some of the many alliances are definite elements of weakness.

The alliance with Chiang Kai-shek, contracted after his flight from the mainland, serves more to provoke than to ward off attack; moreover, it divides the anti-Communist coalition at its core and cements the Sino-Soviet alliance.

The rearming of Pakistan deprived that country of much-needed economic assistance while at the same time forcing a crucially important democratic and pacifist India to divert resources from its Five-Year Plan to rearmament.

The attempt to rearm the Arab states as anti-Communist allies resulted merely in splitting the Arab states into rival factions and increased the already explosive tensions between the Arabs and Israel.

Black Africa was entirely neglected.

United States preoccupation with Europe stood in the way of Latin America's receiving vitally needed economic assistance.

4. While producing little if any military strength, the attempt at physical containment stultified the political posture of the United States. Alliances with anti-democratic and unpopular governments (Franco in Spain, Nuri as-Said in Iraq) placed the United States in the invidious position of defending an outmoded *status quo* in various parts of the world where peoples desired radical change. Concern for its European allies caused the United States either to back the rickety remnants of colonialism (Indo-China) or else to take an ambivalent position (Algeria) which pleased neither the colonial power nor the people seeking freedom and independence. Concentration of American effort upon military containment caused a woeful neglect of the political opportunities presented by almost every part of a rapidly changing world.

E.

The steadily mounting cost of containment and its failure to contain, plus the unexpectedly rapid Soviet acquisition of retaliatory power, led, in 1953, to the adoption of a new set of self-deceiving doctrines:

Item: "More bang for a buck," meaning greater reliance upon the relatively cheap instruments of mass murder and destruction, instead of upon the more expensive conventional containing forces.

Item: "Massive retaliation at points of our own choosing," meaning that, instead of meeting military aggression at the point where it might be committed, the United States would henceforth retaliate upon the presumed

55

sources of that aggression. (And thereby incur counter-retaliation upon American cities.)

Item: "Liberation, not containment," a wholly spurious slogan designed to give an affirmative face to a negative policy—a dangerous promise without substance. (Hungary)

By far the most dangerous was the doctrine that the Communist dictatorships were not strong but weak, and that they were bound to disintegrate by reason of their inner weakness and iniquity.

When President Eisenhower himself assumed the direction of American foreign policy, in the spring of 1959, the United States was no nearer to the establishment of peace than it had been at the conclusion of the Second World War. In 1945 the United States held undisputed paramount power and an impeccable reputation among the world's peoples. In 1959 the United States had little to show for its costly fourteen-year effort except the rehabilitation of Western Europe—a Western Europe restored to economic health but of divided counsel and increasing unwillingness to follow American leadership.

Instead of being the world's paramount power, the United States was engaged in a neck-and-neck arms race with the Soviet Union, with the enormous power potential of China looming over the horizon. Much of the good will of the world's peoples had been lost. The immobilism of the past decade had clearly demonstrated its failure.

F.

It is both profitless and impossible fairly to apportion the blame for this failure among Democrats and Republicans—much less among individuals.

The great constructive actions of the early postwar period were initiated by Democrats but, for the most part, enjoyed Republican support. The Berlin airlift, the intervention in Greece, the NATO alliance, and the whole containment policy were the product of joint leadership. Truman's bold intervention in Korea, though later sharply criticized by Republicans ("Truman's war"), was originally undertaken with bipartisan support.

The Eisenhower administration, in spite of the campaign oratory of 1952, took over the basic Truman foreign policy along with the basic misconceptions which had lain at its root. It negotiated the same truce in Korea which it had damned Truman for attempting to negotiate, adding its own contribution to the Far Eastern imbroglio by "unleashing" Chiang Kai-shek, permitting if not encouraging him to fortify the offshore islands and then releashing him at the cost of entanglement in a mutual defense alliance. The Eisenhower administration carried forward the policy of containment, after denouncing it in favor of a policy of "liberation," by erecting the SEATO alliance and then attempting to link it through Pakistan with the ill-fated Baghdad Pact, in turn linked to NATO through Turkey's membership in both alliances. In Europe its policy was indistinguishable from that of its predecessor.

G.

It is too soon to determine whether President Eisenhower's belated assumption of responsibility will result in any substantial change. Following up the initiative taken by Prime Minister Macmillan early in 1959, the President has taken the first and extremely important step toward breaking the ten-year deadlock between the United States and the U.S.S.R.—at least to the extent of opening the door to negotiations. Given the shortness of time left to his administration, the delays imposed by President de Gaulle and Chancellor Adenauer, and the fact that 1960 was a year of presidential election, it seems doubtful whether more than a beneficial change of atmosphere could have been accomplished.

Moreover, even if President Eisenhower had attempted

a basic policy revision, it is difficult to see how this could have been accomplished by an administration whose thinking was so strongly influenced by the Pentagon, the Treasury, and the Bureau of the Budget.

H.

The people of the United States are ready for a new approach to foreign policy. This, however, will not happen if the Democratic party allows itself to be dominated by those who appear unable to detach themselves from the past or to realize that the policies which they initiated—whatever their merit at the time—are no longer relevant to the changed and rapidly changing state of world affairs.

It is with these considerations in mind that the undersigned present the following statement of principles, aims, and procedural guide lines.

II ULTIMATE AND IMMEDIATE AIMS

We suggest that the *ultimate* aims of American foreign policy should be:

1. The achievement of universal security against military aggression through universal disarmament under adequately enforced world law.

2. The achievement of universal human betterment through world-wide co-operation in economic and social development.

We suggest that the *immediate* aims of American foreign policy should be:

1. To remove by give-and-take negotiation, with due regard to the vital interests of the United States and its allies, as much as possible of the tensions which now exist between the United States and the Soviet Union and between the United States and the People's Republic of China.

2. To maintain, pending the achievement of universal disarmament, a military posture of sufficient strength to

discourage aggression against the United States or against allies whom the United States is committed to defend, it being understood that such commitments are subject to revision as hereinafter set forth.

3. To build and maintain for the United States and nations willing to co-operate with it a position of effective competition in economic development with the Sino-Soviet bloc until such time as universal co-operation can be achieved.

III DISARMAMENT

A. Definition of Ultimate Objective and Its Implications

In September 1959 the United Kingdom and the Soviet Union each laid before the General Assembly of the United Nations a proposal for universal national disarmament. Approval in principle of the aim of total universal disarmament has been expressed by many other nations.

Our own government has talked about various facets of disarmament and control but *has never yet fully defined its position with regard to total universal disarmament.*

We think that the American people as well as all the nations and peoples of the world are entitled to know where the United States government stands.

While we do not believe that universal disarmament alone will assure world peace, we are convinced that there can be no assurance of peace without it.

We believe it illusory to think that peace can be assured by a mere limitation or control of national armaments. So long as nations subject to no supranational law possess any offensive armaments whatever, we believe that wars will recur; and that, once war breaks out, it is inevitable that whatever limitations or controls may have been agreed upon will fall by the wayside.

We recognize that total universal disarmament cannot

be achieved overnight; that a stepwise procedure is necessary, with each step carefully controlled. But it is our conviction that such a stepwise procedure is not only useless but dangerous, unless there is universal agreement that it shall lead to a clearly defined goal of total disarmament under adequately enforced world law.

Past attempts at "disarmament" have, in our judgment, failed because they were either directed merely at the limitation of national armaments (as in the case of the naval treaties of the 1920s), or else because (as in our government's 1957 "package plan") proposals have been put forward as "first steps" without any answer to the question: "Steps toward what?"

We believe that the United States should unequivocally declare that its goal is universal national disarmament down to the level of lightly armed internal police forces; that such disarmament must be enforced under world law; and that the enforcement of such world law must be provided for by universal agreement to endow a supranational world organization with the exclusive right to maintain and, if necessary, to use armed force in order to prevent violation.

While it would seem natural and desirable that a revised and greatly strengthened United Nations Security Council take over the function of enforcement, we recognize that it may be difficult to obtain universal consent to the necessary Charter amendments. We would not, therefore, preclude the creation within the framework of the United Nations of a specially designed *ad hoc* organization of clearly defined and limited power.

The United States will not be in a position to inquire whether the Soviet Union and other nations are actually prepared to accept the full implications of total universal disarmament until the United States itself has answered the same question in the affirmative.

We believe that this question should promptly be laid by the Executive before the Congress and the people of the United States, with a clear statement both as to the necessity of universal disarmament and as to its implications.

Until this question of ultimate goal has been defined and answered by the nations of the world, "disarmament talks" can at best serve only the limited purpose of relaxing extreme tensions and gaining time.

"Universal" Means All Nations

We call attention to the fact that, if the United States declares one of its major aims to be the achievement of universal disarmament under adequately enforced world law, it must be prepared to agree that every nation in the world must be a party to the agreement and participate in the creation and maintenance of the enforcement agency. This requires a revision of United States policy with respect to those nations which are not now members of the United Nations—notably the People's Republic of China, Outer Mongolia, and the presently divided nations of Germany, Korea, and Vietnam.

B. Intermediate Steps

If the three nuclear powers, the United States, the United Kingdom, and the Soviet Union (with the probable addition of France), can agree upon the ultimate objective of total universal disarmament in full recognition of what this implies, then it will become possible to examine whatever immediate steps may be proposed in full awareness of the end toward which they are intended to lead.

Thus, an agreement by the nuclear powers to ban test explosions and to refrain from supplying nuclear weapons or information concerning their manufacture to other nations would logically be accompanied by an agreement on the part of all the non-nuclear nations not to attempt to make or acquire such weapons.

Likewise, since, if stepwise disarmament is to take place, it is necessary that all nations disarm "in full sight of each other," it will become evident that whatever inspection and control machinery is adopted should fit into the ultimate plan of erecting a supranational enforcement agency. The enforcement agency might, in fact, be empirically developed by beginning with the establishment of its "presence" in each of the countries party to the first steps toward disarmament. Thus an embryonic enforcement agency might develop the techniques of inspection and reportage, even before it had been endowed with full enforcement powers.

C. The Maintenance of Balance

The urgent desire to prevent a nuclear war is the chief dynamic of the trend toward disarmament. Yet the present precarious balance of power rests increasingly upon nuclear weapons. The United States and its allies have not only placed their chief reliance upon "massive retaliation"; the United States has also equipped its inadequate conventional forces with nuclear weapons, thus rendering itself incapable of fighting a non-nuclear war. The latest announcements from Moscow indicate that the Soviet Union is following a similar course.

If the proposed reduction of Soviet conventional forces is carried out, there will exist something like a rough balance as between the Soviet Union and the Western powers in nuclear-armed conventional forces. However, unless China undertakes an even more drastic reduction of its conventional forces, the abolition of nuclear weapons would leave the Sino-Soviet bloc in possession of undoubted military supremacy.

Any stepwise plan for universal disarmament must, therefore, preserve at each stage a rough balance between the Communist and anti-Communist orbits in three major respects: (1) in the abolition of strategic nuclear weapons and delivery systems; (2) in the denuclearization of conventional forces (i.e., in the abolition of tactical nuclear weapons); and (3) in the *pari passu* reduction of conventional land, sea, and air forces. (Possibly chemical- and biological-warfare capability should constitute a fourth category.)

The admittedly difficult matter of achieving and preserving a global Communist–anti-Communist balance of capability might, as a practical matter, best be approached regionally. Thus a beginning might be made in arriving at a balanced reduction of the capabilities of the NATO and the Warsaw Pact alliances in Europe. (See Part IV, Section B.) Similarly one might begin in the Far East with an attempt to achieve and preserve a balance in that area between the Communist and anti-Communist forces. This would involve the stepwise demobilization of mainland China's, North Korea's, and North Vietnam's conventional forces offset by a similar reduction of the indigenous anti-Communist conventional forces and a gradual withdrawal of United States nuclear-armed sea and air power. (See Part V, Section C.)

The point to be made here is that a balance must be maintained during the entire period of phased disarmament; and that the sooner the supranational enforcement agency exists and is equipped with adequate power of its own, the easier this problem will become.

D. Preparing the American Economy for Disarmament

In addition to preserving a balance of military power throughout the various stages leading to eventual total disarmament, it is, in our judgment, necessary to take simultaneous action in the direction of preparing the United States economy for conversion to production for peace. Unless this is done, disarmament may cause serious unemployment and a major economic depression; and, unless there is openly discussed planning for peace, the fear of economic collapse may dilute the determination of the American people to achieve disarmament.

63

Such planning must be undertaken co-operatively by government, business, and labor. It must take into consideration what businesses may require help in reconversion, what labor forces will have to be retrained and perhaps relocated, and in what manner the great productive capacity of the United States may be geared not only to the needs of the American consumer but to world needs. Such planning must also take into consideration a revised fiscal policy which will provide for wise public expenditure deliberately calculated not only to supply long-neglected domestic needs but also to stimulate private investment.

It must be recognized that disarmament will probably mean not the end of the cold war but the transference of the struggle out of the military and into the politico-economic arena. Soviet Premier Khrushchev, in fact, said in so many words: "Let us both throw away our arms and relieve ourselves of the burden and danger of the arms race. Then we shall proceed to defeat you by proving to the world that our system is better than yours."

To meet this challenge we must see to it that the healthy growth of the American economy is stimulated and that it not be interrupted by the reduction and ultimate elimination of military expenditures. (The economics of disarmament will be more fully discussed in a subsequent working paper.)

We recommend that the President, proceeding under the authority of the Employment Act of 1946, immediately appoint a mixed commission to begin the necessary studies.

IV REDUCTION OF TENSIONS BETWEEN THE UNITED
STATES AND THE U.S.S.R.

A.

It is claimed by some that disarmament would, in and of itself, eliminate the explosive tensions which have brought the world to the brink of disaster. It is claimed by others that there can be no disarmament until the tensions which have caused the arms race have been relaxed.

We do not accept either view. We hold that it is not a question of which comes first—disarmament or a detente. We believe that simultaneous efforts can and must be made in both directions.

Parallel to the educational effort necessary to bring about universal acceptance of disarmament, we hold that it is essential to proceed by patient give-and-take negotiation to settle the outstanding differences between the rival power orbits. There is no other way to break out of the vicious circle of mutual distrust and fear.

The major tensions between the Soviet Union and the West exist in Europe and the Middle East. The major tensions between the rival power orbits in the Far East exist between the United States and the People's Republic of China.

B. *Europe*

The key to East–West tensions in Europe is Germany, focusing at the moment upon the status of Berlin.

We do not know whether an honorable and just compromise of this question is possible. We do know that, to date, neither side has sincerely attempted to reach a compromise. We think the effort should be made.

We need not concern ourselves here with the events that led up to the partition of Germany in 1949.

For the past ten years the Western powers have demanded at conference after conference and in note after note that the two German states be reunited by free elections and that a thus reunified Germany should remain free to join the anti-Soviet NATO alliance. Throughout the same ten years the Russians have demanded that Germany be reunified on a trick-laden basis which would give the East German Communist apparatus a chance to gain control over all of Germany. Thus each side has demanded the unconditional surrender of the other. Each side pretended to seek the reunification of Germany on its own terms, while actually caring very little about ending the partition. What each side really wanted was the preservation of the *status quo*, although neither was willing to admit it for fear of alienating the Germans. The Western powers were unwilling to relinquish a German military participation in Western defense. The Soviet Union was unwilling to give up one of its satellites for fear of the effect upon the others.

The exception, from the Soviet point of view, was the *status quo* as to West Berlin. Here was a Western enclave, situated in the heart of the East German satellite republic —an enclave which was not only a Western outpost and a showcase of freedom but an escape hatch through which the most useful elements in the East German population were steadily fleeing into West Germany. As Nikita Khrushchev was later to describe it, West Berlin was a "bone in his throat"—a "cancer which must be eliminated."

From the Western point of view, West Berlin is of no particular value, except that the West has incurred a moral liability to protect its 2,250,000 inhabitants from being overrun by communism. Strategically, the Western position is untenable. Economically, it is unprofitable. Legally, the West has foolishly neglected to obtain an ironclad agreement as to its right of access.

In November 1958 Premier Khrushchev cut through the ten-year deadlock with a meat cleaver, summarily demanding that the Western powers get out of Berlin within six months. For the first time, the Soviet leader frankly stated that no one really wanted to reunify Germany except perhaps the Germans, and that, if the Germans wished to achieve reunification, it was up to the two German states to work out the problem.

There followed then the exploratory visit to Moscow of Prime Minister Macmillan, the fruitless meeting of the foreign ministers at Geneva, and, finally, the withdrawal of the ultimatum by Mr. Khrushchev during his visit to Washington and President Eisenhower's consequent expression of willingness to discuss the problem of Berlin.

Both sides have now recognized that the situation in Berlin is "abnormal." The question is: "Can its abnormality be corrected without correcting the abnormality of a partitioned Germany?"

It appears to us that the Western powers must finally face a choice which has all along been inescapable. They must decide which of two things they want most—a German military contribution to NATO or the reunification of the two German states. They cannot have both.

Either choice implies a different sort of solution for the problem of Berlin.

If the Western powers decide that they cannot forego German participation in Western defense, then they must accept the more or less permanent partition of Germany, which implies the recognition of the East German state and acceptance of the *status quo* in Eastern Europe. In that case it would be unrealistic to expect West Berlin to remain as a Western-controlled island of freedom in the heart of the East German state.

The most that could in these circumstances be hoped for would be the reunification of Berlin under United Nations authority, with the United Nations possibly exercising that authority through a re-established Four-Power Kommandatura. Even then, it is difficult to see how a gradually increasing economic dependence of the city upon the surrounding Communist territory could be avoided.

The other alternative would be for the Western powers to decide that they want German reunification more than they want a German military contribution to NATO. They would then put forward a proposal under which the two German states would be enabled to find their way toward reunification without outside interference of any sort. Obviously this would require the withdrawal of Soviet coercive power from East Germany—an end which could not be attained without a countervailing withdrawal of Anglo-French-American forces perhaps no farther than to the west bank of the Rhine.

Were a German settlement to be sought along these lines, the answer to the Berlin problem would be an agreement to preserve the *status quo* in that city, perhaps with some modifications, until reunification had taken place and Berlin could once more become the capital of a reunited Germany.

These, in broad terms, seem to us the two alternatives.

The first would undoubtedly be easier to negotiate with the Russians. We are opposed to it for two reasons:

1. Were the Western powers to accept Germany's permanent partition, they could do so only over the violent objection of the West German government—an objection which would probably be sustained by the majority of the West German population. In that event, we should doubt the value of West Germany as an ally. In other words, by choosing this alternative, the Western powers would, in our judgment, destroy the value of the very thing for the sake of which they had chosen it; namely, the retention of an effective German contribution to Western defense.

2. A rearmed West Germany would in these circumstances not only be an unreliable ally but a serious danger to peace. Western acceptance of partition would almost certainly reawaken German nationalism. Reawakened German nationalism, resentful against both West and East, could lead either to war or—and this seems far more likely —to a German-Soviet deal in which Germany would purchase its reunification and perhaps the return of some of its Polish-held eastern territory at the price of alliance with the Soviet bloc. Such things have happened before.

The Polish Rapacki Plan appeals to us as a point of departure in shaping a Western proposal for reunifying Germany at the price of its military neutralization. The virtue of this Polish proposal is that it provides for the non-discriminatory military neutralization of Germany, since it applies not only to the two German states but to Poland and Czechoslovakia as well. Austria is already debarred from military alliances with either East or West. Switzerland and Sweden are neutral by choice. Hungary and Denmark might well be added to the neutral belt. Thus there would be no question—as there was in the Versailles Treaty —of imposing demilitarization or neutralization upon a single nation. Indeed, there would be no question of imposition at all. The Western proposal, as we envisage it, would be shaped with the full consent of the German people.

Debarment from military alliances would not mean that the states in the neutralized area would be deprived of the right to maintain or enter into whatever non-military association they might wish. West Germany's exit from NATO would not mean that it would have to withdraw from Euratom or the Common Market. Nor would East Germany's, Poland's, and Czechoslovakia's exit from the Warsaw Pact involve the rupture of their political and economic ties to the Soviet bloc. On the contrary, one might hope that the creation of a militarily neutralized belt would tend to increase East–West economic co-operation and thus gradually to restore the European trading community.

There are two major reasons why we think this possibility should be explored.

The first is a conviction that this is the sort of proposal the United States ought to make, in its own interest, in Europe's interest, and in the interest of peace.

The second reason is a belief that a solution of this sort is in Russia's interest no less than in the interest of the West. We are inclined to think that Mr. Khrushchev knows that the Soviet Union's coercive position in Eastern Europe is in the long run untenable—that it will ultimately alienate peoples who might otherwise, of their own free will, choose close association with the Soviet Union. We are convinced that Mr. Khrushchev would gladly liquidate that coercive position if, as a *quid pro quo*, he could obtain the withdrawal of American military power from the continent and the liquidation of American bases on the Soviet periphery.

Obviously the United States cannot, in the present circumstances, withdraw altogether from the continent. Nor can it, overnight, liquidate its bases. But the United States could, we think, recognize that this is what it eventually wants to do, when and if peace in Europe and elsewhere is assured.

The United States could offer to withdraw behind the Rhine, if Russia were to withdraw behind the Oder.

The United States could, pending the forthcoming negotiations, refrain from building new bases such as that which it is now constructing in Turkey.

The United States could, pending the outcome of its efforts to halt the arms race, refrain from spreading nuclear weapons systems around the world and discourage its own war industries from rebuilding West Germany into an arsenal.

Ten years ago our government said that it would never acquiesce in German rearmament. In 1950 our government demanded German troops for NATO but said that it would never allow Germany to rebuild its own war industries. In 1959 our government has agreed to give Germany everything except nuclear warheads and has permitted our war industries to go into partnership with Krupp, Kloeckner, Heinckel, and Messerschmidt in re-creating German capacity to build almost every kind of war equipment.

If we are serious and sincere in wishing to halt the arms race and to reach a European settlement, the least we can do is to call a halt in rearming Germany while we negotiate.

Unfortunately it is true that the approach we advocate would run counter to the wishes of West German Chancellor Adenauer, whose belief in the intransigent policy of refusing to negotiate except from a "situation of strength" remains as unshaken as that of its author, former Secretary of State Acheson.

Even more unfortunately, Chancellor Adenauer's intransigence is supported, for reasons not entirely clear, by President de Gaulle of France, who has no interest whatever in the reunification of Germany.

On the other hand, we believe that the United Kingdom and Canada would support an initiative such as we have suggested.

Great as is America's interest in the security of Western Europe, we believe that the time has come when Germany and France must either assume the major responsibility for the future of Europe or else adopt a less arbitrary and more constructive attitude toward the non-European powers who are at present bearing the major burden of Western Europe's defense.

Finally, we wish to take note of two objections to the creation of a neutralized belt in Central Europe which have been raised in this country.

It is contended by some that a withdrawal of Anglo-French-American forces to the west bank of the Rhine would fatally weaken the NATO defense. To this we reply that no less an authority than the former commander in chief of the United States Army in Europe, General Clyde D. Eddelman, has denied that such would be the case. His view is shared by the distinguished Marshal of the Royal Air Force, Sir John Slessor.

The point is raised by former Secretary of State Acheson and others that a westward removal of the American installations would be extremely costly. This is no doubt true, but even if the cost ran to several hundred million dollars it would be relatively insignificant as the price for substantial progress toward a European peace settlement. (In this connection we raise the question whether it is necessary or, for that matter, suitable that a ready combat force should be accompanied by dependents, and whether the efficiency of the American force in Germany would not actually be greater if troops without dependents were rotated to that theater.)

C. The Middle East

For the purposes of this discussion, the loosely defined term, Middle East, will be taken to include the following areas:

1. The *Maghreb* (Morocco, Algeria, Tunis, and Libya)
2. The Arab states and Israel
3. The non-Arab flank states (Turkey and Iran)

The Maghreb

It is our view that the interests of peace would best be served if Morocco, Algeria, and Tunis (with perhaps Libya) were to unite in a Maghreb Federation, either wholly independent or linked to France in the French community.

Such a federation cannot come about until the status of Algeria is determined—a matter which now seems slowly to be progressing toward a solution.

The United States cannot back Algerian independence without alienating France. It cannot support France in denying Algerian independence without alienating most of the Afro-Asian nations. Moreover, it is not clear to us at this moment whether the majority of the Muslim population of Algeria wants complete independence, a dominion status within the French community, or perhaps only local autonomy.

The United States has a definite interest in the early achievement of an Algerian settlement and in the return of the French army from North Africa to Europe. So long as "pacification" continues, France will remain an almost worthless member of NATO. And, so long as the revolt continues, the unsolved Algerian problem will adversely affect the future orientation of most of the African peoples now emerging into independence.

It appears to us that the most promising course for the

United States to pursue is that of encouraging both sides to negotiate and of keeping in close touch and quietly co-operating with Tunisia and Morocco, whose governments seem best suited to act as intermediaries.

The Arab States and Israel

The proven ineffectiveness of the "Eisenhower Doctrine," the collapse of the ill-fated Baghdad Pact, the existing hostility between the United Arab Republic and Iraq, the unremitting tensions between Israel and its Arab neighbors, and the precarious state of King Hussein's regime in Jordan all clearly indicate that the United States should for the time being pursue a quiet policy of "watchful waiting."

There are at least three lessons to be learned from our past mistakes in this area:

1. That the whole area is in a state of revolutionary change and that any attempt to arrest that change in defense of the *status quo* is self-defeating.

2. That arming the Arab states results only in arming them against each other or against Israel.

3. That alliances with anti-democratic feudal regimes result in alienating the people living under those regimes and tend to strengthen the appeal of communism as an apparent ally of social revolution.

We suggest that the aims of United States policy in this area should be:

1. To reach an agreement with the Soviet Union and all other industrialized nations not to ship arms into the area.

2. To reach a similar multilateral agreement under which all governmental economic aid to the area would be channeled through a Regional Development Authority to be established under United Nations auspices. (See, in this connection, the proposal for a United Nations Development Authority in Section D, of Part VI.)

3. To obtain an agreement between the oil-producing states and the oil companies operating in the area whereby

73

both would agree that a tax be levied upon their profits by the Regional Development Authority, so that all the states in the area would benefit from the area's resources and have a vested interest in their continuous development and exploitation.

4. To obtain the co-operation of the Soviet Union, and of all the other nations which voted in the United Nations for the partition of Palestine, in bringing about peace between the Arab states and Israel. This would involve Arab acceptance of Israel's existence, the permanent fixing of Israel's frontiers, and a fair settlement of the problem posed by the Arab refugees from Palestine.

We fully recognize that these four aims will not be easy to achieve and that, in large measure, their achievement will depend upon a successful effort to relax East–West tensions in Europe. We believe, however, that the open avowal of these aims by the government of the United States would in itself have a salutary effect both upon the peoples of the area and upon the relations between the West and the Soviet Union. Such a declaration of aims would, in our opinion, not be inconsistent with a policy of watchful waiting.

The Flank Countries

Turkey: It is our view that Turkey should be considered more as a member of NATO than as a member of the Middle East area, and that future American policy with respect to this country should be governed chiefly by the success or failure of the effort to achieve a detente in Europe. Specifically, Turkey should be excluded from the arms embargo suggested in the preceding section, the question of Turkey's military position being governed by NATO considerations.

Iran and Pakistan: We question whether these two countries are of any great value as military allies. We are inclined to think that they would benefit more and be of more value to the anti-Communist coalition if military aid were converted into economic assistance.

D. *Cultural and Scientific Relations with the U.S.S.R.*

We regard as highly promising the advance recorded in recent years in the development of cultural and scientific relations between the United States and the Soviet Union.

We believe that the interchange of persons and the sharing of scientific knowledge, as well as all forms of cultural and educational exchanges, constitute one of the strongest antidotes to mutual distrust and hostility.

E. *Trade Relations*

We believe that the time has come when the United States should liberalize its restrictive trade policy vis-à-vis the Soviet Union. We question whether this policy has measurably retarded the growth of the Soviet war potential. We are inclined to think that this policy has actually imposed a greater burden upon the United States and its allies than upon the nations against which it has been directed.

We recommend that a careful study be made of the possible reciprocal concessions through which a mutually acceptable pattern of trade relationships between the United States and the Soviet Union might be developed.

V REDUCTION OF TENSIONS BETWEEN THE UNITED STATES AND THE PEOPLE'S REPUBLIC OF CHINA

A. *Establishing Channels of Communication*

Whereas the channels of communication and negotiation between the United States and the Soviet Union are open, there has been and is no direct contact with the People's Republic of China.

We cannot see how our government can hope to ease tensions, to arrive at fair settlements of disputes, or, above all, to achieve disarmament without establishing direct channels of communication with Peking.

We hold the view that our policy with respect to recognition should be realistic, as defined by the late John Foster Dulles in his book (*War and Peace*) written before he became Secretary of State and adjusted his ideas concerning China to the exigencies of domestic politics. We believe that it should be made clear to the American people that recognition of the Peking regime would not denote or imply approval, any more than our recognition of the Soviet regime implies anything more than the belief that the establishment of diplomatic relations serves the interests of the United States and the interests of peace.

Even if it is by no means certain that the Peking regime would welcome the establishment of diplomatic relations with the United States, this should not stand in the way of our making the attempt to open the channels of negotiation. If the channels are to remain closed, it should not be through the fault of the United States.

Similarly it seems to us utterly absurd for our government to restrict travel to China on the part of American citizens. Surely it is not in the best interest of the United States that its government and its citizens should be kept in ignorance concerning the rapidly changing conditions within a nation whose population comprises one quarter of the earth's inhabitants.

B. Admission to the United Nations

With respect to admitting the People's Republic of China to the United Nations, we again quote the late John Foster Dulles. A year after the Chinese Communists had gained control of the Chinese mainland, Mr. Dulles wrote:

> "If the government of China in fact proves its ability to govern China without serious domestic resist-

ance, then it too should be admitted to the United Nations." (The Peking regime has governed China without serious domestic resistance for the past ten years.)

"Some of the present member nations and others that might become members," Mr. Dulles continued, "have governments that are not representative of the people. But if in fact they are 'governments'—that is, if they 'govern'—then they have a power which should be represented in any organization which purports to mirror reality. . . . All nations should be members without attempting to appraise those which are 'good' and those which are 'bad.' Already that distinction is obliterated by the present membership of the United Nations."

The fact that Mr. Dulles did not follow his own precepts when he became Secretary of State does not, in our judgment, detract from their wisdom.

Furthermore, the now widely recognized need for universal disarmament makes it mandatory for China to be drawn into a universal world organization.

Accordingly it is our view that the United States should offer to withdraw its opposition to China's admission to the United Nations, provided that the Peking regime will reaffirm the renunciation of force which it signed at the Bandung conference of 1955 and which it has since repudiated by its action with respect to the Indian-Chinese border; and provided further that the Peking regime will undertake the obligations imposed by the Charter of the United Nations and agree to co-operate in working toward universal total disarmament adequately enforced under world law. (Note: The Peking regime may likewise be considered to have violated its renunciation of force in Tibet and with respect to the offshore islands, but Peking claims that both Tibet and the Taiwan Strait are internal Chinese affairs. The dispute with India, however, is clearly international.)

C. The Taiwan Strait

Having opened the channels of negotiation, it is our view that the United States should tackle directly with Peking the disputes over Taiwan (and the Pescadores) and over the Chinese offshore islands. These matters will probably have to be settled before Peking will accept membership in the United Nations on the conditions proposed.

We would suggest that the United States begin by recognizing Peking's unquestionably valid claim to the offshore islands (perhaps subject to final determination by the International Court of Justice) in exchange for Peking's agreement to permit the unmolested evacuation of the Chinese Nationalist garrisons and of such of the local population as might wish to be evacuated.

Next we would recommend that the United States propose that Taiwan and the Pescadores be placed for at least five years under United Nations administration, (the People's Republic of China having previously become a member nation); that, during these five years, the islands be neutralized and demilitarized, except for such military, naval, and air forces as might be furnished for their protection by or at the request of the United Nations; and that, at the end of the five-year trusteeship, the native population of Taiwan and the Pescadores be permitted to decide by plebiscite whether they wish to become part of mainland China or to remain an independent state.

This solution will at first appeal neither to Peking nor to the Nationalist regime on Taiwan. Nevertheless, it seems to us the only solution fair to all concerned. We are convinced that, if the United States were to make such a proposal, it would have the overwhelming support of world opinion, especially if the proposal were backed by a declaration of American willingness to withdraw all military forces from Japan and Okinawa at the appropriate phase of universal disarmament.

Korea and Vietnam

In our opinion the United States should seek an arrangement with Peking and Moscow under which all three powers would agree to withdraw completely from these unhappily partitioned countries, leaving the peoples concerned to decide whether or not to seek reunification. A United Nations or other neutral peace force should be empowered to occupy a neutralized belt between North and South Korea and another between North and South Vietnam for so long as partition continues. Eventually the peace forces might be empowered to supervise all-Korean and all-Vietnamese elections.

Cultural and Trade Relations

Our observations concerning cultural, scientific, and trade relations between the United States and the Soviet Union, as stated in the preceding chapter, likewise apply to the relations between the United States and the People's Republic of China.

United States Relations with the Nationalists

In our opinion the United States has more than fulfilled its obligations to the Nationalist regime as a wartime ally. We can see no reason why the Generalissimo should be permitted to keep the United States entangled in his forlorn hopes of reconquering the mainland and thus to keep the United States continuously at the brink of war with the most powerful nation in Asia. The United States could and, in our judgment, should either demand a political amnesty for those of the Nationalist leaders who may not wish to make their peace with history, or else offer them asylum.

Conclusion

United States policy with respect to China has remained static for ten years. In 1949, China was a weak and disorganized nation torn by civil conflict. During the past decade China has emerged into the most powerful and highly organized nation in Asia. Whatever the merit of United States policy when it was initiated, it is now clearly outdated. This obsolete and inflexible policy divides the anti-Communist coalition at its European core, alienates the crucially important uncommitted peoples of Asia, cements the Sino-Soviet alliance, and stands as a road block to any relaxation of tensions in the Far East.

In our opinion the interests of the United States and of world peace demand a drastic revision along the lines here indicated, irrespective of whatever response such a revision might evoke on the part of Peking.

VI BUILDING TOWARD PEACE

A.

The following broad principles should, in our judgment, govern United States policy both toward friendly nations and those which are uncommitted to either side in the cold war:

1. The industrialization of presently less developed countries is in the interest of the United States. (Canada, with its seventeen million inhabitants, buys more from the United States than all of Latin America with a combined population ten times greater.)

2. The industrialization of the less developed countries must go hand in hand with improved utilization of land and water resources so as to create an agricultural base sufficient to supply the nation's food requirements while at

the same time freeing a labor force for basic industrial development.

3. In many of these countries the creation of a strong agricultural base is impeded by feudal or semi-feudal land tenure, resulting in peasant serfdom, poor cultivation, and often in a concentration upon cash crops rather than upon the creation of an adequate food supply. In such countries land reform must precede industrialization. It is to the interest of the United States to help governments to avoid confiscatory practices with their disruptive political consequences by providing assistance to land reform through orderly purchase and redistribution.

4. It is extremely dangerous to help an emerging nation to prolong the life span of its population by the introduction of sanitation, measures of disease control and infant care without simultaneously raising the level of agricultural production. Unless this is done, reducing the death rate will lead to catastrophe unless health measures are accompanied by effective education for birth control.

5. It is to the interest of the United States to help the less developed countries train technical and administrative personnel in conjunction with any effort to promote economic development.

6. Economic assistance should always be planned and financial appropriations for it should be made on a long-range basis.

7. Economic and technical assistance should, wherever possible, be channeled through multinational or international organizations.

8. Economic assistance should be divorced from military assistance. So-called defense-support economic aid to allies should be handled by the Defense Department and appropriations for such aid should come under the military budget.

9. Military and defense-support aid should never be permitted to distort the economy of an allied nation by causing

it to undertake military commitments for which an agricultural and industrial base is lacking.

10. Military aid should not be given to any country whose rearmament evokes countervailing rearmament by another. (E.g., Pakistan and India, or Israel and the Arab states.)

11. It is to the interest of the United States to promote triangular trade among nations and to eliminate wherever possible artificial barriers to the free exchange of goods and services. In this connection:

(a) It is necessary to apply a somewhat different standard to the industrialized nations on the one hand and to the less developed nations on the other; many of the latter temporarily need certain restrictive devices to protect their economic development and to avoid inflation.

(b) It is *not* to the interest of the United States to tie foreign loans or any kind of economic assistance to "Buy American" restrictions; to do so dilutes the aid given, provokes similar restrictions by other industrialized nations, and runs counter to the American interest in promoting world trade.

12. It is *not* to the interest of the United States to discriminate in giving economic assistance in favor of "capitalist" and against "socialist" nations. It is not reasonable to expect a nation in which there is little or no accumulation of private capital to adopt "free-enterprise capitalism."

13. While it is to the interest of the United States to encourage the growth of a middle class and the accumulation of private capital, it is *not* true that individual freedom can be provided only where these exist.

14. In many of the emerging nations it is not reasonable to expect the immediate development of Western-style democracy. India, for example, while in some respects quite dissimilar to a Western-style democracy, provides a high degree of respect and protection for the rights of the individual. It is inevitable that in most of the emerging na-

tions there will for a time be a high degree of concentration of political and economic power in the hands of an elite. The question is: "What sort of an elite?" The case of Pakistan illustrates how rearming and militarizing a newly independent country tends to create a military rather than a civilian oligarchy.

B. The Most Critical Areas

We shall not attempt to set forth a specific application of these principles to each individual nation. We shall, however, emphasize that, in our judgment, not nearly enough has been done to assist the development of India, Latin America, and the emerging nations of sub-Saharan Africa. These seem to us the crucially important areas in the immediate future. To say this does not imply satisfaction with what has so far been accomplished in other vitally important areas such as the Middle East.

C. Stabilization of Raw Material Prices

Much of the economic assistance which has been given to the underdeveloped areas has been offset by the failure of the industrialized nations to stabilize the world prices of primary raw materials. This is of particular importance to Latin America, Africa, and Southeast Asia, where most of the countries depend for their economic life upon the export of a few commodities, sometimes upon the export of a single raw material or foodstuff. The violent fluctuations in the price of these relatively few commodities cause alternate booms and depressions in the raw material-producing countries which they are powerless to prevent.

We recommend that the United States take the lead in studying this question and in eventually calling an international conference to consider what might be done to stabilize the market for the most important raw materials, or at least to cushion the extreme price fluctuations to which they are now subject.

D. A UN Development Authority

With reference to paragraphs 6 and 7 among the principles set forth in the first section of this chapter, we wish to put forward a specific suggestion.

The problem of aiding the underdeveloped countries is not solely one of providing technical advice and capital assistance. What is needed, first of all, is a true, empathetic understanding on the part of those who wish to assist these peoples to catch up to the mid-twentieth century.

Empathy is not the same as sympathy. Sympathy means sharing and, to a certain extent, agreeing with the feelings of others. Empathy means entering into another's state of mind and feeling, *without necessarily agreeing with it*. Sympathy requires merely an emotional identification, often based upon subjective factors rather than upon true understanding. Empathy requires a depth of understanding attainable only through the ability to project oneself fully into the position of another human being.

We, the American people, are long on sympathy, but we are woefully short of the ability to project ourselves into the mental and emotional state of peoples living in distant lands and in circumstances radically different from those to which we are accustomed. Most of us are regrettably ignorant of languages, cultures, religions, and historical backgrounds other than our own. Thus, with all our sympathy, our good intentions, and our abundant resources, we are ill equipped to render the help we desire to extend.

Our shortcoming in this respect is by no means unique. Nations with far more extensive experience than ours in dealing with other peoples, such as, for example, the European colonial powers, have often shown themselves curiously obtuse in understanding the psychology of those whom they call "the natives." What is more, they have frequently abused what understanding they possessed in order to exploit and oppress, rather than to assist and liberate.

True understanding of one people by another exists, broadly speaking, only within certain cultural families. The West Europeans, for example, thoroughly understand even when they do not like each other. The Indians understand the Burmese. The Arabs, disunited and torn though they are by dissension, understand each other. But it is scarcely necessary to point out how little understanding exists between the Arabs and the peoples of the West, or between Europe and Asia, or between us and the Spanish-speaking people of Latin America.

The point of these observations is that the empathetic understanding essential to helpful co-operation exists only collectively. No one nation—certainly not the United States —knows enough about all the peoples of the underdeveloped areas to render them effective assistance, because assistance, to be effective, must be rendered in terms of helping the recipients to realize their own aims in their own way, irrespective of whether those aims or means coincide or correspond with the ideas of those who render the assistance.

To say this is not to say that the countries in need of aid should be given whatever they ask or desire. Obviously sound judgment must be applied to conserve the available resources. The point is that only a collective judgment can in most cases be expected to produce constructive results.

Where can a collective judgment be formed?

The answer should, of course, be: in the United Nations. But here we encounter a serious obstacle.

The history of the development of the United Nations during the first fourteen years of its existence is marked by the unanticipated weakness of its quasi-executive organs and the consequent strengthening of the General Assembly.

The Security Council has been paralyzed not only by abuse of the veto but also through having become a forum for cold-war polemics. The Economic and Social Council has become impotent, chiefly because its deliberations and debates, conducted by relatively low-level representatives, are repeated by higher-level representatives in the General Assembly.

At the same time, the nature of the Assembly has been considerably altered by the admission of new members.

Broadly speaking, the balance of power in the original Assembly lay in the hands of the relatively more developed and wealthier countries of the North Atlantic community. It has now shifted toward the relatively underdeveloped and poorer nations of Asia, Africa, and the Middle East with whom some of the Latin American republics have tended more and more to ally themselves.

The problem which thus arises is that of an imbalance between the nations which will have to supply the greater part of the funds with which the United Nations must be endowed, if it is to act as the channel for aid to economic development, and the Assembly majority consisting of nations which will presumably be the beneficiaries of economic assistance. This accounts in large measure for the present reluctance of the wealthier nations to direct their economic aid through the world organization. It accounts for our own government's unwillingness to contribute to such projects as the proposed Special United Nations Fund for Economic Development (SUNFED).

Our suggestion for solving this problem is to create a United Nations Development Authority, so constituted as to give appropriate representation both to the nations supplying it with funds and to those seeking assistance. This could be done without Charter revision by a two-thirds vote of the Assembly, conceivably accompanied by a decision to abolish the Economic and Social Council, except for its Commission on Human Rights.

We visualize the Development Authority as being constituted somewhat along the lines of the Security Council, except that there would be no veto. Five seats would be allotted to the industrialized nations, to be occupied each year by the five particular nations which in the last year had made the largest contributions of funds. The remaining four seats would be occupied by rotating regional representatives of the underdeveloped nations.

Our concept calls for the creation of four regional subsidiaries of the parent body, one a Middle East Development Authority (previously discussed), the others located in Southeast Asia, Africa, and Latin America.[1] Each of these four regional boards, under an annually rotating chairman, would sift the problems and opportunities existing in its area and would assign priorities to the specific projects of which it approved. Each regional board would then, through its chairman, present its approved projects for consideration of the parent body.

The fixing of priorities among the projects recommended by the regional boards, as well as the allocation of funds, would be determined by the parent body in which the industrialized nations occupying the permanent seats would exercise the decisive influence. A majority of the five nations holding these seats would be required for approval of any project or appropriation.

Thus the ultimate control of the funds would rest with the United States and the four other major contributors, of which the Soviet Union could be one, if it elected to participate in the plan. However, the Soviet Union alone could not obstruct action since there would be no veto; nor could it, in the foreseeable future, control a majority of the permanent seats, even if China were to become a United Na-

---

[1] The existing regional UN Economic Commissions might conceivably be transformed into regional subsidiaries of the proposed UN Development Authority.

tions member and a major contributor to the Development Authority.

Should the Sino-Soviet bloc agree to participate, one of the major aspects of an economic cold war would be eliminated. On the other hand, should the Soviet Union decline to participate, it would lose much of its influence over the mostly unaligned peoples of the underdeveloped areas.

What would be the advantages of such a multinational approach, as opposed to the binational method by which we have been trying to solve the problem?

1. A United Nations Development Authority with its regional subsidiaries would be better equipped than the bureaucratic or legislative machinery of any one nation to understand and evaluate relative needs for assistance and to determine how and upon what conditions assistance should be rendered.

2. Conditions imposed by a United Nations Development Authority would be more readily accepted by beneficiary governments and peoples than would the same conditions, if imposed by any single nation. This would be especially important where such conditions might involve reforms fundamental to progress such as fiscal reform, or land reform, or the creation of credit facilities to displace firmly entrenched, usurious moneylenders.

3. A United Nations Development Authority could more readily make long-range plans and long-range commitments than can most national governments, especially our own. As already pointed out, this is vitally important because successful economic development requires planning for several years ahead and the assurance that capital for approved long-range plans will be available.

4. The suggested proposal would accomplish the purpose of stimulating other industrialized nations to shoulder a greater part of the burden for world-wide economic development and thus relieve the adverse balance of payments of the United States—far more effectively, in our

opinion, than the attempt to tie American loans and grants to purchases in the American market.

To repeat: If the Sino-Soviet bloc agreed to the proposal, the economic aspects of *competitive* coexistence would become *co-operative* coexistence. In that case a fifth region comprising the underdeveloped Communist countries might be added to the structure. If the United States were to put forward the proposal and the Sino-Soviet bloc were to reject it, the competitive position of the non-Communist nations would be improved, while the Sino-Soviet alliance would stand unmasked as being willing to supply economic aid solely in pursuance of its own political purposes.

It may be asked why the same purposes could not be served by the World Bank and its new soft-loan subsidiary, the International Development Association. There are two answers to this question:

1. The World Bank and its subsidiary are creations of the West. Admirable as have been the World Bank's accomplishments, this institution and its subsidiary are exclusively the instruments of the industrialized Western nations. The underdeveloped countries have no proprietary interest in these institutions; they deal with them as suppliants; they have no voice in their decisions. The Communist nations regard these institutions—no matter how unjustly—as tools of Western imperialism. If our purpose is ultimately to achieve world-wide co-operation in economic development, it seems to us desirable to create an instrument which all nations—rich or poor, Communist or anti-Communist—may regard as universal and impartial.

2. In view of the fact that the United Nations may be transformed into an organization capable of enforcing world law prohibiting national armaments, it would seem important in every possible way to broaden and strengthen its powers. From this point of view it would seem to us desirable to make the United Nations, rather than institutions created outside of its jurisdiction, into the instrument

of the widest possible international co-operation in laying the economic foundations for enduring peace.

VII THE FORMULATION AND EXECUTION OF UNITED STATES FOREIGN POLICY

A. *The Executive*

Theodore Roosevelt once said: "In a crisis, the duty of a leader is to lead."

We are living in a time of chronic crisis—a time in which continuous strong leadership by the Executive is essential to survival.

Strong leadership requires the capacity to reach a decision and, having reached it, the capacity to go forward wholly committed to the decision. It requires also a combination of wisdom and intuition which enables a leader to reach right decisions. But, above all, a leader must decide, for better or worse. He cannot afford indecision.

Under the Constitution of the United States, the President is the leader in matters of foreign policy, acting with "the advice and consent of the Senate." In recent times the implementation of foreign policy has become more and more dependent upon appropriations of funds and, for this reason, the House of Representatives has acquired a greater voice in the making of foreign policy than was contemplated by the Founding Fathers. Yet, while their concurrence is needed, neither the Senate nor the House can originate policy. Congress can only approve, reject, or modify the policy laid before it by the Executive.[2]

It follows that the Executive, having reached a decision, must act in close and continual consultation with the leaders of both Houses of Congress.

[2] Nevertheless, there are times like the present when members of the Congress can and should express their views concerning matters which vitally affect the nation's security.

It is our opinion that in recent years such consultation has been sporadic and insufficient; that policy decisions have often been lacking at the highest level; and that, when made, decisions have all too frequently been reversed without adequate explanation and consultation. For example: The Executive has opposed and then favored the creation of a Middle East Development Authority; it has opposed and then favored the creation of an Inter-American Bank; it has favored and then opposed providing the Development Loan Fund with the authority to make long-range commitments. In such cases the Executive has adequately explained to Congress neither its original decision nor its subsequent reversal.

It is further our opinion that the decisions of the Executive have in recent years been too strongly influenced by the Joint Chiefs of Staff, the Atomic Energy Commission, and the Bureau of the Budget.

We believe that foreign policy should not be dictated by the military; that, on the contrary, military policy should be subservient to political aims.

We believe that the people and their duly elected representatives have a right to know the facts upon which to base reasoned judgments; and that the decision as to what information may legitimately be withheld in the interest of national security should not be left to the military or to a quasi-military agency such as the Atomic Energy Commission.

We hold that it is not the function of the Bureau of the Budget but the function of the President and the Congress to decide what the nation can or cannot afford in national defense or in foreign policy expenditure.

Holding these views, we recommend a thorough re-examination of the foreign policy-making process, in which —as we see it—the military-dominated National Security Council and the Bureau of the Budget have far too heavily influenced Executive decisions.

We believe that a Secretary of State functions most effectively when he is in continuous touch with the Department of State and draws continuously upon its resources at home and abroad, as did Secretaries Stimson, Marshall, and Acheson. We do not believe that a Secretary of State should be a roving ambassador.

It is our view that insufficient funds are being provided for the Foreign Service. We recommend: (1) that appropriations for representation of the United States abroad should be adequate to provide that career diplomats or other eminently qualified individuals may fill the important posts throughout the world without having to draw upon private means to eke out insufficient salaries and expense allowances; and (2) that sufficient funds be appropriated *on a long-range basis* to make possible the institution of a long-range program of attracting, training, and holding desirable personnel in the Foreign Service.

B. The Legislative Branch

The effective co-operation of the Congress with the Executive in the making of foreign policy is, in our opinion, impeded by:

1. The overlapping and sometimes conflicting jurisdiction of a multiplicity of committees and subcommittees; and

2. The inadequate staffing of the committees and subcommittees dealing with various aspects of foreign policy.

With respect to the first difficulty, we recommend the appointment by concurrent resolution of the Senate and House of a commission of non-partisan experts whose mandate it shall be to study the existing committee structure and to suggest procedures by which this structure might be simplified and improved.

We call particular attention to the fact that, as matters now stand, foreign policy measures involving the appropriation of funds must pass through two separate processes: the first resulting in enabling legislation; the second resulting in the passage of the appropriation required. Frequently the first process entails prolonged debate which is then repeated in the second, often with somewhat different results.

We further call attention to the overlap between the Senate Committees on Foreign Relations and Armed Services, and between the House Committee on Foreign Affairs and the committees concerned with defense policy.

With respect to inadequate staffing, we suggest the possibility of providing a single, well-staffed and equipped Foreign Affairs Information Bureau which, in co-operation with the Library of Congress, would serve all congressional committees working in this area. Failing this, we recommend that both the Senate Foreign Relations Committee (and its subcommittees) and the House Foreign Affairs Committee (and its subcommittees) be provided with more extensive and better staff facilities.

C. *United States Information Service*

It is our opinion that propaganda can be no better than the policies which it seeks to explain and exploit. Benjamin Franklin once said: "It is hard to make an empty sack stand upright."

At present the basic defect of American propaganda is that it explains *what the United States is against,* but *not what the United States is for.* This is because United States foreign policy lacks a clearly defined affirmative purpose, such as we have endeavored to suggest in the preceding chapters.

In addition, United States propaganda conveys an *inaccurate impression of what we are.* It portrays the United States as an extremely rich country with a government which stands benevolently aside, leaving all planning and all decision to a "free-enterprise economy." This picture is not only one with which other people cannot possibly identify themselves; *it is also untrue.*

It is untrue because the cardinal principle of the great unfinished American experiment in freedom is that which was voiced by Abraham Lincoln, when he said: "The function of government is to do for the people that which needs to be done but which they cannot do for themselves at all or do equally well." It is on the basis of this principle that our government regulates, stimulates, and protects agriculture, industry, labor, and the public services. Upon the basis of this principle we have abolished child labor, established a minimum wage and social security—upon the basis of this principle we have collective bargaining, a free public school system, public housing, and government-financed road and river development.

The principle which Lincoln enunciated has been the dynamic of the American society ever since the nation was founded, even though in recent years the tempo of progress under it has been slowed down by a Republican administration which suffers from myopic vision and addiction to obsolete economic theory.

This—a nation conducting a great unfinished experiment in freedom through the co-operation of a people with its government—is what we are; and with this picture of the United States peoples throughout the world could in the past identify their own hopes and aspirations.

The reason why peoples in foreign lands can no longer identify themselves with us is chiefly because of the slowing down of our momentum, but also because we present ourselves as worse than we really are—as having reached the end of the great experiment, as being complacently satisfied with things as they are, and as being frightened of and hostile to change.

To be against change is to be against the hopes and longings of mankind.

The appeal of communism is that it has identified itself with change. The fact that communism, once adopted, denies change is not evident to those who have not yet lived under its dominion.

For us to present ourselves as merely being against communism, and not as being, above all, the protagonists of a continuous flow of revolutionary change, is to commit psychological suicide.

The Voice of America had better be silent, unless it is able to portray the American people as they really are—a people forever on the march in spite of inevitable temporary setbacks—a nation in which government, private enterprise, workers, and consumers are laboring ceaselessly together in the great, unfinished experiment.

To this end we believe that honest self-criticism is better propaganda than criticism of an adversary; that openly expressed interest in other people's ideas and experiments is better propaganda than glorification of our own achievements; and that the battle for the minds and hearts of men is more likely to be won by visions of the future than by expressed satisfaction with things as they are.

POSTSCRIPT

We stated at the outset that foreign policy inevitably reflects the domestic state of the Union. The recommendations for a new approach to foreign policy set forth in the foregoing cannot be adopted without a basic change in domestic philosophy, especially with respect to fiscal policy. The foreign policy we recommend cannot be based upon private extravagance and public parsimony. It requires not only broader vision of affirmative purpose on the part of leadership but less self-indulgence, harder work, and a greater sense of responsibility on the part of the American people.

We are convinced that, if leadership does its part, the people will respond.

This document represents a general consensus of those who offer it for the consideration of their colleagues and constituents, without binding any individual to every specific recommendation therein contained. Indeed, it is the hope of those who present it that the outline of policy here suggested will be improved by discussion and modified in accordance with rapidly changing circumstance.

THREE

A Liberal Military-Defense Policy

BY WALTER MILLIS

Journalist and writer on foreign and military policy; author of *Road to War* and *Arms and Men*

It is difficult to speak in terms of a specifically "liberal" defense policy. Few of the traditional liberal attitudes in this field—support for disarmament and collective security, insistence upon minimal armament expenditures, upon "civilian supremacy" and a reduction of military influence in foreign policy and domestic economic and social planning—are in themselves of much relevance to present problems. It is useless, for example, simply to inveigh against current tendencies toward the militarization of our polity and economy if these tendencies are no more than symptoms of deeper historic causes to which liberals may have contributed quite as much as conservatives or those of any other persuasion. Rather, one must look first for the sources of the symptoms. And if one does so, I think one is forced to the conclusion that they do not lie in any particular "threat" from outside, in any particularly aggressive or bellicose spirit on our own part, in any specifically "liberal" or "conservative" policies followed in the past. They arise, rather, from the nature of the war system itself.

As long as great nation-states—the democratic no less than the totalitarian, our own no less than the Russian or the Chinese—found their external relations upon the institution of war, they are bound to reap the results, in the form of internal militarization, of fear, of aggression, and of instability, which the war system in the supertechnical age imposes. It is difficult to see how a liberal statesmanship in the modern era can take as its ultimate goal anything less than the abolition of the war system itself. The abolition of war appears to demand, as its minimum requirement (and its minimum consequence) a universal and total disarmament, down to police-force levels, by all the nations of the world. In all its dealings with current issues of military policy, appropriations, organization, national "strategy," this must be consciously held as the final objective of liberalism in this field.

Unfortunately it is as yet a very remote objective. Policy may often be illumined and strengthened by a vision of the future; but it has to deal with the present, and it is as dangerous to sacrifice the present to an ideal future as it is to sacrifice the future to the traditions of the past. It would scarcely be reasonable or practicable to present universal disarmament as the sole guide to a liberal military policy in the present context. Assuming this to be the only rational liberal goal, the liberal must still face hard questions as to why this goal now seems unattainable, as to how the obstacles may in fact be removed, and as to the way in which specific military and defense policies may or may not conduce to its achievement. The defense appropriations (the embodiment of military policy at any given point) have to be adopted every year, and year by year one has to bring to them some more applicable tests than those which can be derived from a generalized enthusiasm for universal disarmament, or for any other revolutionary reorganization of world politics. It would be absurd (as well as quite futile) to attack the next defense budget on the ground that it nowhere provides for universal disarmament. The best one can do is to examine as critically as possible the basic military-defense policies to which it commits the nation, and then to ask whether better or sounder guide lines can be developed which will not hinder, even if they do little to promote, the ultimate goal. To do this it is necessary to look first at the military policies which are currently being followed.

AMERICAN DEFENSE POLICY

The United States appears to be effectively committed to a basic defense policy which is unduly logical and simplistic in conception, at the same that it is inordinately dangerous and difficult in practical application. As repeatedly stated by President Eisenhower and others of authority, it may be compactly summarized. It is: (a) to maintain a nuclear retaliatory mass-destruction force which will prevent ("deter") a resort to mass-destruction war by anybody under any circumstances (as the President has said, this force is "not to be used, but to make certain that the other fellow doesn't use his"); and (b) to retain for the United States a maximum freedom of military threat and military action compatible with the limitations which attainment of the first objective must impose. The more "conventional" military establishments will be kept up, as the President has explained, "to meet situations of less than general war." Finally, (c) in order to overcome the perils and inconsistencies concealed in the first two objectives, we will continue "to work for disarmament," though the kind and scope of the disarmament for which we will work, the effects to be expected of it, or the manner in which we will "work" for it have never been defined with any precision.

So formulated, this basic policy has certain significant features. It is the product not of any coherent and far-sighted plan, but of a confused history. It is a kind of resultant of all the shocks, the disputes, the diplomatic experiments, the technological changes, the budgetary and interservice compromises which have occurred since the first military application of atomic energy in 1945. The loss of the atomic monopoly, the development of the hydrogen bomb, the Soviet achievements in missile delivery

99

have all contributed to it; so have the Korean War, the death of Stalin, the ill success of the policy of "a capacity for massive retaliation," the varying fortunes of NATO, and much besides. As it has presently emerged, it looks less like a rational analysis of the world military problem than a statement of what seems to be about the best that can be done in the situation at which we have arrived.

Again, while the policy has been affected by all these factors, it has at the same time grown in much the same isolation as has characterized most military planning—and especially American military planning—in the past. Starting from the assumption—by no means wholly sound—that the United States will never wish to levy war upon others, our publics and policy makers tend to think of military policy as something specialized, apart from the general run of national policy, simply a kind of "insurance" against unforeseeable emergency. Since 1945 the nation has been at great pains to combine its military, diplomatic, and budgetary policy into a consistent whole, through such agencies as the National Security Council or the hundreds of lesser joint boards and commissions operating in the security field. But the results have not been too effective; and most discussions of military policy, both inside and outside of government, remain compartmented from the practical world of international relations which that policy is supposed to affect and reflect.

These characteristics of the basic policy contribute to its vagueness as a guide in face of concrete questions as to budget levels, the allocation of weapons systems, the arming of NATO and other allies, the specific diplomatic posture to be adopted in such crises as that over Berlin, the proper response to the "missile gap," and so on. They contribute to the undue disproportion between the amounts of heat and of light generated by current argument over defense issues. But the announced basic policy is open to much deeper criticism. It fails to meet or deal with the two central questions which it raises. Does "deterrence" mean the *prevention* of nuclear war, or only its *discouragement* up to that point (sooner or later inevitable) at which it must take place? Does the retention of freedom of military action in "situations of less than general war" authorize us to take military action in any situation which appears adversely to affect our national interest, or does it impose limits on what we can expect to defend by military means? Present policy answers neither question. By that familiar process which has been aptly called "simulopt"—the simultaneous adoption of mutually incompatible or contradictory courses—the only reply it returns to either question is: "Yes." This is not helpful.

DETERRENCE

Throughout, "deterrence" has been a dangerously weasel word, used indiscriminately in either of its senses in accordance with the exigencies of the moment or the pressures under which the given statesman or publicist may be speaking. When a President says that the great weapons "are not to be used," he is talking about the absolute prevention of any nuclear war whatever. But when he says (as President Eisenhower has said) that the United States will not "fight a ground war" for Berlin, he is talking about the discouragement of a nuclear war, yet at the same time calling the weapons to his aid in a situation which might well require their employment.

Yet this is logically impermissible for a policy based upon the prevention of mass-destruction war through the mechanism of retaliatory mass destruction. If the weapons should ever in fact be used, the policy itself would have failed catastrophically, thus demonstrating its tragic inutility for attaining the only object for which it had been adopted. A military policy of mass-destruction deterrence is actually no more nor less than a form of gigantic blackmail, and as with other forms of blackmail its threats are valueless if they ever have to be made good. Unless mass-

destruction deterrence succeeds absolutely in its only rational purpose—to prevent altogether—it is a total failure;
and what might happen thereafter, how the subsequent
war would be waged or who would win or how many
would survive, becomes an almost academic question. The
appalling nature of the weaponry considered necessary to
guarantee that deterrence will succeed—including multimegaton thermonuclear bombs capable of destroying scores
of millions of innocent "enemy" lives in a space of hours—
can insure only that if deterrence does not succeed the
consequences will be intolerable under any rational social
policy.

This situation, an inherent result of the development of
the megaton bombs, is difficult to state and difficult for
anyone, whether a soldier or a statesman or a citizen, to
accept. Yet the dilemma is inescapable, and all the twists
and turnings of the new strategists of deterrence have
failed to evade it. Their efforts to demonstrate that with
proper dispersion and shelter systems casualties could, after
all, be reduced to supportable levels can tend only to trans-
form the military system from one for preventing mass-
destruction war into one for fighting it. The extraordinary
way in which their reasoning compels them to convert
passive (civil) defense into an offensive weapon is a case
in point. The argument runs that if the Russians had prepared a large shelter and evacuation system in advance
they could at a chosen moment put a sufficient proportion
of their people in safety and then threaten to wreak a
devastation upon the unprotected populations of the West
to which Western retaliatory forces could no longer make
a corresponding reply. Passive defense (like "defensive
mobilization" in 1914, of which it has often been said that
"mobilization meant war") thus becomes a weapon of aggression. There is no answer to this fearful form of attack
except to build up Western shelter and dispersion systems.
The West must embark upon still another form of arms
competition—competitive digging in. The argument, of

course, is that by keeping even in competitive protection, the balance of terror will be maintained and nuclear war will still be "deterred." It overlooks the fact that if competitive protection can reduce the probable destruction of nuclear warfare to mutually acceptable levels, it will only make a nuclear exchange once more a practicable military concept. This might suffice to maintain the terror balance. It seems much more likely simply to license a nuclear exchange.

There is no escape through such reasonings from the dilemma that the system of retaliatory mass destruction must serve either to prevent mass-destruction warfare or to make it possible; that the two objectives are incompatible and that, in large measure, to the degree in which policy provides for success in one it must insure failure in the other. Which aim does present policy follow? The only available answer is: "Both."

"LESS THAN GENERAL WAR"

Assuming that the multimegaton weapons can be held in suspense indefinitely, what are the "situations of less than general war" in which the United States can retain its freedom of conventional military action? On this vital question current policy is again silent, or ambivalent. Presumably issues may arise—a military struggle over the Chinese coastal islands comes to mind as a possible example—which would be susceptible to military settlement without evoking a general nucleonic war. For such issues "limited war" seems a possible and appropriate answer. In general they will be of one of two kinds: issues in which the preponderance of one side is so great that it can enforce a favorable decision without more than a partial mobilization of its total power; and issues in which each side recognizes that even an adverse decision, however unpalatable, is to be preferred to the total effort which would be necessary to overturn it. One can find examples of each kind in the many limited wars of the past century or so; interestingly enough, the Korean War—the greatest limited war of our times—was an example of both. Up through the rout of the North Koreans, complete by November of 1950, it was a war limited by the massive preponderance of the United Nations power; from the Chinese intervention at the end of November it was a war limited by the fact that neither contestant preferred total triumph to the costs and effort necessary to achieve it. The first phase of the war ended in a conventional victory for the West; the second ended, as wars limited in this way must almost necessarily end, in a stalemate and a restoration of the *status quo ante*. Limited wars, in whatever sense the term is used, seem possible only in situations in which stalemate is, for each side, preferable to victory.

These are the "situations of less than general war" for which our policy proposes to use the "non-strategic" military, air, and naval forces. But what are they, and how can they be recognized in advance? General Maxwell D. Taylor tells us in his memoirs that he spent much of his four-year term as Army chief of staff arguing with his colleagues on JCS as to whether Western Europe could be defended by limited war. Taylor felt that it would have to be, because if its only defense was the superbombs it would not be defended at all. But to the Air Force this was virtually "treason," because to provide a conventional defense for Western Europe would be to convey to the Russians the idea that we did not, after all, really intend to exterminate them with the megaton weapons, and thus license them to an attack which the conventional forces could not resist. In the specific case of West Berlin, nobody now knows whether even a minor military threat to the city would be a case of "less than general war" or the beginning of a nuclear holocaust. To the question of which sort of situation it presents, present policy again answers simply: "Yes."

And again it is not helpful. General Taylor argues that

by raising the defense budget to about sixty billion dollars we could provide a conventional military system adequate to defend Western Europe without recourse to the thermonuclears. Is the conscientious citizen, or the liberal legislator, to support or oppose this program? The announced military policy affords him no guidance; it tells him in effect to do both—and, one might add, to be damned whatever he does.

SEARCH FOR A FIRMER FOUNDATION

The basic policy as declared not only fails to offer any firm guide in concrete problems of budget limits, force levels, or optimum weapons systems, but presents dangers of an appalling kind. The best it can promise in the long run is a continued, competitive build-up of two colossal time bombs, bound to set each other off sooner or later and already capable of destroying civilization between them. Meanwhile, although it is almost certainly true that no authoritative statesman anywhere is either desirous of, planning, or intending to set off the explosion, we must live in the shadow of the likelihood that it will come sooner, rather than later, through sheer accident or, more probably, through miscalculation. For many, the policy involves another kind of peril. The more careful we are in avoiding, under its terms, the total nuclear disaster, the more it exposes us to Communist erosion of diplomatic, political, and moral positions which seem vital. This is a dilemma which none of the many exponents of "limited war" has as yet successfully escaped. Simple and logical as the basic policy must seem, it is almost impossibly dangerous and difficult when one comes to its practical application.

There must, it would seem, be a better foundation on which to rest American military and defense policy than this. Yet the search for such a foundation must be rightly directed and cannot be too ambitious. In confronting present military and defense policy, one is dealing, as has been suggested, not with a program but with a growth—an outgrowth of many contradictory historical factors. One can hardly hope to devise a completely rational and self-consistent program to put in its place—or one cannot hope to do so, at least, with any chance of its practical acceptance. One cannot ask complete and logical consistency of the modern policy maker, laboring as he is under enormous responsibilities in face of a never predictable future; one cannot expect him to stake everything on any one view of historical causation, or fail to keep open alternative—even though quite contradictory—courses. "Simulopt" has its virtues as well as its obvious vices and is in any case a probably inescapable disease of modern statesmanship. But the individual citizen, even the individual legislator, with a lesser responsibility has an even greater obligation.

The relative roles of the Congress and the Executive in policy formation and decision-making is a subject which raises practical and constitutional questions which need not be discussed here. But whatever may be the appropriate function of the Congress as a body, the function of the individual congressman can never be the same as that of the single responsible Executive. The Executive must declare the final decision; the most that one among many congressmen can do is to influence it. Precisely because he will seldom have to accept sole responsibility, the conscientious legislator, like the conscientious citizen, has both a greater freedom and a more urgent duty to advocate only consistent and rational policies. It is not normally the function of the individual citizen, or legislator, to dictate the critical decisions; it is always their responsibility to create the backgrounds of principle and attitudes and ideas out of which rational decision can grow.

What is set forth below as a possible liberal and rational defense policy is not, therefore, anything in the nature of a program. It does not deal with dollars, or weapons systems, or specific strategies. It attempts to state the underlying attitudes, the approaches to the international problem, the ideas about the nature of our world, which might support more rational specific programs.

BASIC PRINCIPLES

I. Defense policy must be always and immediately related to the actual world in which it operates. Military power, in a multimegaton age, is neither "a form of insurance" nor "a fire department." It is not simply a hedge against hypothetical future possibilities but the one most dominant fact in the world of today.

Acceptance of this principle is essential in order to rescue us from the fantastic world in which we have been involved by the games theorists of "deterrence," obsessed by what the Russians "might do" rather than by what they are likely to do. It is, to be sure, a hallowed principle of military combat intelligence always to base estimates on an enemy's "capabilities" rather than his "intentions." But this principle, however sound in combat—when the enemy's goal, victory, is obvious and his capabilities are both limited and roughly ascertainable—verges on nonsense when carried over into the non-combat relations of international affairs. There the putative enemy's real goals are various, complex, often (like our own) self-contradictory; his "capabilities" are so numerous that a valid estimate is almost impossible or, if attempted, is bound to open so wide a range of possible action as to be not only a useless but a misleading guide to statesmanship. The only practicable guide must be in the best possible estimate of the intentions of the hostile statesmen based on the pressures to which they appear to respond, the motives that can be deduced from the actual situations which they occupy.

Current arguments over the alleged "missile gap" are a case in point. They usually rest on the assumption that as soon as the Russians' superiority in missiles gives them a "capability" of reducing Western retaliatory forces to a level at which they could inflict no more than "acceptable" damage to the U.S.S.R., the Russians will immediately employ the missile for this purpose. But this assumption not only involves so many imponderables (what is "no more than acceptable damage"? what level of missile superiority will the Russians consider necessary?), it also leaves out so vast a range of other calculations, motivations, purposes that would actually control Russian actions as to become a fantastically unreal basis for American policy.

In the grim literature of the subject one encounters a frequent nightmare. The Russians have "knocked out" our retaliatory force (or conversely put their population in safety against it); they then make their "demands" on the United States on pain of nuclear extermination. The United States, thus rendered "helpless," has no course save to acquiesce. But few stop to picture the concrete circumstances under which such a situation would in fact arise, even less to ask what good the Soviet threat would be if it were simply rejected by the United States. Would there be any reason why the actual annihilation would follow?

These extreme calculations of possibilities should never be allowed to confuse the probabilities of the actual world we inhabit. We can never guard against all *possible* risks and in a megaton age can only raise greater risks by attempting to do so. It is enough if we can take care of the probable risks.

In another way, policy (and the public attitudes toward it) should be restrained to the actualities of today rather than dubious nightmares about a putative future. Though commonly attempted in military and armament debates, no successful military policy can be constructed on a consideration of abstract possibilities. There is only a certain number of armed nations in the world; there is only a finite (and in fact rather small) number of potentially dangerous situations. In all the talk about "brush-fire wars," it is seldom recognized that today there are only a few spots in which a "brush-fire war" could in fact take place and probably even fewer in which there is any likelihood of one occurring. Official spokesmen may often find it difficult to be specific because of the diplomatic consequences; but those whose part it is to support them in rational courses are under no such limitation; and the more specific, the more concrete the terms in which the real world problem is approached the better will be the results.

II. The sole purpose of the nucleonic mass-destruction arsenals is to prevent their use by anyone under any conditions. They do not, as President Eisenhower has said, exist to be used but to make "certain" that they are not used by anyone, and unless they can achieve a very high degree of certainty the policies we are now basing on them should be rebuilt.

A clear and unequivocal recognition of this principle and its emphatic enunciation to the world should greatly simplify the whole problem. It is the principle already declared by the Soviet Union as well as by the United States. The United States has been unwilling to make a formal undertaking to the effect that it will never resort in the first instance to nuclear weapons, for prudential reasons which may or may not be valid. But there should be no question that American policy is firmly based on this principle; and those whose attitudes and utterances may affect policy should never lose sight of it.

Once it is commonly accepted that the one object of deterrence is to deter—that is, to *prevent*—the problem should become more manageable. Oskar Morgenstern has pointed out that the theoretically ideal situation for deterrence is one in which each of the two nuclear powers possesses completely invulnerable retaliatory striking forces to which the populations and cities of the other are completely exposed. If A's retaliatory force is invulnerable, it offers no temptation to B to try a surprise "first strike" against it; if B's population is completely exposed, B cannot risk opening of mass-destruction war. The situation is the same whether looked at from the Soviet or the American view. In place of present pressures to get in a surprise first strike at all costs, the pressure would all be the other way—to withhold the nuclear strike as long as possible. Once *both* sides are armed with missiles, invulnerable on their launching pads but unstoppable once sent on their way, the supposed present need for first-strike action and hair-trigger reaction would disappear; a genuinely deterrent situation would have been established in which all the pressures would be toward caution and restraint.

Actually, despite our more feverish current imaginings, such a situation very largely exists today. The pressures toward caution on both sides of the Atlantic are obvious. Few Western Europeans really believe in the "credibility" of the American threat to defend them with mass-destruction retaliation. They do not believe that in a crisis we would really lay New York or Chicago or Los Angeles open to total devastation in order to defend West Germany or France or Denmark. Why, then, are they not more alarmed? Probably because they no longer believe that such a crisis is ever likely to arise. They believe that deterrence has deterred, that it will continue to do so, and that there is no hedge against the possibility for its failure.

The French General Pierre Gallois has drawn a significant distinction between "the strategy of operations," which has dominated military thought through the millennia, and still too markedly dominates American military thought, and "the strategy of means," which has actually come to dominate history in the modern era. Actual military operations accomplished only a small part of the vast results of the modern wars, which would have ended much as they did regardless of the brilliance or stupidity of the operational strategies employed. What ultimately counted were the politics, the logistics, the great balances of forces and resources. Eisenhower was not a general; he was a general manager. Those who conduct the contemporary military policies of great states must be general managers in a much wider sense, planning, not successful military operations but successful results, in which international operations will have only that modicum of importance which can be attached to them. Military operations with multimegaton bombs can have no importance in practical policy, because no conceivably desirable results can be produced with them. The absolute prevention of their use is all that can properly concern a strategy of means.

Approached in this way, there are many possibilities for insuring that deterrence really deters, which seem difficult to explore today. It would seem to follow from Morgenstern's suggestion that a genuinely deterrent policy would require the United States to co-operate with the Soviet Union in insuring that their retaliatory force was as invulnerable as ours and that our population was equally exposed to attack with theirs. This will, of course, seem fantastic as a serious policy proposal. Yet if this is the ideal end of a deterrent system, it is likely to be the end toward which the two forces would tend—indeed, it is the end toward which they actually have been tending since the Soviet rejection of the Baruch Plan and their determination to develop a nuclear deterrent of their own. Is it impossible that tacit understanding could be developed into more and more explicit undertakings?

There are possibilities of arriving at a clearer mutual understanding of the kind of situations in which resort to a multimegaton exchange must be accepted, and the kind in which it will not occur. One admits all the difficulties in the way of such understanding. It is quite clear that there exists today a tacit Soviet-American understanding that there will not be a nuclear exchange over West Berlin; yet to reduce this to firm statement, even more to determine what measure of force can be applied to the West Berlin situation, seems presently impossible. A rational approach to defense policy can only insist that the more clearly all sides recognize the basic principle that the great weapons exist *only* to prevent their use, the more avenues will in practice open up through which they can be made to serve that end. And whatever risks may be run by a policy grounded in this principle will be less than those entailed by the extreme and mathematical calculations of "operations analysis," based upon assumptions as to the elements involved in the present power struggle for which there is little foundation in fact.

III. On the postulate that the great weapons not only must but can be neutralized (as they appear to be today) military policies must give constant and careful scrutiny to the remaining functions of the armed forces.

A rational approach to military policy has a right and duty to insist on far better answers than are commonly given to innumerable questions concerning the size and purpose, the weaponing, the organization of the non-retaliatory forces. Is it possible to distinguish, in advance, "situations of less than general war" in which such forces would be used from situations of general war? We have endowed all our "conventional" forces with a so-called "tactical" atomic capability. How are these weapons expected in fact to operate? Are there situations in which to employ them would almost certainly precipitate general nuclear war? In which they could be employed without this risk? In which the conventional forces would not employ them at all?

Do such forces in fact have any military uses in the existing world context, and if so, what are they? It is possible to think of some—to act as a "trip-wire," to prevent or repel minor raids and aggressions, to control suddenly unfavorable local developments (as in the Lebanon landing), and to fight even a fairly large-scale peripheral war, such as might come about through a renewal of hostilities in

Korea or in Southeast Asia. But such possibilities are of a definitely limited order.

Do such forces have other primarily political or even propagandist uses? This is perhaps true. Some time ago a combined maneuver involving some 5000 men, including small contingents from half a dozen Latin American states, simulated a "defense" of the Panama Canal. The military unreality of this exercise was so apparent that it could only be explained as a political maneuver, valuable simply for expressing the political solidarity of Inter-American defense. Again, General Lauris Norstad, in announcing the proposed formation of a mobile multinational NATO brigade with "atomic capability," indicated that its value was mainly political. A congressional committee, after assuring itself that the "atomic capability" would remain in the hands of the United States component of this force, appears to have had no further interest in the military consequences —in what the force would be expected to do, in how it would affect the balances of deterrence in Europe, or in any other of the rather serious military questions it might seem to raise.

In the presence of the two great retaliatory arsenals it seems almost inconceivable that the fate of Germany and Western Europe could be decided by a conventional war— especially one in which both sides would be armed with "tactical" atomic weapons. Is there any reason, therefore, in re-creating an essentially World War II type of military mobilization system (such as has been recommended by General Taylor) to attempt such a decision? But if the answer is in the negative, is there any reason for special concern over the large Soviet superiority (which, incidentally, the U.S.S.R. is proposing unilaterally to reduce) in conventional forces? The existence of such forces cannot, obviously, be wholly neglected by Western military policy. They raise possibilities of minor or peripheral conventional warfare which must be considered. But if the West never intends to meet them in all-out struggle on their own terms, their size is no particular measure for Western conventional strength. What must concern the West is not the "strategy of operations" but the "strategy of means," in which military operations have in fact been reduced to a strictly secondary role.

A rational, or "liberal," attitude toward defense policy must begin, it would seem, by testing all specific programs, all arguments for this or that type of weapon system or this or that degree of military preparedness, against the probable actual function of military violence in the world to which we have been brought by the megaton retaliatory arsenal. The history of the past fifteen years—which includes the neutralization alike of the Soviet conventional preponderance and the American atomic monopoly while it lasted; which includes the stalemates in Korea and Indo-China; the fiasco in Suez; the near farce in Lebanon; the immolation of the Hungarian Revolution; the tragicomedy of Quemoy and Matsu—indicates that while military forces still have a significant part to play in the world's gropings toward world order, it is, and is likely to remain, a quite minor part. We appear to have reached quite definite limits as to what can be accomplished by slaughtering nationals of other powers, destroying their productive capacity, or even forcibly occupying their territory. The liberal or rational attitude toward military policy must find its deepest foundation in an appreciation not simply of the costs and cruelties of war but of the essential irrelevance of the military problem to most of the real issues of the world we inhabit.

IV. *It is useless, as well as misleading, to pursue "disarmament" in the abstract as if it were, in and of itself, a remedy that could rescue us from the contradictions involved in accepted military policy. The reduction of the perils, as well as the burdens, of armaments must remain a primary goal of rational policy. But it is a goal which must be sought more rationally than in the past.*

Through the past ten years in which the effort has been pursued, no real progress has ever been made with "disarmament" as such; and despite the earnestness with which the effort is today being renewed, there is little hope for progress in the proximate future. This, it may be said, is because it has never been possible to correlate the various proposals for arms limitation or reduction to the real functions which arms can or cannot discharge in the contemporary world. To be hopeful, any disarmament proposal or program must, it would seem, be adjusted to the uses which military force is expected to serve. If disarmament seems a more promising goal today than it was after 1898 (when the Czar of Russia first called for a disarmament conference), or in the early thirties (when the League of Nations wrestled exhaustively with the problem), or after 1945 (when the UN confronted the issue), it is not because any of the nations has really changed its motivations. It is because the uses of military force appear to have declined so drastically in the contemporary international system.

It seems most unlikely that any policy of disarmament can succeed so long as it is based only upon an uncomplicated desire to reduce the levels of armaments. It must, surely, begin with some serious analysis of the true role of military force in the contemporary world; and this must, it would seem, begin with the principle enunciated above. Admittedly an approach of this kind might lead to some seemingly quite fantastic results. Current disarmament policy appears to be directed toward two main objectives: the "control," considered as leading toward the ultimate abolition, of nuclear weapons, accompanied by a balancing, *pari passu* reduction of conventional arms. Since there is little presently visible prospect of achieving either, one may ask what a different approach might yield.

The great nuclear weapons appear to have introduced whatever measure of military stability exists in the present world. Clearly it is a present stability purchased only at the price of a frightful future risk; but it seems to be to the great weapons, more than any other one factor, that we owe the fact that we are not now tearing ourselves to pieces in a third global war. Can we, then, contemplate a policy which would not begin by trying simply to abolish them, but rather by trying consciously to balance them, to conserve the stabilities which they do provide while reducing or eliminating the appalling instabilities implicit in their competitive technical development?

The great weapons have already rendered most of the conventional armaments meaningless. The U.S.S.R.'s reported 175 conventionally armed divisions have little greater effect on world policy today than the exiguous NATO divisions or the fourteen United States Army divisions. A rational disarmament policy might well forget the whole lot on either side of the line; it might then concentrate not on abolishing the nuclear arsenals, but on keeping them in a reasonable deterrent balance, and leave the conventional forces to rise or fall according to whatever internal exigencies might determine their fate. As a program of "disarmament" this must seem grotesque. It is clear that to make any progress with it a much better communication must be established between Western, Soviet, and Chinese leaders than any which has existed since 1945. This is not to say that we must learn to "trust" the Russians, or they to trust us, but that each must arrive at a better understanding of the true motivations operable with the other. This seems extraordinarily difficult to do—and certainly cannot be done through any number of summit meetings or UN debates. Yet it is through processes of this kind that arms and armaments seem in fact to have waxed or waned in world history.

A LIBERAL DEFENSE POLICY

The conscientious citizen, and normally the conscientious legislator, does not bear final responsibility for policy formulation. Relieved of the obligation to decide, he has, as has been said, only a deeper obligation to bring rational and consistent criticism to the decisions which are made, to discern the meretricious and support the valid in the determinations of the policy makers. The above has been an attempt to outline the principles which he might bring to this task.

It is not believed to be an appropriate function for a paper of this character to try to develop from these principles a specific program. The programs will no doubt continue in the future as in the past to be hammered out under contradictory influences and countervailing pressures; they will never be completely consistent, and the more logically one tries to plan, the more likely one is to produce an impossibly artificial structure which in some important respect or other will fail to fulfill the expectations.

What follows is not, therefore, offered as a program but rather as a personal prediction of the results to which a maximum of rationality in defense planning could be expected to tend. It is the writer's belief that a rational military establishment would not differ very greatly—in size, cost, or organization—from what has in fact been hammered out through the compromises and controversies of the Eisenhower administration. Some present excrescences and extravagances of concept would be pruned away; some continuing survival from outmoded tradition would be dispensed with; some organizational improvements in command and policy-making agencies would be effected. But, broadly speaking, it seems that the present military program is a generally moderate, reasonable, and sufficient answer to the real military problem, and one would not expect it to undergo drastic change.

One would expect the military establishment to be clearly, consciously, and sharply divided into the retaliatory force or apparatus—charged with the sole function of insuring that it would never in fact be used—and the non-retaliatory or conventional apparatus to meet all other military requirements. There seems little merit in the suggestion to abolish the three existing services, to replace them with a retaliatory, a non-retaliatory, and a "defense" service. But it does seem dangerous and rather grotesque to have high-yield nuclear weapons—good only as preventives —scattered through three or four different service-command systems as well as the ambiguous command relationships of NATO. If it is undesirable to amalgamate the services, it seems essential to put all retaliatory weapons under a unified command, comparable to the unified theater commands familiar since the Second World War, and clearly instructed in its mission.

A single continuing command is less necessary for the conventional war forces—which one would expect to be put together under temporary theater commanders as occasion served. The probable development here seems obvious— in the direction of comparatively small, long-service professional forces, well armed, but with some better understanding than exists at present of the relation between the character of the weapons and the military responsibilities of the forces. At the time of the Lebanon landing, it is said that an Army rocket team was not permitted to land because all it had was tactical atomic weapons; there is also a story that the Navy carriers were embarrassed to rid themselves of their atomic weapons so as to carry in only old-fashioned "fire power." Such contretemps are absurd. It seems probable that the "conventional" forces will be relieved of the responsibility either to wage or to prepare for a mass war of the Second World War pattern. There is little question that a great deal in the present conscription and mass mobilization system is sheer anachronistic waste of time and effort. Most of it is maintained today, not because the military services feel any real need for reserves, but because they are terrified lest they could not get a sufficiency of volunteer recruits unless the compulsions of the draft were maintained. The obvious answer seems to be either a pay scale that will produce the volunteers or a genuinely selective service system that will choose the men required without endlessly wasting the time and morale of thousands who will never be required and for whom compulsory service has become simply a meaningless chore.

A genuinely retaliatory nuclear force, a real "limited war" force, professional and long-service, like the police forces of our cities, seem the obvious indications for the future. What about "defense"? Again, reasonable precautions must undoubtedly be taken. But to make civil defense (whether active or passive) into a military weapon of aggression seems to pass the bounds of common sense. The great nuclear arsenals exist only to prevent attack. The degree to which this preventive function can be strengthened by digging the civilians into the ground and preparing to evacuate our "*A* country" (this is Herman Kahn's concept) into a cowering existence in our "*B* country" seems grossly exaggerated. The reasonable view will hope that our retaliatory deterrent will in fact deter and will plan no further. If it does not deter, no plans will amount to much, anyway, and none—certainly—will operate as they are supposed to do.

A "liberal" military policy must probably be constructed in the same way as liberal policy in any other field—by as exact and realistic an analysis as possible of the factors concerned, and thereafter by a large skepticism as to all programmatic extremes, an understanding that all human history is fluid and unpredictable and that the moderate course, even if illogical, is likely to turn out best in the end.

FOUR

The Theory and Practice of Deterrence

BY ARTHUR WASKOW

Member of the Senior Staff of The Peace Research Institute, Washington, D. C.; author of *The Limits of Defense*.

In recent years "deterrence" has become the fundamental concept in all official proposals for the protection of American national security. At the same time there has developed more and more disagreement on the meaning of "deterrence." In the last several months we have attempted to clarify these various meanings, to spell out the full implications of the sometimes incoherent proposals of various defense experts, and to assess the practical worth of the major alternatives now presented by various spokesmen in the Department of Defense.

In addition to published materials, our chief sources for the various opinions expressed have been interviews with a number of policy-making officers and civilian officials in the various services, in the Department of Defense central organization, and in other government agencies involved in the problem, such as the Office of Civil and Defense Mobilization.

We focused on such questions as these: what kinds of wars does the Department of Defense expect to deter?; what weapons systems would be involved in various methods of deterrence; what is the role of civil defense, as a component or a complement of particular weapons systems, conceived to be?; what types of service reorganization are considered necessary to support any given notion of deterrence?; and whether particular branches of the services of particular agencies espoused particular versions of deterrence. We also tried to explore the varied theoretical explanations of how the psychology of deterrence would operate.

Finally, after examining the theories themselves, we have examined the kinds of practical action the Congress can take in regard to them.

THE COUNTERFORCE THEORY OF DETERRENCE

A number of officers and administrators, mainly in the Air Force, are convinced that thermonuclear war is possible, conceivable, acceptable, and that it will be "won" or "lost" in the classical sense. These men agree that it would be preferable to prevent such a war from taking place, but they think the only effective prevention is the establishment of a force capable of winning such a war and accepting the surrender of the enemy. Against the common belief that thermonuclear war is inconceivable, they have tried to construct a rational model of the probable course of such a war—rational in the literal sense that they expect the highest rationality to be maintained by fighters and governments on both sides. Counterforce theorists assume that the authorities who engage in thermonuclear war will, at least, attempt to restrict as far as possible the great damage that would result from thermonuclear war.

This group conceives that war might come in one of two major ways: the Sino-Soviet bloc might launch a major atomic strike at the United States; alternatively, the bloc might act against some area other than the United States in such an intensely provocative way—for example, by invading Western Europe or Japan—that the United States might decide to make a first atomic strike[1] against the Communist bloc.

[1] All segments of the Defense Department seem to assume that the United States will not be the first to take a warlike act. But some segments would want a Sino-Soviet act of low-level

In either case this group expects the action of the United States to be "counterforce" action. They would expect American attack to be directed not against populations or industry but against the atomic capability of the enemy. They come to this conclusion through two alternative chains of reasoning. One hypothesis is that if the enemy makes a surprise attack with nuclear weapons his first target would be American atomic forces. An American counterattack directed against enemy cities would be suicidal, since it would invite enemy retaliation against American cities with unscathed atomic forces. Hence, American atomic forces which survive the initial attack should be directed at enemy atomic capabilities, in the hope of destroying them. In the second chain of reasoning, the United States would respond to a major provocation by attacking enemy atomic capabilities with thermonuclear bombs. Only in this way would there be hope of preventing a Soviet atomic strike against our cities, on the theory that the Soviets would have nothing left to strike back with.

The counterforce theorists argue that both United States and Soviet atomic-striking forces are sufficiently remote from population centers; in consequence, war between THESE atomic forces would not absolutely destroy the American and Russian peoples. These theorists estimate that up to thirty million Americans might die in such a war, but they regard this as an acceptable loss. They believe that after absorbing such a blow the United States and Soviet governments would still be able to act by rational calculation in attempts to minimize destruction. They assume that capitals would not be destroyed nor governments annihilated, simply because such annihilation would not be to the advantage of the attacking power. Both sides, they believe, would want governments left intact to minimize conflict and simplify surrender.

---

war (such as conventionally armed invasion or even subversion) answered by a high-level American act, even the first use of nuclear weapons.

When mobile land missiles like the Minuteman are in operation on both sides, counterforce theorists recognize the need to pin-point the atomic forces one was trying to destroy; therefore, they suggest that an atomic war of this nature would not be a matter of mere hours. Protracted air reconnaissance would be necessary to hunt down and destroy mobile missiles. During this period civilian populations would wait (either in their home cities or in specially prepared underground "city" sites) for days and weeks while thermonuclear attacks on thermonuclear forces went on around them. This desperate war of attrition will end when the nation that had begun with the larger, more protected, and better-directed atomic force has some atomic-strike capacity left, the other having exhausted its capacity. The nation that had been ahead would demand and receive the surrender of the other.

In the event of a major Soviet provocation short of direct attack on the United States, American populations might be evacuated to previously prepared gigantic shelter areas. Such evacuation would free the United States to demand a withdrawal of the Soviet provocative act on pain of atomic attack upon the Soviet Union. Thus, whether in their cities (theoretically remote from the missile sites and air bases that would be the focus of attack) or in such mass shelters, American populations would be rescued from annihilation.

The chief weapons systems necessary to fight such a war would be the Strategic Air Command (SAC) with its B-70 bombers, the Atlas and Titan liquid-fuel ICBMs, and the mobile solid-fuel Minuteman ICBM—all of which systems are under Air Force control. In addition, to complicate the enemy's problem of discovering the American atomic-striking force, such sea-based systems as Polaris would be valuable components of over-all strategy. But because Polaris missiles are too small to destroy enemy missiles in underground, concrete silos and more difficult to aim accurately, the Polaris could be only secondary in counter-force strategy.

Two essential elements of this strategy are as yet undeveloped. First, we are several years away from an atomic-powered plane capable of the hovering reconnaissance necessary to track down mobile missile sites. Even more difficult, what is being done to create huge underground cities for evacuation, to prepare populations for evacuation and for underground life, to build in our cities effective anti-fallout shelters? These last would be necessary to keep casualties below the thirty-million level while enemy thermonuclear bombs and missiles were dropping on the rockets and planes based in the United States.

Counterforce theorists feel little need for large Army and naval forces as part of their strategy. Counterforce strategy, through its threat of atomic retaliation, is considered a sufficient deterrent against limited war initiated by the enemy.

The counterforce system would act not only as a deterrent to such minor wars, according to its supporters, but would be the only way of deterring general war. In many ways, counterforce theory is an outgrowth of the classic assumption that the best deterrent to enemy attack is being strong enough both to live through the attack and to accept the enemy's surrender. Thus, in this view, "deterrence" is the building of an overwhelming force capable of winning the war if it should come and of leaving the winner in a viable position.

Objections to the Counterforce Theory

Major objections have been posed to this whole theory from a number of sources. Many of these objections have come from the two armed services that counterforce theory would downgrade—that is, the Army and the Navy. These objections have been directed, first, against the hypothetical model of thermonuclear war devised by counterforce theorists and, second, against the kind of American society that would result from acceptance of the counterforce system.

To deal first with the imaginary thermonuclear war, the possibility of actually separating atomic forces and great populations has been questioned. Several U.S. bomber bases are near cities. It seems likely that such situations as now exist in Tucson, Arizona, where Titans have been built close to the city, would become more rather than less the practice. There can be little doubt that Nike bases presently established close to American cities would have to be major targets for atomic destruction if air reconnaissance were going to be free to sniff out mobile or hardened missile sites. Thus it seems likely that atomic attack would have to be centered on targets quite close to our major cities, resulting in casualties far beyond the estimated "acceptable" thirty million. A similar pattern is likely to develop in the Soviet Union, thus lessening the likelihood that the Soviets could accept nuclear attacks on nuclear-force targets and make rational and controlled responses. If even a few cities are destroyed on either side, it is unlikely that the return fire will be selectively directed against military targets only. In such a situation, the national agony would be likely to demand an all-out attack.

Indeed, such a war might easily destroy some vital link in the national chain of command, leaving small groups of atomically armed forces bewildered, fearful, and free to attack at will. Such disintegration would be a likely result of the intense pressure of continuous atomic attack lasting several weeks. If such a breakdown occurred, the war would not be fought along the lines of counterforce theory.

The feasibility of civil defense preparations that would fit counterforce theory is open to serious question. Aside from the problems of expense, if the huge underground city shelters proposed were built, it is questionable if they would be usable. For example, what would an enemy conclude if American evacuation to such shelters were ordered? Might he not expect our attack and therefore attack us pre-emptively? Or, once war had started, would he accept defeat so long as he might hope people in such shelters were running out of food and water and would have to emerge, becoming vulnerable to attack? Such questions point up the impossibility of basing counterforce deterrence even on the future effectiveness of such shelters, let alone the unlikelihood of their construction.

The Minuteman missile, on which much of the counterforce strategy depends, may not be a workable weapon. The special conditions necessary for the long railroad trains that support Minutemen can be found only in the West of the United States, where there are so few railroad tracks that high aerial bursts of thermonuclear weapons in a pattern above the tracks could knock all the Minutemen in the area out of operation. If the Minuteman trains were to leave the scattered tracks of the West in order to travel the complex Eastern railroad systems, they would be more likely to approach metropolitan areas and thus confuse the vital distinction between atomic forces and civilian populations.

It seems likely that as mobile, hardened, or secret missile sites proliferate on both sides it will become more and more difficult to find and destroy atomic forces. This is particularly true of the American capability to find and destroy Soviet bases, since the U.S.S.R. exceeds the United States both in secrecy and in space. Even if counterforce strategy is conceivable in some sense today, it may not be possible ten years from now.

To summarize and clarify these objections to the feasibility of counterforce deterrence, it is useful to look closely at the concept of "rationality" in military planning. As the United States builds a counterforce system that is more subtle, more hidden, more mobile, the temptation increases for an enemy to make an overwhelming and undiscriminating attack. Rationality *to the Soviets* might dictate the use of high-burst pattern bombing to destroy the entire American society; otherwise, some of the American striking force might escape.

The history of twentieth-century war suggests that as one side uses its armed might more effectively, the other's reaction is to strike back with greater strength. We know this process well enough to have called it "total war"; there is every reason to believe that the final step in the process would result from applying counterforce theory. A serious look at what *each* side would consider "rational" thus shows that counterforce deterrence will not work out as counterforce theorists expect, and the counterforce war is not possible.

Counterforce strategy has been attacked as not only impossible of practice in war but as overwhelmingly dangerous to the preservation of peace. If both sides hope to be able to destroy the atomic forces of the other, both sides are under enormous pressure to be quick on the trigger. Striking at empty missile pads is absurd; split-second calculations designed to outshoot an enemy nation may lead to madness.

With the pressure so enormous and the stake so high, there can be little doubt that each side would be forced to attempt to pre-empt the other. In any period of major international crisis the fear of a planned attack could only lead to preparations for attack which might be strictly defensive in intent. But such acts of self-defense must appear as offensive threats to the other side, which would be forced to prepare its missiles. The sequence would lead directly to hair-trigger responses and could scarcely avoid leading to war. The chances of accidental war through some remote crisis developing into a larger threat, partial mobilization, and mutual fears of attack would be enormously increased.

Accepting counterforce strategy would also mean accepting an arms race without end. More and more mobile missiles, more and more underground missiles—the attempt to achieve ever newer counterforce weapons would prevent the achievement of any halt in the arms race. The system is based on the goal of having the larger atomic force to begin with, so as to have more left after attack. Thus neither side can ever stop adding to its atomic-weapon stockpile. The costs of continued stockpiling and of the search for and production of more powerful weapons would be enormous both in human terms and in money and would extend indefinitely into the future. The costs simply of building huge underground evacuation centers might be expected to run into several hundred billion dollars. An American society that would become accustomed to such evacuation shelters, to recurrent evacuations, to the possibility that whole populations would cower in shelters or in cities while atomic strikes went on around them, and to the expectation of thirty million deaths, would to free men be alien and unwanted, even unworthy of protection.

In fact, counterforce theorists admit privately that the United States might, if it fell behind in the counterforce arms race, have to surrender in such a war as they imagine. Since they seem fully to expect that an atomic war of some sort is inevitable if the United States were to fall behind in such an arms race, they must regard as an important possibility that all the sacrifices they demand in money and in human feelings might not prevent our defeat.

Counterforce theory thus seems to be bankrupt. Its hypothetical war between atomic forces is so improbable that there is little possibility of convincing an enemy that preparations for such a war are a credible deterrent. Even if such a war were possible, counterforce strategy seems more likely to bring it on than to prevent it. Far from deterring, counterforce strategy might press both antagonists toward pre-emptive attack. Finally, even if counterforce strategy did not bring about the war it is intended to win, constructing the weapons systems and shelters to support such a strategy would distort the free society we are pledged to defend.

THE COMBINED-DETERRENT THEORY

Some American officers and administrators, centered in the Army and the Navy, have decided that "to win" or "to lose" a thermonuclear war is inconceivable. They believe that such a war must be prevented and they do not believe that preparing to fight it is the way to prevent it. They prefer to make the outbreak of such a war as unlikely as possible by means of sharply increasing its terror. The result of such planning will, hopefully, be the elimination of all but the old-fashioned, conventional wars, for these members of the older military services want basically to work out a way to return to the older fashions of making war.

This theory of deterrence, not surprisingly, is based on a combination of the particular weapons systems and skills of the Army and Navy. For the theorists of this combined deterrent the first question is how to make thermonuclear war sufficiently terrible that it cannot and will not be fought. The mission of accomplishing this ennoblement of terror belongs to the Navy, which claims to have developed an "invulnerable deterrent."

It is the Navy's theory that if both the United States and its chief enemies have great masses of the population open to atomic attack (in a sense being held as hostages) and that if on both sides the forces to mount such an attack are themselves invulnerable, the attack will never be mounted. The theory is that any nation which under such circumstances struck first would be condemning its own population, its economy, its government, its very existence to death. For any nuclear attack would fail to destroy its enemy's invulnerable capacity, and that capacity would then be used to destroy its own cities.

The theorists of combined deterrence argue that the existence of such an invulnerable striking force would bring all the pressure of hope and fear to bear against any idea of a first atomic strike. They thus argue that the invulnerable deterrent with vulnerable populations would stabilize the international situation. Instead of pressing both sides toward a pre-emptive attack, the invulnerable deterrent would press both sides to think long and hard before attacking.

In addition, the argument runs that this situation would constitute a plateau in the arms race. It is suggested that when both sides reach the level of the invulnerable deterrent they can tacitly agree to arrest the arms build-up while they attempt to negotiate understanding difficulties. In fact, many of the proponents of "arms control" are looking to the establishment of this state of affairs as an end in itself, rather than as a way station on the road to disarmament.

The Navy believes that the "invulnerable deterrent" is to be found in its Polaris submarine, driven by atomic motors and armed with thermonuclear missiles. The argument runs that the Polaris can cruise the oceans of the earth in secrecy, ready to strike but with every incentive not to do so unless the United States is struck first. By its very separation from the land masses and population centers of America, the Polaris would avoid attracting an attack against the continental United States. For such an attack would have no purpose if it left the Polaris still capable of striking.

The Polaris itself is not believed to be a provocative weapon, because it can be so managed as to be incapable of attacking an enemy's atomic force. This is thought to be true because the megatonnage of the Polaris missile is too small to crack through hardened missile bases or to kill a hidden base with a near miss. Nor is the Polaris, launched at sea with all the difficulties of precisely accurate aiming that a ship encounters, capable of direct hits on mobile missiles.[2] The only way in which the Polaris could be made

[2] Some Navy men, however, in arguing their case to Congress, claim "pin-point accuracy" for the Polaris. If true, this claim

capable of a counterforce strike would be to mass so many explosions in the territory of the enemy that by sheer salvo technique atomic capability would be destroyed. Most Navy theorists believe that the crucial point in this massing of salvos would be at the number of forty-five Polaris submarines. To avoid turning the Polaris into a provocative counterforce weapon the Navy would like to restrict the number of its Polaris submarines to no more than forty-five.

As the Navy realizes, the form of deterrence based on the Polaris's ability to kill whole cities can only be a deterrence of all-out thermonuclear war. If an enemy were to take any action less emphatic than a thermonuclear attack upon the United States, the United States would certainly hesitate long before mounting a thermonuclear attack upon Soviet cities. For, of course, so long as our cities were intact, they would serve as hostages against the initiation of such an attack by the United States.

Theorists of the invulnerable deterrent therefore have to propose some way in which lesser provocations than all-out war can be deterred. It is in this context that the Army and Navy feel that what is necessary is a combination of deterrents. For major provocations less than all-out war, and in fact for minor provocations as well, the Army and Navy look to tactical forces as the chief deterrent.

Such major provocations might be invasion of Western Europe by the Soviet Union or of Southeast Asia or Japan by Communist China. The question would be how to throw back such an attack without involving the world in a thermonuclear war.

The theorists of the combined deterrent argue that the answer to this question is modernized ability to fight on the fringes of the Communist world. They believe that if the United States and its allies have such ability, it will act as a deterrent and will never have to be used; in other words, *this* kind of war can be won or lost and the way to

would gravely weaken the argument that Polaris is not provocative.

prevent it is to prepare to win it. War may still be "a continuation of politics by other means," but only if the chances of a thermonuclear war are eliminated by balance-of-terror techniques.

The Army and the Navy believe that the old-fashioned foot soldier and fleet are the keys to deterrence, provided that infantry and naval equipment are modernized. Two important factors compel such modernization: first, compared with the Sino-Soviet bloc, the United States and its allies are short on men but long on machines; second, the West must defend a far-flung frontier on which tactical attack might come at any place and at any moment. In consequence, the mobility and the fire power of Western tactical forces should be increased; and, if possible, their numbers should be increased as well. On the question of mobility and numbers, there is general agreement on the need for an air-lift capability that could transport within hours sizable forces of infantrymen to any part of the world.

Sizable fleets, floating off the shores of critical areas, must also be ready to land American marines at short notice. Finally, every attempt should be made to increase the numbers of allied soldiers available to integrated Western commands; hence, emphasis on the need for a strong German army and for increased military subsidies to nations on the Communist periphery that cannot afford to build up their own armies.

Both the Army and Navy believe that increased tactical readiness will not only deter actual military invasion by Sino-Soviet forces but that it could check internal subversion and revolution. For the presence of the fleet "showing the flag" all across the globe, the availability of air-lifted infantrymen, and the existence of powerful indigenous armies, all are thought to work against the possibility of internal Communist revolutions. The three techniques of intervention to stop invasion, intervention to halt subversion, and aid to strengthen an indigenous army against either subversion or invasion were exemplified by American action in Korea, Lebanon, and Greece. In each of these cases the Army and Navy believe that they frustrated the Communists' immediate plans and, by demonstrating American military capacity, reduced the prospects of similar Communist expansion elsewhere.

The one issue in which there is considerable disagreement among theorists of the combined deterrent concerns increased fire power for tactical forces. Some argue that because the West can never, despite mobility and military aid, match the Sino-Soviet bloc in numbers of available soldiers, the West's presumed technological superiority must fill the gap. Atomic, chemical, or bacteriological weapons must be placed in the hands of Western armies to be used against "hordes" of Sino-Soviet invaders. Unless this is done, they believe that Soviet expansion cannot be checked. On the other hand, some combined-deterrent theorists believe that atomic, chemical, and bacteriological weapons could only spread tactical war into general war. These men argue that the only observable limits are defined by the so-called conventional weapons, that once beyond this limit there is no way of stopping one side or the other from employing still more powerful weapons up to and including the H-bomb.

But with this exception on the question of fire power, theorists of the combined deterrent are agreed on their system. They believe it can prevent the thermonuclear war that they believe is absolutely unacceptable to mankind. They also believe it can probably prevent both tactical wars and internal subversion. Even if it fails to prevent them, it can make possible American or Western victory in such situations.

Objections to the Combined-Deterrent Theory

To this whole theory, as to counterforce theory, there have been many objections on various levels. Again, some of the objections question the possibility of building a credible deterrent along these lines and, again, some of the objections dispute the belief that a society and international order based on such a deterrent would be stable or tolerable.

The question of military possibility rests squarely on the alleged "invulnerability" of the Polaris submarine, but the invulnerability of the present Polaris even against existing methods of anti-submarine warfare has been seriously questioned. The Polaris missile has an effective range of some 1500 miles. Most Russian cities are so far from navigable oceans that, to be capable of hitting them, the Polaris submarine must circle quite close to Communist coasts. It cannot literally "hide beneath the oceans," because only a fraction of the world's oceans are within striking distance. If this were all, the protection of the seas might be sufficient; but should the submarine launch one of its missiles, its position would immediately be revealed to enemy aircraft. It is possible that the submarine could be destroyed before firing more than one or two of its sixteen missiles.

Refinements of the Polaris may, of course, add to its range and to its ability of self-concealment, but there will undoubtedly also be refinements in the techniques of anti-submarine warfare. The Polaris system is not a technological plateau. To be a credible deterrent it must be improved, and this improvement will undoubtedly call forth improvements in anti-Polaris systems. This "invulnerable" deterrent cannot stand still; it cannot halt the arms race. It can only give rise to a slightly different kind of arms race in which first anti-submarine warfare and later the anti-missile missile would be the chief direction of arms improvements.

By its nature the Polaris would add to, rather than reduce, one of the major problems of effective deterrence. That problem is the so-called "Nth-country question." Silent underneath the ocean, the Polaris submarine is unidentifiable. If a Polaris-type missile is fired against a city, no one can know for sure who fired it. If nuclear technology proliferates across the world with the result that many nations can build atomic submarines, no one will ever be sure what nation might deliver *or might even have delivered* a thermonuclear blow. If nuclear knowledge spreads, it might even be in the best interest of the Soviet Union and the United States to clear all atomically armed and atomically powered submarines from the sea, so as to prevent a case of mistaken identity or disguised attack. This view shows the difficulty of using the Polaris in the approaching situation when much of the world will have atomic weapons.[3]

In addition to these criticisms of the feasibility of using the Polaris as a deterrent, there have been criticisms of its moral and political implications. Air Force theorists in particular have pointed to what they call the absolute immorality of planning the total destruction of civilian populations, compared with their own acceptance of a "limited" war bringing only thirty million deaths. There is no doubt that if the Polaris deterrent were to fail, the result would be a universal holocaust.

Finally, Polaris has been criticized because of the impossibility of continued governmental control over the acts of the submarine commander. Since the Polaris has to be free to act if governmental centers are destroyed—otherwise, in case of the assumed enemy first strike there would be no way for it to act at all—there is no sure way to prevent independent action by Polaris crews, even in the absence of a first strike. While an American submarine crew, fearful of retaliation against their homeland, would be unlikely to take such independent action, the crews of some lesser power might seek to upset the world balance by

[3] Another curious ramification of the Nth-country problem could develop from the Polaris strategy. By nature the Polaris must be ready to fire if communication with the mainland is cut off. But if communication is cut off, how can the submarine be told on whom to fire? Might it fire on the wrong country, or even fire thinking war had begun when there was only a communications failure?

means of provoking an all-out war. But even in ships of the major powers the chance of an irresponsible or irrational attack should by no means be ruled out.

The other element of the combined deterrent, "tactical readiness," has also been severely criticized. The criticisms directed against the high fire-power wing of theorists have already been described. High fire power in terms of atomic, chemical, or biological weaponry is clearly capable of leading upward into a thermonuclear war. Certainly few powers would want atomic or biological wars fought over their territory and they would be likely to respond to such weapons by pressing for the use of thermonuclear weapons in their own defense.

But many who fear that such escalation would result from unconventionally armed tactical forces are also convinced that in sheer numbers the West can scarcely cope with Sino-Soviet capacities. The costs, both human and economic, of universal and lengthy military conscription would be extremely hard to bear, especially if no end to the struggle can be imagined.

The limited-war lessons that matter most are those which can be drawn from Korea and Algeria; and the lessons apply both for the domestic reactions to such wars and the results in the countries defended. Both the United States and France, during each of these prolonged and stalemated wars, experienced great difficulty in limiting the theater of the war and in preserving their civil liberties. Demands either to abandon the war or to expand it were enormous in each case. Pressures that in the United States showed up as a nightmare episode of attack on civil liberties, in France developed into an actual overthrow of the republic. Thus the effects at home of future involvements in limited wars are not to be dismissed lightly.

In other countries the effects of limited wars would be equally unhappy. Constant readiness to use military force against invasions or revolutions thought to be Communist-directed will not prevent such violence, for its causes are far deeper than Communist manipulation. The political, economic, and social origins of unrest in Africa, Asia, and Latin America cannot be eliminated by Western armies. Such armies can only ally themselves with privileged minorities who are interested in maintaining the *status quo* of poverty and ignorance, trying to hold down or hold back the violence born of desperation. Thus the policy of large Western armies would not only weaken the West but tend to frustrate the necessary development of the hungry nations.

The substitution of Western-aided native "anti-Communist" armies in the hungry nations for actual Western armies meets the same objections. Massive military aid to such nations distorts their economies and interferes with orderly economic and social growth. In fact, heavy military aid to such countries and heavy support for the military classes in such countries often intensify discontent and revolution. Such internal rebellions are frequently deflected by undiscriminating Western opposition to social change into an alliance with the Communist bloc. In some nations (such as Cuba) we have already seen the disturbing effect of such a series of events. In others it may be possible for continued military aid to the ruling groups to suppress any upheavals; but the upheavals will not end, and instability will become a chronic factor in precisely the places where stable allies are most hoped for.

The notion of the combined deterrent thus seems to be only a temporary expedient. The "invulnerable" deterrent seems impossible to make permanently invulnerable, and hence it will not be permanently credible. Large-scale military conscription and tactical readiness would place such a strain upon the economies and the political systems both of developed and underdeveloped countries that it seems an unwise goal. The combined deterrent also seems likely to increase the chances of Nth-country attack and of internal subversion and chronic instability in the poor countries. The plateau promised by the theorists of the combined deterrent is illusory. Though adopting the theory might give the great powers a few additional years to think out new solutions, the combined deterrent promises no permanent "arms control" and is in itself no goal for achieving peace.

THE THEORIES CONFOUNDED

Although we have discussed the major arguments for and against each of the central theories of deterrence, there remain some general considerations to be raised on the nature of deterrence and the nature of the kinds of deterrence so far discussed. Among these is the difficulty of distinguishing operationally between "counterforce" and "combined-deterrent" strategies.

The blurring of the two strategies has been dignified as a theory by some elements of the Defense Department and labeled the "mix," or the "middle course." It is now almost automatic even among those who believe in the combined deterrent to say that there should be a "mix" of weapons and strategies available to the United States. In fact, the services in which the combined-deterrent theory is dominant (the Army and Navy) say specifically that they do not hope or intend to eliminate the weapons systems that fit into a counterforce strategy. In other words, the Titan, Minuteman, the B-70 are all to continue to exist alongside the Polaris and a limited-war capability. This position is politically inescapable for the various services, since each fears it would hurt only itself by attacking the institutionalized prerogatives, industrial allies, and political supporters of the others. But the position is rationalized on the basis that the United States must be ready for whatever kind of war the enemy initiates—must, in short, be ready to fight either a counterforce or counterpopulation war.

Yet there can be no doubt that a potential enemy would view the American military system as a whole. He would doubt that a combined-deterrent policy had been clearly adopted, if weapons systems alien to such a policy were continued. In such a situation the advantages claimed for the combined deterrent—stability during a crisis—would not exist. So there is no point to choosing the combined deterrent, no chance of reaping the advantages claimed for such a system, unless the United States eliminates weapons that do not fit that concept—that is, scraps most of the Air Force. No such intention seems to exist either in the Department of Defense or in the Congress, and certainly not in the missile industry.

On the other hand, if the United States chooses counterforce theory, it must eliminate all semblance of city-busting techniques. For if, in addition to counterforce weapons, we insist on building weapons that can only be used effectively against populations rather than forces, we will make impossible the development of a war according to counterforce theories. If the enemy watches us building a force (for example, Polaris) that is obviously intended for use against cities because it would be of little use against atomic-striking forces, they could only conclude that the intention was to strike against both cities and forces. Once that conclusion is fixed in the mind of a potential enemy the rational calculations will be different from those the counterforce theorists assume. Assuming that it must forestall a general attack, the only rational action open to an enemy is to attack our capital, leadership, population, economy, and industry as well as our atomic force. Thus the war would not develop in the rational ways counterforce theorists propose. If counterforce theory is to be adopted, weapons like Polaris must be scrapped.

Furthermore, if an enemy is to believe that the United States will respond to major conventionally armed provocations (such as an attack on Europe) with an atomic strike it seems necessary to scrap our own limited-war capabilities; otherwise, the enemy will not be convinced that we really mean to use the atomic strike. Pure counterforce theory means that most of the Army and Navy would have to be scrapped, just as pure combined-deterrent theory would mean that most of the Air Force would have to be scrapped.

An exclusive commitment would have to be made to one of these theories for either of them to be believable. But the United States is such a rich country that, instead of making hard choices between costly alternatives, we try to build everything we think of. If that pattern of the past is to be continued, then attempts to argue for either the counterforce or the invulnerable-deterrent strategy are meaningless.

Confusion in an enemy's mind between counterforce and combined-deterrent strategy could be brought about in another way. Even if our choice were made in favor of a combined-deterrent strategy, there is a limit to the size of the invulnerable-weapon system that could be built if the system were not to look like a more subtle counterforce weapon. For example, the Navy theorists suggest that if we build more than forty-five Polaris submarines, that force would no longer appear to the Soviets like a second-strike, deterrent-only weapon system; more than forty-five atomic submarines would suggest that a saturation-bombing technique was to be used. The "value" of having a not too accurate, not too powerful missile would disappear if salvos of such missiles were to be massed. Such a massing could turn the Polaris into a counterforce weapon, and therefore the building of a huge fleet of Polarises would seem to be an adoption of counterforce strategy. This limit is understood by the Navy men, but they do not generalize this concept to apply to the multiplication of weapons systems. If only forty-five Polarises are built, and a Minuteman intended as an "invulnerable" deterrent is also built, and a series of similar invulnerable deterrents are built in addition, the resulting mix of weapons systems will scarcely seem to fit the combined-deterrent theory. Thus, again the potentialities of American wealth could turn what seems to be a choice of a particular strategy into a confusion between the two strategies. But this view is little understood in the Department of Defense and seems scarcely likely of acceptance by the political forces that would determine budget and basic plans.

Finally, there is a third way in which a confusion between the two strategies could arise: if the invulnerable deterrent, even in its most carefully limited form, and alongside it a major civil defense shelter program, were to be built. The theory of the invulnerable deterrent works only if populations are vulnerable and forces are invulnerable. If either the Soviet Union or the United States were to give a clear indication of an all-out program of shelter building, the assumption on the other side could reasonably be that a city-busting attack was expected and was being guarded against. Such an attack would only be expected, according to combined-deterrent theory, in retaliation for an attack by one's own forces against cities. By these assumptions, the reason to guard against such an attack would be to free one's invulnerable deterrent to make a first strike against the cities of one's opponent.

A shelter-building program on either side would therefore contribute greatly to the instability that the invulnerable deterrent is supposed to alleviate. It would raise the specter that the deterrent was to be used for a first strike and would force the opponent into developing a counterforce strategy. Unlike the other two confusions discussed above, this one does not seem as yet built into the political structure and assumptions of the United States. No commitment has yet been made here to an all-out shelter building program. But it is noteworthy that no service, not even the combined-deterrent theorists of the Army and Navy, is willing to suggest that civil defense be abandoned, to uphold the purity of the combined-deterrent theory. So long as even the present ineffective civil defense is continued, notions of a commitment to an all-out shelter program will endure. Such a commitment would have to be prevented for the future, if the United States decided to adopt the invulnerable-deterrent strategy.

We have discussed the ways in which the United States refuses to choose between the two major strategies and thereby may bring about the worst aspects of each. Neither from this confused "mix" nor from either pure theory can we expect a halt to the arms race. Instead, we believe that present military strategies would result in a rising crescendo of destructive capacity—a crescendo in which there would be plateaus, but only plateaus like the steps of an escalator that quickly and insensibly merge into the next step up.

We suggest that there would develop, indefinitely into the future, a rising series of alternations. First there would be a period of high instability tied to a counterforce strategy. Then, as one side or the other caught up in the techniques of making its weapons invulnerable, there would be a period of moderate stability and the dominance of combined-deterrent strategies. During this period research would continue in ways to nullify invulnerability. At our present weapons level, for example, this would mean the development of anti-submarine warfare and anti-missile missiles and reconnaissance satellites. When one side or the other had achieved a break-through in one of these techniques, a new period of extremely high instability would result, and again the counterforce theorists would dominate. But in the second period the destructiveness of the weapons, the hostilities of the peoples, the speed of reaction would all have been heightened.

Thus it is clear that the "stability" proposed by the combined-deterrent theorists and the rationality proposed by the counterforce theorists are only true on a superficial level. Short-run stability would lead to long-run increases in the chances of war. Short-run rationality would only accomplish its own replacement by an irrational spiral.

For these reasons it seems extremely unlikely that either form of deterrence that we have discussed, whether in its pure form or in mixture with the other, can accomplish the ends that are claimed for it. In addition, there seems to be some evidence that such theories of deterrence as those discussed do not apply when deterrence is most needed—at the height of an extreme and vital international crisis. At such times deterrence disappears—not because the weapons systems cease to exist, but because their psychological impact upon the opposing nations disappears.

Deterrence can operate only in the minds of leaders of the nations deterred. There is evidence that under conditions of extreme and growing tension the major decision-makers in every great power become unable to pay attention to the warnings, the threats, the deterrents of their potential enemies. Such a development took place in summer 1914 when the Allies and Central Powers tried, by mobilizing their full strength, to deter each other from going to war. But in 1914 the only information that officials had time and energy to accept was the information about their own nation's capabilities and preparations. When attention could no longer be fixed on the threat of retaliation, deterrence failed. In neither of the views of deterrence presently held by American military experts is there any realization of the necessity to deal with this problem of the height of crisis. Still less is there any proposal for a deterrent that would work in such conditions.

From discussions with policy-makers in the Pentagon it is clear that there has been no adequate exploration of the nature of deterrence. The inadequacy is traceable partly to the rigid quasi-scientism of strategists who have attempted to plot undeviating results from particular actions. The complexity of the hour-to-hour decisions may result in any of the myriad failures of theory that we have here detailed. *But to the theorists who have worked out these strategies, human decision-making seems a one-track operation.* The strategists have further failed to examine the non-military factors—economic, propaganda, psychological, among others—that will condition the responses to any military strategy. An adequate theory of deterrence must be far richer and more flexible—must take in many more factors and allow many more deviations from expectations.

The inadequacy of present deterrent theory may also be traced partly to a basic misconception of deterrence in the international field. Deterrence as a military, international concept claims its roots in the notion of the internal police force as deterrent against crime. But the basic assumption of the police force as deterrent does not exist in international relations. In the world at large the situation is analogous to what has been happening in the Congo. Police forces exist in the Congo, but they do not deter violence because they do not act under agreed sanctions, under one effective national law. The police force in this context is provocative rather than stabilizing. Similarly, in the world at large, armed forces acting in the absence of internationally agreed law can only be provocative, no matter what theory of deterrence they are seeking to carry out.

For accurate and adequate notions of what deterrence can mean we must consider the effective deterrent achieved by a police force under law. From this analogy it would seem that only international arrangements for effective arms reductions and control leading to disarmament could be an effective deterrent. Once laws against national armaments have been promulgated and effective police forces to enforce such laws have been established, then deterrence as municipal policemen now practice it can come into being.

It is essential to examine the conditions under which such a result can be achieved. An international agreement effectively policed can conceivably deter any would-be aggressor. An international police force does not have to be all-powerful to be effective; it is the probability of discovery and punishment that restrains criminal action. Any national leader who attempted to breach an international disarmament agreement would have to face an international police force supported by world opinion. It seems to us that only in this way could the theory of deterrence be adequately reconciled with the facts of international military and technological life.

Often it is argued against the chances of effective disarmament that the West cannot "trust" the Soviets to keep their agreements, and that the risks of "cheating" would be too high. It is important to remember that counterforce and combined-deterrent theory both put enormous "trust" in the Soviets. Both theories trust the Soviets to react "rationally"—that is, as our theorists want them to act—to control their own reactions, and to abide the arms race without growing impatient, unstable, or irrational. The irony of the cold war is that we think of the Communists as irrational for having started it, and yet trust them to act in a rational manner in prosecuting it. As we have shown, the risks of such trust are enormous, for either by accident or through "cheating" on our expectations the Soviets might well help military deterrence to fail and war to come. The risks would be far less if an international police were exerting the controls and enforcing the deterrent.[4]

The idea that a disarmament agreement might be the *only* workable deterrent has not been explored by branches of the armed services, by the Department of Defense itself, or by any other branch of the government so far as we have been able to determine. This idea seems to us a hopeful avenue to pursue. We would urge upon decision makers that this view of deterrence by explored as soon as possible.

NECESSARY PRACTICAL STEPS FOR CONGRESS

The notion of an effectively policed disarmament agreement as the most likely adequate deterrent is so far distant

[4] Soviet disarmament proposals have, at least rhetorically, accepted the idea of careful inspection and enforcement. The rhetoric should be taken seriously long enough to find out whether the Soviets seriously mean it.

from present international realities that it may weary those who want to take practical action. But there are practical actions available to the Congress to deal with the present inadequacy of deterrent theory.

There are four major areas in which the Congress can affect deterrent policy: through budget allocations, through setting organizational forms in the Department of Defense, through the creation of new agencies, and through the treaty power the Congress could act to support its own views of how best to protect American security.

In budgeting for the armed forces, the Congress chooses between weapons systems, whether it intends to do so or not; and by choosing between weapons systems Congress chooses a particular theory of deterrence, whether it intends to do so or not. If the Congress tries to support with funds all the proposed weapons systems of all the services, it gives America the confused "mix" of deterrents which, as we have pointed out, marries the worst of all possible worlds.

The Congress ought deliberately to determine what theory of deterrence it believes most adequate for the nation's security: counterforce deterrent, combined deterrent, or disarmament as deterrent. We recommend that the relevant congressional committees, including the House Appropriations Committee, begin at once the investigations necessary to back up such a decision. Depending on its findings, the Congress will know whether it wishes to increase funds for the B-70 and the Titan and abolish the Polaris, or to increase funds for the Polaris and for a mobile infantry while abolishing the counterforce missile systems, or to take a more complex action that would support the theory of disarmament as deterrent.

Such support would begin by taking seriously American negotiations on disarmament with other powers. Congress should provide for budgetary changes to go into effect if disarmament agreements are reached. Provisions in the budget for reductions in particular areas of defense, according to an internationally agreed plan for disarming, could be accompanied by provisions for redirecting the money to non-defense expenditures or for reduction in taxes. Thus the machinery would be ready for the economy shift in new directions if a disarmament agreement were to be reached.

In the area of civil defense the Congress will want to decide whether to increase enormously the amount spent and to build great underground cities, as would fit the counterforce deterrent, or to scrap all civil defense, as would be logical either to complement the combined deterrent or to move toward disarmament. The present halfhearted expenditure of funds on clearly useless plans for evacuation and partial shelter makes sense for no plan of deterrence. For protecting whole populations against counterforce attack, only entirely new shelter cities or antiradiation shelters for every city resident would be of any use. For protection of the cities themselves against countercity attack, no civil defense of any kind can be useful; H-bombs will kill cities and ICBMs will allow no time for evacuation. For a policed disarmament, the shelters would be unnecessary, and building them would cause great distrust of any avowed disarmament. Our immediate recommendation to the Congress is that it abandon the present half-baked arrangement called civil defense, rather than go further into a program that would end in costing hundreds of billions, destroying liberty, and failing in its purpose anyway.

In examining the question of Defense Department organization, the Congress must take into account factors other than "efficiency." It must examine arguments for reorganization in the light of what theories of deterrence they actually support.

At present the Air Force is by all odds the most powerful single service. Its connections with heavy industry, its long monopoly of the most "glamorous" weapons, and its willingness to plunge deep into the most advanced weapons and theories of twentieth-century war have given it the highest prestige and the largest budget in the Defense Department. So long as it retains this power, the Air Force believes that it will dominate any true unification of the armed forces, ensuring its theory—that is, to counterforce deterrence—the victory in Defense Department debate. This expectation is shared by the Army and Navy, which have therefore opposed unification in the fear that their services, their weapons systems, and their theories would be submerged.

In the present practical situation, therefore, if Congress pressed for total unification of the armed forces it would probably enthrone the counterforce deterrent. We have heard serious fears expressed that this kind of unification might result in some loss of civil and democratic control over the military. Officers in the Pentagon themselves expressed the fear that a single chief of staff over a single service might concentrate so much power, both over publicity and defense contracts, that civilian department heads, the Congress, and the public would be unable to question or to oppose his decisions. In such a unified military service the fears expressed by former President Eisenhower of the growing interdependence of an enlarged military and an enlarged arms industry would be likely to become real and present dangers. But that is not to say that by keeping the forces separate the Congress is effectively choosing the theory of the combined deterrent. For, as has been shown above, so long as the American arsenal contains weapons obviously chosen for their counterforce capability, so long is the "purity" of the combined deterrent compromised and its actual goals thereby made impossible of attainment. Continuing the present system would therefore be a deliberate choice of contradictory theories.

Deep inside the present system, however, certain officials could in fact choose between counterforce and combined-deterrent theory. At present, the key to such a choice may lie with the interservice Joint Targeting Center, in which military officers are attempting to integrate the enemy targets to be selected by various branches of the American armed forces. In planning for missile and airplane strikes, such targets must be arranged ahead of time; and which targets are selected—cities or atomic forces—could decide the struggle between the Air Force and Army-Navy views. For such a choice to be made without the knowledge and understanding of the Congress or the people would amount to surrender of civilian control over basic defense and foreign policy. It would be a complete Defense "reorganization" without congressional sanction.

A similar form of "silent reorganization" so constructed as to benefit one theory of deterrence may be attempted under the cover of foreign policy and the NATO alliance. In many ways the proposal for a NATO force of Polaris submarines looks toward establishment of the combined-deterrent policy under NATO control. Building the deterrent under NATO would side-step the present Air Force dominance in the Defense Department, and for that reason the Army and Navy have supported the proposal. Quite aside from accentuating the problem of the spread of atomic weapons and probably forcing the Soviets to take similar action, the grant of Polaris to NATO, by diluting both American and civilian control over atomic weapons, would tend to deny Congress any continued power over basic defense policy.

One kind of formal reorganization has been proposed that could conceivably fit into the combined-deterrent theory. That is the suggestion that the services should be reoriented into two functional commands: one to fight tactical and limited wars, the other to act as the great deterrent. If the Congress clearly directed and by practical provisions made sure that the great deterrent command was dominated by Navy men and ideas, the two commands would together make up the combined deterrent that the Army and Navy now support. But if the great deterrent command were to come under the control of counterforce theorists, the Navy's ideas and the weapons systems to carry them out would be abandoned. If Congress wishes to choose this method of reorganizing the Defense Department to apply combined-deterrent theories, it must carry through by overseeing arrangements within the tactical and deterrent commands.

If the Congress decides that the view of disarmament as deterrent is indeed a correct one, a rather different view of Defense Department organization would be necessary. The goal would then clearly be the gradual dismantling of the whole defense organization and its replacement with an international police.

To move in this direction would obviously require a writing of contingent legislation by Congress, rather than a single sweeping act of reorganization. Changes in the defense structure and transfer of some personnel to an international police force would have to be made contingent upon successful negotiations with other world powers to establish such a police. The difficulties would be novel, but they would not be impossible of solution.

It is in dealing with these difficulties and attempting to work out a way toward a disarmament agreement that would act as a deterrent that Congress might effectively bring into play another of its powers—the power to create a new agency in the federal government. For the difficulties in the path of an effectively policed world disarmament agreement are so complex and possible solutions so unexplored that it would be most useful to have a new agency confronting these difficulties.

The far-reaching results of basic and applied research have in the last fifteen years become obvious in the field of weapons development. But never has the United States attempted to apply the techniques of research to the questions of how to achieve disarmament, how to reduce the international tensions that stand in the way of disarmament, and how to deal with the gaps in our society that disarmament would make.

To mobilize the techniques of social and natural science in the search for disarmament, it has been suggested that the federal government create a National Peace Agency. The proposed agency has been compared to the National Institutes of Health, in that scholars of all sorts would be encouraged to deal with the myriad questions of reducing tensions in political, economic, military, and other fields. In addition, it has been argued that the Peace Agency might include the corps of men designated by the United States for international service to police a disarmament agreement. In this fashion the agency would make use of the manpower, the knowledge, perhaps even some of the individual men that would have been previously used by the Department of Defense.

The creation of such a Peace Agency, with its potential both for finding the steps that could bring disarmament and for dealing with the actual enforcement of disarmament, we recommend as a practical step to the Congress.

Finally, the Senate's treaty powers could be brought into play. An actual experiment could be set up in the possibilities of international inspection and enforcement, in an area not crucial to American security, if the President signs and the Senate ratifies a treaty for an atomic test ban. Atomic testing is not vital to American military security because it involves only a marginal addition to fire power and no addition at all to delivery capability. It is equally true that a ban on testing is not vital to American security as approached via disarmament, because the test ban will not stop or reverse any of the important parts of the arms race. But as an experiment in international policing the test ban would give Congress and the nation a chance to assess what steps in true disarmament would be possible.

POSTSCRIPT

It is sometimes said that public discussion of and decision on the issues we have raised is unwise: that it is best to "keep the enemy guessing." But only by preventing all enemy guesswork can we hope to make deterrence work. If the United States intends to deter by a counterforce strategy, the Soviets must know this clearly in order to be deterred; if by combined deterrence, then again there must be no doubt. And, of course, negotiations for disarmament could be successful only if we and the Soviets were each convinced the other was totally serious about deterring war through disarmament.

Not only is the policy of "keeping the enemy guessing" unwise, it is impossible to square with the democracy that we are trying to preserve. For ultimately the policy means that we keep ourselves guessing—our people, our Congress, logically perhaps even our President. Refusing to discuss and decide the greatest question of human history means abandoning the very assumptions of the Constitution. Congress, for the safety of the nation and the preservation of democracy, must face the issue of deterrence.

The use of "we" and "our" in this essay is purely the result of editorial convention, and connotes no one's responsibility for the opinions expressed, except the author's.

FIVE

Reciprocal Initiative

BY CHARLES E. OSGOOD

Professor of Psychology and Director of the Institute of Communications Research, University of Illinois

Today we are faced with a potentially lethal combination of weapons against which there is no defense and international tensions from which there seems to be no respite. We are close to the point where either of the two major world powers will be capable of wiping out the other in almost less time than it takes to read this paper. This grim assessment of our situation is the consensus of men who have thought and written about problems of policy in the nuclear age, regardless of their role in our society.

We thus find ourselves in an unprecedented situation completely novel to human experience, requiring radical innovation in policy. Yet today relations among nations are still governed by traditional policies that are deemed "realistic" simply because they are habitual. National leaders talk about achieving peace and security through increasing military strength, when reason shows that the peace thus attained is ephemeral and the security illusory. The truth of the matter is that both Russia and the United States are now almost immobilized by the very power they possess for destruction.

Recent developments in communication, transportation, and other forms of human interdependence—to say nothing of weaponry—have made some form of world government not merely feasible; they have made it essential if our civilization is to survive. But the problem is this: How can we move from the present situation of competing sovereign nations toward a situation of international law? How can we halt, and then put into reverse, the tensions/arms-race spiral in which we are caught, thereby creating an atmosphere of mutual trust in which steps toward world government could be taken?

It will be the primary purpose of this paper to suggest a way out of the tensions/arms-race dilemma, a strategy that would allow a nation to take the initiative by inducing reciprocal tension reduction, yet always operating within tolerable limits of security. It is a strategy that would use mutual capacity for nuclear annihilation to support actions designed ultimately to eliminate this very capacity itself.

Both the justification of this strategy and the main opposition to it will be found to lie in matters of human nature and human relationships. This may come as a shock to many who have conceived of our policy problem in terms of scientific and military technology. Nevertheless, although the debate so far has been carried on more by physicists and generals than by social scientists and intelligent laymen, I think it can be easily shown that military technology merely exacerbates the problem—it neither explains our dilemma nor offers any solution. My own argument will require a careful analysis of the cold-war mentality, including the questioning of some psychological assumptions that have been taken on faith and the assertion of others that have been largely overlooked.

My proposals for policy will be offered in the broadest possible terms. I do not believe that the ordinary citizen —whether he be a college professor or a businessman—is equipped by knowledge or by experience to develop specific and detailed policies. What the scholar can best do is raise questions about the assumptions underlying policy and ask that they be re-examined rather than simply taken for granted. He can also offer what may be novel ways of viewing policy problems, in the hope of contributing to the discovery of alternatives not previously believed to exist.

MINIMUM CRITERIA FOR EVALUATING POLICY ALTERNATIVES

If the long-term goals of a society are not made explicit, decisions are likely to be made opportunistically in defense of the *status quo*. What are our goals? What are we "fighting for"? Certainly we have no expansionist ambitions in South America, Europe, or Asia; we do not wish to annihilate human beings on other portions of the globe; nor do we even desire to impose our way of life on others, except as they observe our model, try it on for size, and find it good. But we do want to *preserve our own way of life* for ourselves and our progeny. And to accomplish this *we must at least stay alive*. To these two minimal objectives of policy in the nuclear age we must add a third, practical criterion—any policy must be *feasible* within the existing system of competing sovereign states.

In discussing these criteria it is necessary to distinguish between two quite different wars and opponents. Most people think of "war" in terms of soldiers and guns, military victories and defeats, destruction and death wreaked by each side on the other. In this sense of the term we are in danger of becoming involved in a catastrophic war with Russia as a nation, and it is here that the criterion of biological survival is primary. A broader conception of "war," and one that is even held by many military men (e.g., King-Hall, 19), is that it is an attempt to change the system of beliefs held by some other group of people, particularly when these beliefs seem to engender behavior which threatens one's own security. In this sense we are presently engaged in a "war" with communism (but equally with other totalitarian systems), and it is here that the criterion of preserving our own beliefs and way of life is primary. We have been waging this "war" for a long, long time; it goes on steadily in the minds of men, and it is fought as much within the borders of nations as across them. Victory in a military war with Russia—even granting that victory in a nuclear war is conceivable—would not mean winning the war against communism. Indeed, it would be possible for us to "win" a short-term military encounter at the expense of losing the long-term ideological conflict—that is, by adopting a totalitarian way of life as a means to military power.

Biological Survival

First things first. I take the physicists at their word when they say that there is no adequate military defense against nuclear attack. I am vaguely impressed when I read in the National Planning Association's report, titled *1970 Without Arms Control* (25), that "one thermonuclear bomb in the low megaton range releases more destructive energy than that released by all of the bombs dropped on Germany and Japan during World War II." But somehow words do not carry the impact of the events they represent —which is one reason why most people in Europe, Russia, and Japan are more deeply pacifistic than most Americans. I am sure that just one ordinary atomic bomb dropped on New York City, with complete television coverage, would do more to convince us of the utter horror of nuclear war than all the statistics one could amass. Nevertheless, I ask those who doubt if the advent of nuclear weapons has in any way changed "the old game of international politics" to hold in mind the *details* of shattered bodies and plans, of disintegrating human culture and even human protoplasm—and then read further in the same report: that in a full-scale nuclear attack we could expect by the sixtieth day seventy-two million dead and twenty-one million seriously injured, with only fifty-eight million relatively unscathed. Computations based on relatively minor and localized disasters show that this proportion of the population surviving could not adequately care for the injured and bury the dead—to say nothing of maintaining a complex civilization.

Now, as a psychologist, I am fully aware that threatening people with hell-fire without offering them any solution does more to reinforce complacency than to shake it. People try to avoid and forget information about fearful things over which they have no control; at the same time they welcome and rehearse information that seems to reassure them and reduce their anxieties. This has been the trouble with most of the pacifist criticisms of present policy —they have offered believable threats without acceptable solutions. But those concerned with the security of the nation cannot afford to depreciate the threat to our biological survival which these new weapons represent; rather, this vision of hell-fire must be kept in focus while we search for ways to escape it.

Suffice it to say that, without arms control, in the very near future warring nations will be able to destroy each other many times over. This availability of nuclear weapons with awesome capacities for destruction—to say nothing about biological and neurological weapons which are even easier to produce and harder to control—may not alter the nature of the underlying conflict or its goals, but it certainly must change radically the weights we use in evaluating alternative strategies.

Preservation of Our Way of Life

Stripped to its essentials, the way of life we wish to preserve for ourselves and our progeny is one in which the state is subservient to the individuals who compose it. In the language of the Declaration of Independence, governments are created to preserve the rights of individual citizens, and not vice versa. All of our most cherished institutions—the democratic form of government, our economic system, a legal system which guarantees individuals the right to education and freedom of expression—flow from this pervasive underlying notion. Even though practice may often fall far short of theory, the theory itself is important. The development of such a political philosophy, based on the essential dignity of the individual human being, was a most remarkable step along the path to becoming civilized; it was hard come by, yet it may be all too easily lost.

The basic philosophy of communism, as we see it, is quite the reverse of this. In essence it holds that individuals who compose the state are subservient to it. The individual has no "rights"—to dissent, to be educated, to be informed, to compete for a share in the economy equal to his ability and effort—except in so far as serving the best interests of the state may be considered a right. But again practice doesn't jibe with theory. Just as technological and other developments have produced modifications in our way of life, as practiced, so have the industrial revolution, universal education, and the race to catch up with the United States in material wealth produced deviations from Communist theory.

Although the cold war is waged in terms of rival theories, flexibility and rationality in foreign policy require that we take account of similarities as well as differences in how the systems operate in practice. In this connection, I am impressed with Ralph K. White's argument (38), based on international studies of beliefs and attitudes, that the common people in both the East and the West are steadily converging toward a "modal philosophy" which values political freedom, believes in free economic enterprise, but sides with the economic underdog. Nevertheless, there *are* substantial differences between our way of life and the Communist way, both in the trend of practice and the theory which supports it, and any acceptable policy must serve to preserve our own way rather than subvert it.

There are, of course, case-hardened statesmen who believe that our conflict with communism lies primarily in disagreement over who is to control the great and increasingly important uncommitted areas of the world, rather than in ideological conflict per se. There are also many well-disciplined political scientists who will say that the underlying source of international tensions is still, as it always has been, the struggle for power, and in this struggle weapons are simply instruments for effecting a change in the balance of power—whether the weapons be clubs or atomic warheads. Admitting the risk of alienating some influential readers, I will nevertheless dub this "the Neanderthal Conception of International Relations." Even though the manifest behaviors of nations may often conform to this image, I suspect that the Neanderthalic bluster has nearly always masked a deeper anxiety. Today, probably more than ever before in history, *mutual insecurity* rather than struggle for power is the major source of international tensions; elite groups now accept national security as their primary responsibility and base their decisions upon it.

Survival of Our Species or of Our Way of Life?

Disagreement over the relative importance of biological survival vs. preserving our way of life is one of the main sources of divergent opinion about policy in the nuclear age. This was made particularly clear in the debate between Bertrand Russell and Sidney Hook on the pages of the *New Leader* (May 26 and July 7, 1958). Russell maintained that a Communist victory would certainly not be so great a disaster as the extinction of human life, whereas Hook maintained just the reverse. I, for one, would have to side with Lord Russell in this calculus of human values—not only is survival a prerequisite for the attainment of all other more lofty goals but where there's life, there's hope. And, furthermore, it seems more than a little arrogant and presumptuous for a small segment of one generation to make such a decision for all people and for all future time.

However—fortunately—this is *not* a decision we are called upon to make at this time. Those who would pose the policy problem as a choice between abject surrender to communism or continuing our present policies to the point of no return have already given up trying to solve it. Such extreme positions inhibit the search for fresh policy alternatives, strategies through which we may be able to both survive *and* preserve our way of life.

Feasibility

But the criterion of feasibility places severe restrictions on the choice of alternatives. These restrictions stem not so much from the unmodifiability of human nature—it is highly modifiable, given time—but from the particular shaping of human behavior that we call *nationalism*. The external manifestations of nationalism are power competition, accompanied by mutual suspicion and aversion to compromise; the internal manifestations are intense patriotism, identification with national symbols, and similar phenomena.

Now it may be true that complete unilateral disarmament by either the United States or Russia would induce reciprocal adjustment by the other side, and it is quite possible that in the long run Gandhian passive resistance would preserve our way of life—but under existing nationalistic conditions, both internal and external, it would be impossible for a government to initiate such steps or long remain in power if it did. This is not to say that the policies we accept as traditional and now pursue are feasible either. In the next few pages I will try to show that neither our basic policy of mutual deterrence nor our attempts at mutual agreement by negotiation are really feasible under present conditions.

EVALUATION OF OUR PRESENT POLICY

The dominant theme in American international policy for a long time has been "peace through strength." The basic idea is that the only way to secure peace and security in a threatening world is to make one's own nation so powerful that no combination of enemies would dare to attack. This theme is accompanied by the assurance that we would never use this power unless provoked by aggression from outside—which does more to support idealism at home than to reduce anxiety abroad. This is still the basic policy espoused by political and military leaders responsible for our security in the present age of nuclear technology. Is our security increased by this policy? Let us evaluate it against the minimal criteria we have established.

Biological Survival

In a world that has resolved itself into two competing groups with roughly equal power, "peace through strength" becomes "peace through fear of retaliation," and with the advent of thermonuclear weapons we are rapidly approaching the point where it becomes "peace through fear of annihilation." The underlying hope behind our present policy of mutual deterrence is that, with either side capable of practically destroying the other by reflexive retaliation, a prolonged, if uneasy, "peace" can be maintained by the balance of terror. What are the actual dynamics of this situation?

It is clear, in the first place, that this is not a situation designed to promote feelings of security on either side. There is no elimination of the threat of nuclear destruction and all that it entails in the way of personal human suffering; quite to the contrary, it is this mutual terror that is supposed to guarantee the peace. Responsible people on both sides, in government, in the military, in science, feel themselves to be "walking on atomic eggs." The consequences of a mistake, of an error of judgment, become incalculable. Furthermore, it is difficult to maintain just the right degree of threat—not so little that an enemy is encouraged to aggress through confidence and not so much that he is encouraged to aggress through fear. I submit that this is an intolerable state of affairs, as much for nations as for the individuals who make them up.

The responses to such a situation of insecurity, anxiety, and conflict are complex and varied, but they are all designed to reduce these unpleasant states. One response is to support demands for research, development, and stockpiling of new and better armaments. But every step that serves to decrease insecurity at home serves to increase insecurity abroad. Thus we see that the policy of mutual deterrence through fear of retaliation leads inevitably to an armament race.

This inevitability is not rational but psychological—being able to annihilate an enemy once probably deters him almost as much as being able to annihilate him ten times over. Brown and Real, in their recent paper titled *Community of Fear* (2), have characterized the competitive psychology of the proponents of the arms race in this way: "Can gigaton bombs be built? We must do the work and see. Can climate over the Soviet Union be altered? We must experiment. Can the earth be burned, broken, kept from rotating? . . . All these questions must be considered. If we don't consider them, the Russians might, and if successful they would have us at a disadvantage." It is clear that, driven by such human suspicions and anxieties, the essential character of an arms race is continually shifting advantage and disadvantage. We do *not* have the stably poised balance of deterrence that mathematicians and chess players are fond of envisaging; rather we have a highly unstable, teetering imbalance in which either side may believe itself so far below as to strike out defensively or so far above as to strike out offensively.

The final degradation of human intelligence, and surrender of our right to decide our own fate, is to be found in proposals—seriously being considered because the Russians might be considering them—for "a push-button for the dead man's hand" and for "a Doomsday Machine." Since a surprise attack could well wipe out a major portion of the defending personnel, the argument goes, we must provide automatic devices that will react to blast, heat, or radiation levels by releasing our own retaliation. The "Doomsday Machine," which it is said (Kahn, in *Daedalus*, 14) could be built by 1970 for well under 100 billion dollars, would be such an automatic, deeply buried device capable of literally fragmenting the planet. One can imagine the hollow pleasure our dying civilians would take in the sure knowledge that enemy civilians were suffering the same final torment. The *purpose* of such machines, of course, is deterrence, and the *assumption* is that they would never be used, but as long as they exist would it be possible to talk rationally about their guaranteeing our biological security?

Feasibility

Is the policy of mutual deterrence a feasible one for the United States? The answer here seems to depend on whether we think of mutual deterrence in terms of a rationally sufficient minimum or in terms of a continually expanding arms race. Certainly it is feasible in the near future for this country to develop a system of "hardened," nearly impregnable intercontinental missile bases—a deterrent, second-strike force. Given the existing national and international situation, this is almost certain to happen on both sides, and therefore it is something which must be taken into account in any serious consideration of policy. As I shall try to demonstrate later, it is crucial that this nuclear force be explicitly conceived and designed as a second-strike, retaliatory system and that it be the minimum necessary for effective deterrence.

But, as we have seen, competitive military psychology leads not to the minimum necessary for effective deterrence but to the progressively expanding seesaw of an arms race. Is it feasible for this country to maintain a favorable balance in such a race? Although we have the initial advantage in a balanced technology and a wider economic cushion, in my own attempt to weigh this question objectively I come to the somber conclusion that we would ultimately lose in such a competition.

Why? In the first place, ours is the smaller nation in terms of both area and manpower—particularly if we place China on the scales. Our natural resources have been more fully utilized to date than those of China and the Soviet Union. Our traditional isolation by virtue of the two oceans which separate us from potential enemies has lost its significance in an age of ballistic missiles. We used to be confident in our greater supply of educated young people, our greater mastery of science, and our greater technical know-how—but surely only those who are incapable of reading the signs in our skies can cling to such confidence now.

But the biggest factor leading me to this conclusion is the difference in our "ways of life." The totalitarian system seems better able to wage a conflict on these terms than a democratic system: where the Communists have been able to channel the energies of their people into military preparations at the expense of civilian needs and comforts, we have been trying to maintain both a massive military establishment *and* the luxurious civilian economy depicted by Madison Avenue. Where the Communists have been able to order their young people into mathematics, engineering, and the physical sciences, our democratic system allows youths to choose their own careers—and most of them choose the business world where our free economy provides the largest rewards. Where the Communists are able to make quick decisions and abrupt changes in policy without continuous reference to the will of the people, democratic systems require the consent of the governed (even if indirectly through an intricate system of checks and balances among their representatives) and therefore display greater inertia in both launching new policy and terminating old. If I am right, the longer mutual deterrence works and the arms race continues, the more likely we are to fall behind.

Preserving Our Way of Life

It would seem, then, that to pursue the policy of mutual deterrence *successfully* will require us to give up as rapidly as possible a system of beliefs and practices which ill fits us for the race. As I have defined the nature of the real conflict with communism, this would mean losing what we are really fighting for in the course of fighting for it.

The signs of erosion in our way of life are already becoming apparent, despite the gradualness of the process: maintaining deterrent pressure demands a unified front in the eyes of the enemy, so the very diversity of opinion on which democracy thrives becomes dangerous (and we find one presidential candidate asserting that the other should not debate our foreign policy while Khrushchev is at the UN). An arms race demands secrecy, so the information citizens need is kept from them (and newspaper reporters try, usually in vain, to pierce the fog of secrecy). Maintaining our balance on the slippery seesaw demands quick decisions and commitments, so we find increasing pressures being brought to side-step the democratic process in determining policy (and policy-executing agencies like the military and the AEC assume policy-making roles, while elected senators and congressmen rubber-stamp their decisions).

Whether or not one considers these changes in our beliefs and practices necessary under present world conditions, they nevertheless must be recognized as weakening our democratic institutions. Some will argue that it has always been necessary to give up our freedoms in time of war in order that, in the long run, we might preserve them. But, not only does the ideological conflict between democratic and totalitarian systems have no foreseeable conclusion, the policy of mutual deterrence in itself says nothing about when it will be over. Our "way of life" is a set of learned habits of thinking and behaving which can be just as easily unlearned and forgotten by another generation. Prolonged subjection to a totalitarian set of beliefs, *particularly and perhaps only if self-imposed,* would probably result in a thorough distortion of our own sociopolitical philosophy.

But we have been considering only the effects within —what about the effects of this policy elsewhere? The usual argument has been that the Communist system will somehow naturally crack if the stalemate persists long enough. It is true that there are now operating in Russia strong liberalizing pressures that have become most evident in the shift from Stalinism to the present regime. These pressures are generated by education, by a gradually expanding civilian economy, by an increasingly self-conscious technological "middle" class, and other developments. The same pressures are being felt in the satellite countries. But the external threat produced and maintained by the arms race "keeps the totalitarian cap on"—it creates precisely the conditions under which human individuals are willing to forfeit their rights, are willing to sacrifice both physical luxuries and intellectual freedoms. The Communist concentration on the good world of the future, while slaving in the present, is in considerable part maintained by their perception of overwhelming external threat.

In other words, mutual deterrence fosters the very conditions, both in the United States *and* in Russia, which support a totalitarian way of life. In the most basic sense, then, this is a weapon turned against ourselves. Quoting again from the National Planning Association report: "Retaliation plans . . . promote a spirit of indifference to the widespread subjection of civilians to the horrors of warfare. In the seemingly logical pursuit of an idea we may thus lose sight of the prime goal of a war plan—namely, the best defense of our national values, ethics, and institutions."

Waning Initiative and the Concept of Limited War

Massive retaliation is clearly to be employed only as a last resort. Only if our heartland were endangered, only if our very survival were threatened, would we be willing to unleash such a holocaust. Both our allies and our enemies know this—the former finding little comfort in it and the latter little immediate threat. Therefore, it is completely unwieldy as an instrument for dealing with the everyday skirmishes of foreign policy that have less than survival significance.

Despite our overwhelming superiority in nuclear weapons at that time, we did not use them to conclude the Korean War—instead it fizzled to an inconclusive stalemate. The present state of unstable balance in nuclear retaliatory capacity has produced an almost complete "freeze" as far as foreign policy initiative is concerned. Neither side dares do anything boldly—except talk—for fear of starting something it doesn't want to finish. The prompt damping of Anglo-French initiative toward Egypt and the Suez by this country is one example; another is the indecisiveness of Russia in the Congo; yet another illustration of this new state of affairs is the way in which the Cuban mouse has been able to caper with relative immunity about the toes of the American elephant. To borrow Robert Colborn's apt image (4), international relations now display the massive apathy of people moving about under water.

The complete failure of deterrence through massive retaliation to provide a workable framework has led some people to search for ways in which ordinary war could be preserved as an instrument of foreign policy. Proposals usually take one of two forms: (a) implicit agreements to ban strategic ("saturation") nuclear weapons while still using tactical nuclear weapons; (b) implicit agreements to restrict wars to the use of conventional, non-nuclear weapons. The first version is essentially the Kissinger Plan, as developed in his *Nuclear Weapons and Foreign Policy* (20), but which has since been modified (cf. Kissinger's paper in *Daedalus*, 14). The second version, involving increased reliance on conventional weapons, seems to be the present trend in policy. Both proposals assume that international conflicts can be conducted as "gentlemanly wars" in which certain codes of conduct will be adhered to by the military and in which adequate, but not "survival state," morale can be generated and maintained in civilian populations.

In the first place it is clear that as long as strategic nuclear weapons are available and stockpiled, even though there may be explicit or implicit agreement not to use them, there always exists the possibility of their use. Therefore, limited war cannot be said to eliminate the threat to our biological survival. Indeed it is the presence of massive-retaliatory capacity in the background that is supposed to provide the graduated deterrence necessary to keep wars localized—the very horror of full-scale nuclear war is supposed to prevent antagonists from unleashing it. But, by the very same reasoning, this same horror already should have led us to nuclear disarmament, promptly agreed to by all sides—yet it obviously hasn't. If the horror of nuclear attack has not had this effect in a time of relative peace, what hope can we have that it will during a time of war?

Proponents of limited war see it as a strategy which will not only allow us to protect the perimeter of our sphere of interest by countering aggression wherever it may occur but one which will also allow us to take the initiative. The use of tactical nuclear weapons is considered advantageous for the United States because it substitutes highly mobile fire power for sheer manpower. How valid are these assumptions? In the first place, we can now expect the Russians quickly to cancel out the advantage of tactical nuclear weapons with similar devices of their own. Second, one can understand how countries being "protected" might take a dim view of being the sites of localized devastation, since the whole concept of limited war is to keep conflicts localized *elsewhere* than in the heartlands of the two major powers. Finally, what about initiative? Both Russia and the NATO powers have had conventional weapons available in great magnitude for a long time, but there has been little initiative—nor is there likely to be as long as the only protection against full-scale nuclear war is fear of it.

The particular danger in the limited-war conception is what the experts have come to call *escalation*. However appealing the notion of "gentlemanly war" may be to military men, it seems hardly feasible, given the attitudes and emotions generated in wartime by the frustrations of a war economy, the injury and death of loved ones, and the identification with far-flung symbols of victory and defeat. Modern ideological wars are waged by whole populations, not by a few champions following rigid codes of honor. Victories and defeats are viewed passionately, not with the indifference of peasants watching a tournament of knights. The will to sacrifice and fight is a monolithic energy, not easily guided in its course. Even though a conflict might begin as a localized affair, waged with conventional weapons, each side soon finds reasons to increase the violence of its attack. Reversals under conventional weapons lead field commanders to employ tactical nuclear weapons against what they conceive to be military targets —but humans are fallible, and what was thought to be tactical by one side is easily seen as strategic by the other.

When facing a disastrous defeat, full of the hatreds generated by war, people who would ordinarily shun the very thought of nuclear bombing of whole populations may clamor for it.

When and How Does Mutual Deterrence End?

Our political and military leaders have been virtually unanimous in public assertions that we must get ahead and stay ahead in the armament race; they have been equally unanimous in saying nothing about what happens *then*. Suppose we achieve the state of ideal mutual deterrence—capacity to annihilate each other completely from hardened land bases or elusive submarines—*what then?* Surely no sane man can envisage our planet spinning on into eternity, divided into two armed camps poised to destroy each other, and call it "peace" and "security"! The point is that *the policy of mutual deterrence includes no provisions for its own resolution.* Since nothing lasts forever, particularly anything constructed of such unstable components as the balance of terror, we must ask ourselves how this state of affairs is likely to be terminated. We have already seen that *escalation* from little war into big war is one possible resolution.

Another possibility, but rather remote, is *preventive war*. The decision to wage preventive war implies a sufficient lead in the armament race to minimize the probability of punishing reprisal or a sufficient frenzy to take the gamble. In either case, such a war would necessarily begin with a surprise attack that would make Pearl Harbor seem like a tea party in slow motion. This means that preparations would have to be made in secret and the final decision reached through other than democratic processes. In a country like ours this would probably mean a military coup. In considering this possibility, it must be kept in mind that the "lead" need not be in terms of superior weapons or defense—a cleverly designed infiltration of our "hardened" bases and submarines would serve just as well. It must also be realized that the longer a deterrent stalemate persists, the greater become the internal pressures to escape from the intolerable situation in one way or another.

A more likely possibility is *pre-emptive war*. If at some time a nuclear war appears inevitable, the advantages of striking first are very great. This means that unless there is rapid and full communication between opponents at times of crisis, to dispel what Schelling (34) has called "the reciprocal fear of surprise attack," either side may choose what seems to be the lesser risk of attacking first —convinced that the other is about to reach the same conclusion. The situations that *could* give rise to reciprocal fear of surprise attack are innumerable, e.g., an accidental nuclear explosion, rebellion in one of the satellite countries, United States action against Cuba, and so forth. As we shall see, the cold-war mentality fosters the conviction that the enemy—being unlike us in both morality and rationality—is likely to strike first in time of crisis. This conviction justifies our acting immorally and irrationally to beat him to the punch!

The possibilities of *accidental war* are many. They have been described by many writers, of science and of science fiction, and need not be detailed here (however, cf. Herman Kahn in 14). Although the absolute probability of accidental war may be small, particularly given the elaborate safeguards being devised for both men and materials, this is no basis for security. Suppose that the probability of throwing "snake eyes" twice in a row is only one in a thousand; if one keeps throwing dice long enough, this particular sequence is *certain* to come up sooner or later. By the same argument, the longer the state of mutual deterrence persists, the more and more probable becomes the eventual occurrence of the kind of accident that would precipitate full-scale war. And the consequences of double "snake eyes" in this case are so catastrophic that no odds are really acceptable.

Furthermore, in considering accidental war, we must keep in mind *the unpredictability of human behavior under stress*. The entire notion of mutual deterrence as a means of preserving peace is predicated upon the assumption of rationality on both sides. But, as the speed with which missiles can be delivered increases, the response time for retaliation decreases; and, as retaliation response-time decreases, so does the time available for rational thought and considered action. There must be dispersion of decision-making away from central authority toward more and more people whose fingers are closer to the "buttons" that must be pressed, and this increases the chance that *someone* will be psychologically unstable (irrational). Furthermore, we must accept the fact that there are people with suicidal tendencies who, in destroying themselves, have no compunctions about destroying others. The stresses of prolonged mutual deterrence can be expected to increase the numbers of such people, in high places as well as low.

Finally there is the matter of *dispersion of nuclear weapons to other nations*. The probabilities of accidental war will increase geometrically with the number of nations possessing nuclear weapons. It is estimated that by 1970 at least ten countries will have nuclear weapons—unless controls are instituted (25). Just as the Colt .45 brought big men and little men to common stature in the days of the Old West, so will nuclear weapons become "the great equalizer" among nations. A Cuba armed with nuclear weapons *could* devastate the United States as completely as could Russia. We cannot expect the smaller nations to forego the security and power that such equalizers seem to offer; to the contrary, we can expect them to beg, borrow, and steal the necessary know-how and materials. Recent developments have made it easier and less expensive to produce fissionable materials, and chemical weapons are even easier to produce. The period of international "blackmail in a suitcase" may not be far off. Furthermore, since the source of an ICBM attack or of a chemical invasion would be very difficult to pin-point in the short time available, it becomes possible for an aggressive Nth power to touch off a full-scale nuclear war between the major powers. Then, surely, would the meek inherit the earth—or what's left of it.

Negotiating Agreements for Mutual Disarmament

We have been considering only aggressive resolutions of the unstable balance of deterrence. Are there any non-aggressive possibilities? The traditional way of resolving international conflicts other than war has been through negotiating mutual agreements, pacts, or treaties governing armaments. If disarmament included nuclear weapons, there is no question but what the threat to biological survival would be at least temporarily alleviated. Such agreements would also serve to reduce the external threat felt by both sides and thereby create conditions favoring our way of life. But the problem here is *feasibility*.

It is unfortunate but true that the history of negotiations reveals an inverse relation between urgency and achievement—the greater the need for disarmament, the less seems to be the prospect for successful negotiation. This is because both sides bring to the conference table precisely those attitudes and beliefs which generated the tensions and arms race to begin with. Yet success in negotiation requires an awareness of the greater threat, a trust in the essential humanity of the enemy, and hence a willingness to compromise. As Bertrand Russell has so wisely (but, I'm afraid, naïvely) said, it requires both sides to accept a course in which neither gains and neither loses. Let us look more closely into the dynamics of this situation.

Human perceptions are easily influenced by previous conditioning, by existing attitudes, by dominant motives. If the larger of two moving dots on a screen is shown behind the smaller, it is perceived as "chasing" the little one; if the larger is shown in front of the smaller, it is "leading"

175

the little one (but rarely being chased!)—our previous experience with size in interpersonal relations influences our perception of this neutral event (cf. Heider and Simmel, 12). The objectively impassive face of a man in a picket line looks "threatening" to a representative of management, but "determined" to a representative of labor—their attitudes toward him differ. Elsewhere (26) I have summarized a great deal of experimental evidence which shows how momentary motives affect our interpretation of both words and events. Men who have just experienced failure become sensitized to words signifying failure; hungry men are prone to perceive food objects where there are none; ambiguous words are given interpretations that suit one's purposes and expectations. And as a person's drive level goes up—as he becomes more hungry, more angry, more anxious, as the case may be—the more rigid and inflexible become his ways of perceiving and interpreting (which is one reason why prospects of successful negotiation decrease as cold-war tensions increase).

One experimental demonstration of perceptual bias in which I participated myself many years ago seems particularly relevant here. Two bars of light arranged in the shape of an X (see the accompanying figures) are illuminated in rapid alternation, so that what the observer sees is a single bar rotating from one position to the other—the familiar "phi phenomenon" used in animated neon signs. Now if the two crossing bars are aligned at right angles to each other (Figure A) when the observer first sees them, he will be about equally likely to perceive either a "rocking" or a "teetering" motion. If they are originally aligned in the vertical plane (Figure B), he will always see "rocking"; if they are originally aligned in the horizontal plane (Figure C), he will always see "teetering"—in other words, the apparent movement ordinarily tends to occur over the shortest distance between lights. But now suppose we start the observer with the bars in position (B) and, *while he keeps watching*, we gradually shift the bars through the point of objective equality and into position (*C*). Rather than change his mode of perception, the observer will persist in seeing the original "rocking" movement far beyond the point of objective equality, more and more wildly "rocking" (*D*), until suddenly, at some point of gross *in*equality, it breaks into a mild, normal "teetering."

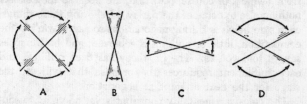

A   B   C   D

Now what has all this to do with disarmament negotiations? It provides a scientific background for one of the major dynamics operating in negotiations of all types, which I shall call *the biased perception of what is equable*. Bertrand Russell's rule about both sides accepting a course in which neither wins and neither loses may be logical, but it is not psycho-logical. East and West behave like two naïve observers of this phi phenomenon, trying to agree on the angle of objective balance—when one always starts from the vertical orientation and the other always from the horizontal. What one side perceives as equable (fair, balanced, just) is likely to be perceived by the other as inequable. The same American overseas bases that we see as "defensive" the Russians see as "offensive." The Soviets want nuclear disarmament first and inspection second (they have a closed society's traditional fear of espionage); Americans want inspection first and disarmament second (they have an open society's traditional fear of secrecy).

The second major dynamic working against successful negotiations is what has been called *the self-fulfilling prophecy*. This is one of the outcomes of the cold-war mentality. Both sides approach disarmament negotiations with the conviction that the other will prove obdurate, unreasonable, and entirely self-interested. Prior to each conference the press in each nation warns its readers to expect no progress because the other side really doesn't want peace. Each side believes the other is really using the negotiations to gain an edge in the cold-war propaganda front (which, of course, they both are because they expect nothing else to come of the parley). Believing these things, each side behaves during negotiations so as to "win" in the competition, little or nothing is achieved, and both parties say, "I told you so." The prophecy has been fulfilled, and each fulfillment reinforces the premise that will set the stage for the next attempt at negotiation.

The cold-war mentality contributes yet another psychological block to successful negotiation—*distrust in agreements*. Since the other fellow is the enemy, and enemies are evil, it follows that he will cheat where we would not —and one of the deepest American anxieties concerns being "taken advantage of," "hornswoggled," "hoodwinked." An example of this kind of thinking appeared in "A Second Open Letter to the Presidential Candidates" (released Friday, November 4, 1960) written by Thomas E. Murray, ex-chairman of the AEC. In this letter he argues for the resumption of testing nuclear weapons by the United States, particularly of a new "third generation" nuclear weapon primarily anti-personnel in nature. He says, "Nuclear technology does not stand still or stand pat, certainly not in the Soviet Union, which restlessly and in all secrecy seeks the means of military advantage." And later, "I take it for granted that the Soviet Union is actively developing nuclear technology along this revolutionary line. I must assume that they have done some preliminary tests of the new 'fantastic' weapon. Such tests could easily have been carried on without detection." In other words, there is no hard evidence that the Russians have been cheating on their self-imposed testing ban, but we must "take it for granted" that they are. (A cynical psychiatrist might comment on the similarity of this reasoning to the mechanism of projection he often sees in his patients.) No inspection system is ever going to be 100 per cent foolproof, and therefore some degree of mutual trust is essential. As long as the prospective signatories have no faith that agreements will be kept, we cannot expect them to negotiate in earnest.

We have behind us a long and dismal history of unsuccessful negotiation. It is easy to blame it all on the Communists, but the mechanisms we have been discussing operate on both sides. Judging from the woefully inadequate technical preparation of negotiators and the almost complete lack of government support for studying peaceful solutions (cf. papers by Humphrey, Davis, and Wiesner in 14), it would appear that neither side holds much hope for reaching agreements on arms control. And there are, of course, influential factions on both sides that firmly believe in the inevitability of war in some form and do not want the arms race terminated. The crucial point is that *mutual agreements on arms control require commitments prior to action,* and in the present climate of fear and distrust it is hard to see how bilateral commitments of any significance could be reached.

THE COLD-WAR MENTALITY

Most Americans who think about it at all, and I'm sure most Russians as well, are aware of the danger in our present course. Yet they feel impelled along it with a certain *sense of inevitability.* "We must learn to live with it," our newspapers tell us; editorials complain about the cost of military preparations, but conclude that "we must grin and pay it." What produces this sense of inevitability? What dynamic processes in human thinking operate in times of controversy to force ordinary disagreements toward mutual destruction? In order to understand the cold-war mentality, and also to lay the groundwork for what I hope will be the more constructive aspects of this paper, it is necessary at this point to inquire into several cognitive mechanisms that are well documented in the psychological laboratory.

Social Relativity

"Man is the measure of all things," it has been said—but this is true, I think, only to the extent that his science is primitive. One can trace in the development of science a progressive freeing of man's measurements or observations from the arbitrary platform of his own senses. Copernicus removed our planet from the center of the conceptual universe; Darwin removed our species from the center of God's creative intentions; Freud removed man's reason from the center of control in determining his behavior. We have yet to remove man's *ethnocentrism* from the central role in determining his social judgments.

Social judgments are also made relative to our own "position" as an observer. What a person perceives as "neutral" or "normal" on any dimension of judgment depends upon the range of relevant objects to which he has been exposed. These norms, taken together, constitute his "frame of reference" for judging subsequent objects. What is "big" for the child may be "little" for the adult; what is obviously "loud" and "risqué" to a New England grandmother may be "stylish" and "conservative" to her teenage granddaughter. Consistent shifts in the range of experience produce gradual "drift" in our norms—what was "big" for the child gradually becomes "little" as he matures. In the process of judgment, stimuli which deviate only slightly from our norms tend to assimilate with them, and the differences are minimized; conversely, stimuli which deviate a great deal produce a contrast effect, and differences are exaggerated. Scientific support for these notions can be found in classic psychophysical investigations and in more recent studies by Helson (13) on adaptation level, by Johnson (18) on the generalization of reference scales, by Hovland and Sherif (16), Peak (31), and others on the phenomena of assimilation and contrast in social as well as physical judgments.

We are seldom aware of our own norms—they are projected outward as the natural design of the universe. For my teen-age son to wear his trousers barely above the midline of the buttocks is *obviously* sloppy; for Khrushchev to pound his desk at the UN with his fists (and worse, with his shoes!) as a sign of displeasure is *obviously* boorish. Nor are we ordinarily aware of drifts in our norms—it is always the things and people "out there" that are shifting while we remain the bedrock of constancy and stability. It is always the younger generation that has changed, not us; we thought and felt at eighteen just as we do now at forty-five! And so it is with objects of overwhelming threat or distaste. During the past decade we have steadily but imperceptibly adapted to the horror of indiscriminate civilian extinction and to the threat to our own survival, to the point where we can now read with perfect equanimity a feature article telling how a certain general has been assigned the task of selecting precisely the strategic (not tactical) targets in Russia at which our nuclear missiles will be aimed—and the certain knowledge that we are being similarly pin-pointed by some Russian general hardly ripples the pool of our complacency.

To fully appreciate the location of our own social norms it is necessary to get outside the mass of cultural stimuli to which we have adapted, to get away from the pervasive frame of reference provided by our own mass media. Spending time in other countries—particularly if one breaks free of the protective "American bubble"—is an excellent way to accomplish this. During the past year I have spent considerable time outside this country in connection with some cross-cultural research we are doing. I have found the foreign press full of refreshing heresy! And, for both ourselves and the Russians, I have been moved to wish, with Robert Burns:

> O wad some Power the giftie gi'e us
> to see oursels as ithers see us!

But while the cold-war haze is lifted, and East-West relations are treated with balance and objectivity in, say, Bombay and Teheran, one also needs to see the snarling, fist-shaking treatment of Pakistan-Indian relations in the Bombay newspapers and of Egyptian-Iranian relations in the press of Teheran! The difficulty of getting outside one's own social conditioning has already been illustrated in my analysis of bilateral negotiations; what I called *biased perceptions of what is equable* is simply a special instance of the relativity of human judgments.

As a matter of fact I think one could describe at least three stages in the development of clear social thinking—or of "becoming civilized," if you will. At the simplest, most primitive stage *we unconsciously project our own frame of reference onto others.* Since Ego assumes Alter to be using the same norms as himself, it follows that when Alter sees as "straight" what to Ego is obviously "crooked," when he judges to be "tasteless" what to Ego is obviously "tasty," and so on, he must be deliberately malingering, must be evil in some sense, or perhaps sick or abnormal. A classic example of this is given in Hans Reusch's anthropological novel about the Eskimo, *Top of the World:* the hero, Ernenek, plies his white guest with his most savory delicacies, like fermented bear brain, and is insulted when they are turned down with disgust; his wife, Asiak, makes the final gesture of Eskimo sociability, prettying her hair with urine, greasing her face with melted blubber, and then offering herself, giggling and blushing, to their guest; the poor man tries to flee, whereupon Ernenek, outraged, dashes him against the ice wall until he is dead (32).

The second stage is where *we recognize the relativistic*

nature of Alter's frame of reference, but not our own. This produces a more humanitarian approach to social problems, a "forgive *them* for *they* know not what they do" attitude. This is the level of understanding at which we account for disapproved behavior in others as being due to the conditions under which they happen to develop. Thus members of minority groups are "pushy," "aggressive," or "immoral," because they grew up in an atmosphere of prejudice or without as much education as we've had. This is "the White Man's burden" idea, and at least it leads to less punitive reactions than Ernenek's.

The third stage, and one that is arrived at with great difficulty and maintained with even greater difficulty, is where *we realize the equally relativistic nature of our own frame of reference.* Here Ego seeks to understand the nature and location of his own "platform" as well as that of Alter. This is the parent who is able to see that maybe his own idea of how high up the trousers "look right" is essentially arbitrary. This is the sensitive—not "ugly"—American who realizes that his own neutral points on the clean-dirty, tasty-distasteful, or even moral-immoral scales of judgment are no more "natural" than those of the Mexican or Hindu. This is also the student of international affairs who sees our own policies to be as relative to our own cultural heritage as the enemy's are to his.

There are some people who feel that accepting the notion of relativity in human social judgment is tantamount to claiming that there are no absolutes, no goods or evils, no rights or wrongs. I would conclude just the opposite —it is precisely *because* human perception and judgment are so liable to bias, so subject to the prejudice of experience and motivation, that we need continually to strive for valid and objective external criteria. Certainly there are criteria external to cultural experience that bear upon such significant matters as the conditions for health and disease, medical practices, population control, agricultural techniques, how to control floods, and even how to build better bridges. To understand, and thereby discount, the cold-war mentality, it is particularly important that we substitute objective for subjective criteria and try to see ourselves and others more clearly.

Psycho-logic

Over the past two decades a great deal of social psychological research—by Heider (11), Festinger (7), Abelson and Rosenberg (1), Osgood, Suci, and Tannenbaum (29), and many others—has been converging on a conclusion about human thinking that common sense had already isolated as "the consistency of little minds." Unfortunately, as we shall see, the same pressures toward consistency affect big minds as well as little, in high places as well as low. I have detailed the theory and evidence elsewhere (28), but for our present purposes the following summary statements will have to suffice: Whenever cognitively inconsistent elements are forged together in assertions (in news items we read, in interpersonal situations we observe, etc.), psychological stress toward consistency is produced; this stress resolves itself in a variety of ways (denying the truth of the assertion or event, changing one's attitude toward one of the elements, etc.), but typically the resolution is one which requires a minimum of cognitive restructuring. In other words, human beings generally react to events which do not fit their expectations, to propositions which are inconsistent with their existing attitudes, with mental adjustments designed to preserve as simple and stable a "world view" as possible. Each of us has a set of highly intense values—concerning our self-image, our family, our religion, our nation, our job—which serve as anchor points for our cognitive structure, and these exert a pushing-pulling effect upon all other ideas we encounter.

What results is a kind of pseudo-logic, or psycho-logic, to which we are all susceptible to some degree—particularly when we are emotional, are not alert, or are dealing with matters outside our own areas of special training. Psycho-logic underlies the oversimplified "two-valued orientation" stressed by General Semantics. Thus, if we like Ike, and he happens to praise some congressman from Timbuktu, this relatively unknown congressman tends to rise in our estimation (it is consistent for us to favor things favored by people we like and respect); but let Mr. Khrushchev comment on this congressman's sound ideas—a type of assertion popularly known as "the kiss of death"—then psycho-logically, but not logically, we find ourselves distrusting this man (it is consistent for us to be against things favored by those we dislike). It is not logical for us to conclude that a man who beats his wife is a worse poet therefore, but it is psycho-logical. The fact that psycho-logic may sometimes lead to logical conclusions does not validate the process.

Psycho-logic runs rampant in the area of international relations, where the usual corrective process of reality testing is difficult to apply. It fosters what Robert Colborn, an editor of *Business Week,* has called (4) "the corrupting myth of an apocalyptic world struggle between Communism and some indescribable side of the angels." It is what leads many people to conclude that Nehru is pro-Communist because he insists on India's neutrality ("If you're not with us you must be against us"). It is the dynamism behind the self-fulfilling prophecy: It is consistent for us to expect the Soviets to cheat on any arms-control agreement and to use any negotiation for cold-war propaganda. Psycho-logic has made the enemy in every past war into a bogy man—the Simon Legree of the Civil War, the murderous Santa Anna of the war with Mexico, the Kaiser of the First World War, the cruel, bucktoothed Jap of the Second World War—even though not long before the war, and soon after, he may have been our friend and ally. Here again, of course, there may happen to be elements of logical validity in these images, Adolf Hitler being a case in point, but the process is independent of validity.

What are the dynamics of bogy building? Given the belief by each side that WE are *good, kind, fair,* and so on —a necessary and generally valid belief as far as everyday human relations are concerned—and given also the logical opposition between WE and THEM, between FRIEND and ENEMY, psycho-logic dictates that THEY, THE ENEMY, must be *bad, cruel, unfair,* and so on through the opposites of all traits we attribute to ourselves. This conception serves both to justify aggressive behavior by WE against THEM and effectively to nullify any non-aggressive, conciliatory ploys by THEM as being deceptions. But what happens when WE are exposed to real live THEMS—when we visit their homes and farms, or vice versa, and find them *friendly, sociable,* and in many ways *just like us?* The cognitive line of least resistance in this case is to further discriminate among THEM—it is the ENEMY LEADERS who are the *bad, dangerous* fellows, and we begin to wonder psychologically why the *good* RUSSIAN PEOPLE don't overthrow their *bad* COMMUNIST LEADERS (just as, no doubt, the Russian man in the street wonders why the *good* AMERICAN WORKERS, *just like him,* haven't yet begun the revolution against their *bad* CAPITALIST LEADERS!).

Once the fundamental evaluative polarity has been established, then psycho-logic operates subtly but continuously on the interpretation of all subsequent incoming information. One effect is to push both sides down reciprocal *paths of self-delusion.* In our own case, observe the alacrity and near universality with which our media people jumped on the "blame it all on Khrushchev" bandwagon even before the dust of the summit fiasco had settled—in the face of evidence of a good share of culpability on our own side and at the expense of healthy self-criticism. Or witness the ease with which we have accepted the official interpretation that the demonstrations in Japan were Communist-inspired; the intensely pacifistic attitude of many people in that country and their legitimate concern about again being the target for atomic bombs because of American bases there has hardly been mentioned.

Another effect is the setting up of *double standards of national morality*. Exactly the same behavior is moral if WE do it but immoral if THEY do it. Why? Because different *motives* are attributed to WE and to THEY in keeping with psycho-logic. Witness the debate over the U-2 spy-plane incident. It is legitimate for us to spy on them in order to defend ourselves against treacherous surprise attack; but since they view themselves as peace-loving, not treacherous, our justification is incredible in their eyes and our insistence on continuing such flights aggressive. Or observe the conclusion of an editorial in a local newspaper on the downing of a C-47 in East Germany: "It was not to be expected that the Americans would receive the courtesies and comforts showered upon those Russian sailors who . . . were rescued from their open boat . . . and given the grand tour in this country. There is satisfaction here that the C-47 incident had a happy ending, even if the Russians were actuated by propaganda motives and hope to profit from their action."

We expect the normal human being to defend himself against attack, including mental attack. We expect him to refute any suggestion that he is wrong or immoral. But we also expect him to be accessible to facts, pleasant or unpleasant. If he is not, if he refuses to accept reality, then we place him in an institution. Unfortunately there are no institutions for nations. If whole groups of people, including their leaders, refuse to accept reality, if their communications media consistently paint self-righteous pictures in disregard of facts, then there is no court to dispel the dangerous process of self-delusion. Both Russia and the United States, along with all other nations on this globe, have been steadily manufacturing their own versions of reality in absolute blacks and whites. As those of us who deal with individual human beings under stress realize so well, there are seldom, if ever, absolute blacks and whites. But in the behavior of nations we are asked to think like worms. Both sides need thoughtful self-criticism from within, but the psycho-logic of mass self-justification makes this very difficult to apply—and support once it has been applied.

Finally it must be emphasized that such psycho-logic constitutes the deepest resistance to any non-aggressive, co-operative strategies in foreign policy. To illustrate this point, let us recall the good philosopher Socrates from his grave and ask him to apply his method of questioning to a typical American—realizing full well that the philosopher would reach similar conclusions if he appeared on the streets of Moscow.

Suppose, says Socrates, that Russian Man were to decide that war under present conditions is intolerable and were publicly to destroy all of his weapons—would you, American Man, leap to destroy him in a nuclear holocaust? Of course not, replies American Man—we are only concerned with protecting ourselves, not destroying others. Would you overrun the Soviet Union, asks Socrates, and enslave the Russian people? For goodness sake, American Man replies with a grin, *we* have no imperialist ambitions—and, in any case, a world unified under our way of life would be as good for them as for us. To tell the truth, he adds, we'd welcome the chance to get rid of our weapons and live in peace. Very well, then, says the wise Socrates, do you think that Russian Man would leap to destroy you with his nuclear missiles if you were to lay down your weapons and render yourself defenseless? Here there is a long pause. Finally American Man replies that maybe the Russians wouldn't, but he can't afford to take a chance on it—and, in any case, he adds, they would certainly take advantage of our helplessness by overrunning the world and making Communists out of everybody. You apparently wish me to conclude, says Socrates, that Russian Man is intrinsically different from American Man. But can you support your opinion with reason?

I can almost hear the objections of many readers at this

point. It may be true that Americans would react to a defenseless enemy in humane ways, but the Russians are another matter altogether. As Sidney Hook (15) has said, men like Stalin, Bulganin, and Khrushchev—the whole crew in the Kremlin—are power-mad fanatics. "Today, a Communist world would be a tightly knit despotism of fear without sanctuaries, without interstices to hide, without possibilities for anonymity. . . . A Communist world could easily become a scientific Gehenna . . . our children and grandchildren may curse us for turning them over to the jailers of a Communist 1984 in which, brainwashed and degraded, they are not even free to die until their masters give them leave." Now I certainly do not claim any exclusive possession of the truth, and it could be that Hook is more nearly right in this than I am. But I can show how such bogy-man conceptions of the enemy develop naturally out of the dynamics of human thinking—when little minds seek simple consistencies in a complex world, or big minds like Hook's operate under intense emotion, as I suspect was the case. The admonition to "know thyself" is *a propos* here; only to the extent that we understand the workings of our own minds can we arrive at policies which satisfy the requirements of reason and reality.

Cognitive Stereotypy

As we trace the course of evolution, and more particularly the development of the cortex, we find higher species capable of maintaining longer delays, employing more extended foresight, and striving for more remote goals. Within each species the more intelligent members display these capacities to a greater degree than the less intelligent. But intense emotion has the effect of primitivizing this capacity, and the motivational conditions of controversy (e.g., our present tensions/arms-race dilemma) are precisely those designed to restrict our perspective and foresight.

The basic psychological notion here is that, beyond some optimum level for facilitation, increased motivation serves not only to energize the organism but also to restrict its capacity to select among alternatives at all levels of behavioral organization. The result is that heightened emotion and drive tend to produce stereotypy, in perception, in interpretation, and in association, as well as in overt behavior. When emotionally driven, we tend to see things in terms of our most probable expectations, to decide things along the most habitual lines, and to act most predictably. The scientific underpinnings here are implicit in Hull's behavior theory (17) and explicit in the more recent work of Spence and his associates (36); Hebb (10), Malmo (23), and others have provided tie-ins with the neurophysiology of the activation systems; I have utilized these notions in analyzing the motivational dynamics of language behavior (26). The expected stereotypy effects were demonstrated, for example, in a comparison of suicide notes with ordinary letters to friends and relatives (30) and in a comparison of word association under high and low drive conditions (3)—in both cases the more driven subjects displayed less spontaneity, less diversity, less flexibility.

One effect of drive-produced stereotypy is that it reduces capacity to solve problems. Rational problem solving requires that one understand his own ultimate goals, weigh the consequences of alternative means to these goals, and then select among the alternatives in terms of their success probabilities. And, of course, problem situations are more or less defined by the fact that the dominant, habitual responses don't work—if they did, there obviously wouldn't be any problem. Yet, as we have seen, the effect of heightened emotion is both to reduce awareness of available alternatives and decrease the probability of any novel responses. A normally intelligent raccoon trying to get out from under a stinging shower will persistently bang its head against a locked door that used to be open, completely ignoring free passageways to left and right.

In strictly analogous fashion, nations today are lumbering down the one habitual path to "security"—bigger and better weapons—gathering as they go tensions which make it less and less possible to conceive of any other alternatives. This has always been the dominant response to external threat, and, being habitual, this course is felt to be "realistic." Unfortunately "realistic" is usually equated with what is familiar, "tried and true." Anthropologists have described cultures that, through blind adherence to practices that once were realistic, have gradually committed suicide. I think that we are in exactly the same spot. We are continuing to practice rites and rituals of international relations that were developed in and appropriate to the past—firmly believing them to be realistic—in a nuclear present that renders them suicidal.

Foreshortening of perspective is another result of heightened emotion and motivation. A monkey that has been trained under ordinary levels of drive to delay his opening of a drawer for several minutes will, when made very hungry or frightened, reach for the drawer right away and therefore lose his peanut. Similarly, in this age of awful military power, people feel driven to reach for immediate security, however illusory it may be, and are also in danger of losing their peanuts. The truly magnificent achievements of human science—achievements that soon may free us from earthly bondage and catapult us toward the stars—seem to have significance only within the petty framework of the cold war. Our leaders, almost without exception, seem fixated upon the immediate goal of passing or staying ahead of the Russians in total military power, in numbers of engineers produced, in economic growth, in prestige—as if we were engaged in some back-alley foot race. The larger goals of the human species and the civilization which it has built together, not separately, are lost in the scuffle.

The Sense of Inevitability

Most Americans are filled with the basically irrational conviction that the only way to avoid military conflict with the Communist world is to prepare for it. Now we are in a better position to understand this conviction. Unconsciously projecting our own norms and values, we feel threatened when they are not adhered to and attribute it to the essential boorishness and deceit of others. By encouraging self-delusion and condoning a double standard of national morality, our psycho-logic has created an over-simplified world inhabited by angels and bogy men. Everything becomes channeled into this one overwhelming polarity of good and evil—Cuba is seen as a Communist outpost (when there is probably nothing more Communist about Castro Cuba than there is democratic about Franco Spain) and even school integration in the South is viewed by some as Communist-inspired! Faced apparently with such powerful and expanding evil, mounting anxiety narrows our perspective, robs us of our problem-solving capacity, and forces us into the most stereotyped and traditional responses to external danger—maintaining a threatening posture and building weapons as fast as we can. Now *if* the enemy is in truth inhuman and completely unlike us, then we have no choice but to kill and be killed. Or, if the enemy is entirely human and much like us, *but* we and he continue to hew inflexibly to present policies, then nuclear holocaust is equally inevitable.

INITIATIVE THROUGH UNILATERAL ACTION

Nuclear deterrence has frozen initiative in foreign policy along traditional lines. Paradoxically, the very capacity for destruction which nuclear technology represents, the very power it confers, serves to inhibit freedom of action by those who possess it. Is there any solution? Can't we get rid of these new weapons and go back to the almost friendly pattern of "war as usual"? No, we can never go back—the scientific knowledge that yields the nuclear technology is irreversible. Can't we somehow reach mutual agreements with the Russians on disarmament? The prospects are not good, as we have seen. The same forces that have created the arms race militate against success in mutual negotiations—and it is not only the Russians with whom we must negotiate. Unilateral acts of an aggressive, tension-*increasing* nature have become prohibitively dangerous, and therefore the whole notion of power politics has now become anachronistic. We stand with terrible power but shorn of initiative. What about unilateral acts of a tension-*reducing* nature? Abject unilateral disarmament is unfeasible; it asks American Man to act in a uniquely civilized way and to assume that Russian Man would respond in kind—but human culture is not ready for such a big step. However, there are other forms of unilateral, tension-reducing action, and these we must now explore in the hope of discovering some way out of the Great Freeze.

The Arms Race in Reverse

Imagine two husky men standing facing each other near the middle, but on opposite sides, of a long and rigid seesaw balanced over an abyss. As either man takes a step outward, the other must compensate with a nearly equal step outward on his side or the balance will be destroyed. The farther out they move, the greater the unbalancing effect of each step, and the more agile and quick to react both men must become to maintain the precarious equilibrium. To make the situation even worse, both of these husky men realize that this teetering board has some limit to its tensile strength—at some point it is certain to crack, dropping them both to destruction. So both men are frightened, but neither is willing to admit it for fear the other might take advantage of him.

How are these two men to escape from this dangerous situation, a situation in which the fate of each is bound up with that of the other? One reasonable solution immediately presents itself: Let them agree to walk slowly and carefully back toward the center of the teetering board in unison. To do this they must trust each other. But these men do not trust each other, and each supposes the other to be irrational enough to destroy them both unless he (Ego) preserves the balance. But now let us suppose that it occurs to one of these men that perhaps the other is just as frightened as he is and would also welcome some way of escaping from this intolerable situation. So this man decides to gamble on his new insight and calls out loudly, "I am taking a small step *toward* you!" The other man, rather than have the precarious balance upset, also takes a tentative step forward, whereupon the first takes yet another, larger step. Thus they work their ways back to safety by a series of unilateral, yet reciprocal, steps—very much as they had originally moved out against each other.

As a form of international behavior, the arms race is a case of graduated, but reciprocal, unilateral action. It is obviously unilateral, in that the nation developing a new weapon, increasing its stockpile, or setting up a new military base does not make its action contingent upon any agreement with the other side. It is reciprocal because each increment in military power by one side provides the stimulus for intensified efforts by the other to catch up and get ahead. The arms race is necessarily graduated: first, by the irregular and somewhat unpredictable pace at which scientific technology develops and second by oscillating national moods of fear and relative complacency. Is it possible that the arms race provides a model for its own reversal? Graduated and reciprocated unilateral action of a tension-*reducing* nature is certainly conceivable—but is it feasible under present conditions? In the remainder of this paper I will try to show that, given the same dedication and effort we have been pouring into the arms race, its reversal is certainly feasible; more than that, given existing capacities for nuclear retaliation, some policy of this sort may well be the only avenue left for positive foreign policy.

Graduated Reciprocation in Tension Reduction

Perhaps the most general characterization of my proposal would be that it asks for a deliberate "peace offensive" designed to induce reciprocation by an enemy. It is an offensive in deeds rather than words, but the deeds are carefully graduated in magnitude of risk so as to maintain tolerable levels of dignity and security. The actions we might undertake would be highly diversified and an opponent would not be able to predict their time and place, but all our actions would be intended to reduce tensions. The range of acts envisaged is much broader than "disarmament" and even broader than "disengagement," as usually conceived, since much more than arms control is involved, and even "engagement" in certain co-operative activities would be included. The goal is reversal of the tensions/arms-race spiral and creation of an atmosphere in which steps toward a more permanent solution of the problem of survival in the nuclear age can be taken. The following principles are intended to guide us to this goal.

Inducing Reciprocation

1) *Our unilateral acts must be perceived by an opponent as reducing his external threat.* To be most effective in inducing an opponent to reciprocate, the initiator must attempt to reduce his opponent's level of tension so that the opponent, in turn, acquires increased freedom for ac-

tion. This means that the acts must not be advantageous to the initiator in terms of military aggression; they may or may not be militarily disadvantageous—although, of course, militarily disadvantageous actions have an additional degree of "bonafideness." As we shall see later in a hypothetical example, the ways in which perception of external threat may be reduced are many and varied.

2) *Our unilateral acts must be accompanied by explicit invitations to reciprocation.* In the recent history of Russo-American relations there have been many instances of unilateral, tension-reducing actions on both sides, but they have been largely abortive—because they were not announced in advance as part of a consistent policy, were not explicit as to expected reciprocation, and were therefore never disentangled from the cold war. It is the fact that reciprocation is expected which must be made explicit. Reciprocation might be the same or different in kind, depending on the nature of the initiating act and it need not be objectively balanced in quantity; as Fisher (8) has pointed out, the burden of an identical rule may be quite different in two countries (e.g., openness of inspection in the United States and the U.S.S.R.). In some cases the invitation to reciprocation may be entirely open-ended, leaving the selection of appropriate response up to the opponent, or we may merely intimate what we hope for in return for our concession. Explicit invitation to reciprocate serves several purposes: it encourages the opponent actively to consider tension-reducing alternatives; it assures him that we will correctly interpret his action; and it indicates that we believe his motives parallel, if not identical, to ours.

3) *Unilateral acts must be executed regardless of prior commitment by the opponent to reciprocate.* This is the characteristic that distinguishes this policy most clearly from mutual negotiation and allows a reasonable degree of initiative. We have already seen how attempts at negotiating agreements under conditions of high tension are

bedeviled by biased perceptions of what is equable and by self-fulfilling prophecies. As long as we remain chained to the requirement of prior commitment by the opponent, our freedom of action is greatly restricted, as is his. Furthermore, our execution of a previously announced action serves to contradict cries of "cold-war propaganda," and the opponent's prophecy is *not* fulfilled—which is a significant learning experience for him. Furthermore, as Fisher (8) has also pointed out, unilateral action has distinct advantages where perceptions of what is equable are biased or where the same rule might be unequally burdensome on two countries—it is more flexible in that it allows for equality of intent and spirit despite inequality in specific performance.

4) *Unilateral acts must be planned in sequences and continued over considerable periods regardless of reciprocation by an opponent.* Where the announcement of an initial act may be greeted with cries of "propaganda" by an opponent, particularly since it would be small in magnitude of risk, and where even its subsequent execution could still be considered a cold-war "trick," the announcement and then execution of the next—and the next, and the next —makes it harder and harder to maintain this interpretation. Not only is the self-fulfilling prophecy being repeatedly denied, but the bogy-man conception of their enemy (ourselves) is becoming less tenable—the machinations of psycho-logic (ordinarily reinforced by the threatening posture of the enemy) must become more and more complex and ludicrous until they fall of their own weight. This, again, is a forced learning process we are able to induce unilaterally. Maintaining a series of unilateral, tension-reducing acts produces a cumulative pressure toward reciprocation.

5) *Unilateral acts must be announced in advance of execution and widely publicized to ally, neutral, and enemy countries as part of a consistent policy.* Tension-reducing acts are likely to lose some of their impact if

announcement and execution are coincident. Rather, time intervals between announcement and execution should be planned, these being just sufficient for rational consideration by an opponent, for his preparation of reciprocative action, and for world opinion to mobilize. This means that the time interval will necessarily vary with the nature of the act. However, the announcement of each act should include the proposed time of execution; otherwise, both the announcement and the execution would lose much of their force. General public announcement should be made for several reasons: first, many of our acts would invite reciprocation from several or even all other countries; second, one of the major pressures toward reciprocation by the opponent would come from favorable reactions in the neutral or uncommitted nations; third, we would be interested in offering a new model of international behavior to all nations. Linking each announced action with a consistent policy of tension reduction through graduated and (hopefully) reciprocated unilateral acts would serve both to disentangle it from the cold war and to augment its cumulative impact by explicit identification with other actions, past and future.

Maintaining Security

1) *Unilateral acts must be graduated in risk potential, should they not be reciprocated or should they be exploited by an opponent.* Being a highly unconventional international policy, because of both its unilateral and its non-aggressive nature, graduated and reciprocated tension reduction is liable to suspicion abroad and resistance at home. Therefore, its initial phases must be viewed as a learning experience on both sides of the fence. If the correct national behavior is to be acquired, the probabilities of reward must be considerably higher than the probabilities of punishment. In general, earlier unilateral acts would be smaller in magnitude of risk than later acts. Further-

more, the initial series of acts would be so designed as to maximize the likelihood of clear reciprocation being obtained (e.g., involve issues where we know the opponent is eager to move positively) and minimize the likelihood of resistance at home (e.g., involve issues where security seems to be less concerned than general human welfare). Whatever scoffing there might be at the insignificance of our initial acts would be resolved in the continuation of the program. Another basis for graduation throughout would be whether or not reciprocation for previous acts had been obtained; failure would be followed by acts of lower risk potential and success by acts of higher risk potential. This stresses the need for extraordinary intelligence, information, and flexibility in the design and maintenance of such a policy—which should be viewed as a challenge rather than a flaw.

2) *Unilateral acts must be diverse in nature and unpredictable (by an opponent) as to locus of application and timing in series.* The only thing that binds together the separate actions envisaged in this policy is their tension-reducing impact upon an opponent (and, indirectly, upon ourselves). Their nature and area of application can and should be diverse. This is in order that reduction of tension and pressure toward reciprocation on the opponent can be maintained cumulatively without progressively weakening ourselves in any one area. Thus, an act in one area (e.g., inviting diplomatic exchange with Communist China) would be followed by a number of acts in quite different areas (e.g., on controls and inspection vis-à-vis Russia, on joint provision of technicians for the Congo, etc.) before we would return to another step in the China area again. The locus of application and timing of our unilateral acts must be unpredictable by the opponent to prevent his usurpation prior to our announcement of intention. I submit that the likelihood of an opponent taking an aggressive initiative (e.g., Communist China invading the islands of Quemoy and Matsu), and his support by

world opinion if he does, is much less if we have already announced that we intend to take the relevant action as of a certain date.

3) *Unilateral acts must never endanger our "heartland" or reduce our fundamental capacity for retaliatory second strike.* I take it for granted that in the very near future both Russia and the United States will have ready an effective second-strike nuclear force, whether consisting of "hardened" land bases or of mobile nuclear-powered submarines armed with Polaris-type missiles, or both. This is an awesome fact of life which may have redeeming features; it may offer the psychological support for tension-reducing actions within tolerable limits of security—*provided that* (a) the retaliatory, second-strike nature of this power is continually emphasized and (b) the minimum power necessary for effective deterrence, rather than an arms race, is maintained. This minimum capacity for effective deterrence should not be reduced by unilateral action (even though other forms of armament could be), but rather its elimination should be arrived at through negotiation, in the atmosphere of greater confidence and trust produced by the policy we are discussing. The reason for preserving our retaliatory capacity while continuing a program of tension reduction is that it is this capacity for near annihilation on both sides that both encourages reciprocation and prevents overstepping. The reason for not initiating actions which might endanger our "heartland" is again that, if taken advantage of, we would be likely to release full-scale retaliation and thereby write "finis" to this chapter of the human book. This proposal for "nuclear deterrents last" is novel and quite the opposite of most disarmament proposals, which ask for "nuclear disarmament first and popguns last." I firmly believe I am right in this—as long as nationalistic tensions and technical know-how exist, popguns can start conflicts that end in nuclear devastation.

4) *Unilateral acts of tension-reducing nature must be accompanied by explicit firmness in all areas.* This may

sound like a bit of fine sophistry, but it is no more so than the way a wise parent encourages spontaneity in his child in prescribed situations but without letting down the bars all over the house. In the present case this means that announcements of unilateral actions would be accompanied by explicit warning that encroachment in this or any other area would be resisted firmly. Indeed, should such encroachment occur—and one can be certain that under present conditions of nuclear deterrence it would be partial, tentative, and probing—we would have to deal with it firmly, just as if the policy of tension reduction were not in effect. Here yet again we would have a kind of learning experience for any opponent as well as ourselves—learning that unilateral action does not mean "softness" or "surrender." However, just as the wise parent does not take away all privileges from his child and forever lock him in the cellar for a single misdemeanor, so the action we would take for a specific encroachment should be pin-pointed to that event in both word and deed, i.e., designed to restore the *status quo*. And once the *status quo* was restored, the program of graduated tension reduction should continue as before, without reprisals. It is apparent that this policy represents something quite different than the traditional "Neanderthal" conception of international relations; maintaining the initiative would require both firmness of purpose and exercise of self-restraint, by the government, by the military, by the mass media, and ultimately by the public at large—but the stakes are high and the policy is appropriate to the nuclear age.

A *Hypothetical Program*

Selecting the particular unilateral acts that might be available for such a policy and ordering them as to risk potential is a complex task. It would require specialists in many areas, government and non-government, and a great deal of information not available to the ordinary citizen, such as myself. This is why the illustrative program described below must be purely hypothetical. However, I am sure that if only one cent out of every defense dollar were put into an intensive effort to design and evaluate series of graduated tension-reducing actions, effective and flexible programs could be devised. Is this too much to invest in the search for alternatives to nuclear war and a way out of the Great Freeze on policy? Judging from the almost complete lack of such support in the past, perhaps it is; but, on the other hand, perhaps policy makers are beginning to see more clearly the nature of our situation.

The following hypothetical program of unilateral actions assumes several broad areas of application (A. Science and Secrecy; B. Communist China; C. Controls and Inspection; D. Socio-economic; E. Military) and several levels of risk potential or significance (1, 2 . . . N) within each area. It is assumed that the periods of various actions (between announcement and execution) may overlap and that an opponent may or may not reciprocate in any particular instance. It is also assumed that our announced actions are executed on schedule.

> *April 1:* We announce that, as of May 1, we intend to make public all medical information we have been gathering concerning man in space; reciprocation invited from all nations; nature of general policy indicated (A1).
>
> *May 1:* We announce that, as of May 15, all discriminatory trade and travel restrictions with respect to Communist China will be lifted, and we will entertain diplomatic exchange; reciprocation in kind is invited and general policy stated (B1).
>
> (*A1 reciprocated by Russia and most other countries.*)
>
> *May 20:* We announce a unilateral test ban that will be continued indefinitely and invite reciprocal announcement from Russia, England, and France

(C1); we also announce that we are making technicians and professionals in various fields of specialization available to the UN for work in the Congo
and other areas; reciprocation from other "have"
nations invited and general policy again stressed
(D1).

(*B1 not reciprocated by Communist China.*)

June 1: We announce that at the next convening of
the General Assembly of the UN (June 20) we will
move the seating of Communist China; we again
indicate our willingness to entertain diplomatic exchange and the general nature of our policy (B2).

(*C1 reciprocated by Russia, England, and
France; D1 reciprocated by England, France,
and others, but not Russia.*)

June 15: We announce that, as of July 15, one of our
overseas bases in Japan will be publicly denuclearized, and we invite UN and Russian inspection;
reciprocation is invited but left open-ended, and our
general policy is again stressed (E2).

(*On June 16 bombardment of Quemoy and
Matsu increases abruptly and invasion preparations are observed; U.S. naval power concentrates
and firm warnings about what our policy does
and does not imply are given; Russia makes nuclear threat; on June 20 we nevertheless move
seating of China in UN; one invasion attempt is
repulsed [but no counterattack on Chinese mainland occurs]; Russo-Chinese conferences are followed by Chinese delegation seated in UN;
Quemoy-Matsu hostilities peter out; D1 reciprocated by Russia.*)

August 1: We announce that, as of the next September, student exchanges will be offered in proportion
to the populations of the countries involved; reciprocation is invited generally (A2). We announce
that, as of August 20, the DEW Line (early warning system) will be made bidirectional (warning of

our flights toward Russia as well as vice versa),
and we invite the Soviets to "plug in" (NOTE: I
am told this is technically feasible; it emphasizes
our reliance on second-strike rather than first-strike
strategy; if we have no intention of surprise attack,
there is no reason why this shouldn't be done);
reciprocation in kind invited (C2).

   (*Russia announces that, as of September 1, its
   armed forces in East Germany will be reduced by
   one third and reciprocation in form of denuclearization of West Germany invited; we interpret
   this as indirect reciprocation of E2; an envoy
   from Peking arrives in Washington for talks.*)

August 15: We announce that, with agreements from
some of the major mass media, beginning September 1, material on contemporary world affairs prepared by Russian sources may appear on Sundays
in special newspaper sections and certain TV and
radio programs without censure; reciprocation in
kind invited (D2).

   (*We announce that, as of September 1, NATO
   forces are being reduced in West Germany but
   that no denuclearizing is contemplated at this
   time; East Germany announces relaxation of
   transit regulations between West Germany and
   West Berlin; B1 reciprocated by Communist
   China.*)

September 1: We announce that, as of January 1, we
will be prepared to have all launchings of flights
into outer space supervised by a new agency of the
UN which we propose be established (A3).

   (*Russia announces an expanded program of inviting scholars and scientists for advanced study
   in Soviet institutes [which we interpret as indirect reciprocation for A2]; Communist China invites joint teams of Russian and American scientists to Peking for conferences on technical*

problems; C_2 and D_2 still not reciprocated by Russia.)

September 15: We announce that, as of October 15, the islands of Quemoy and Matsu will be publicly demilitarized and turned over to proper authorities from the mainland, and clear statements about the unchanged status of Taiwan are made (B_3); we announce that surpluses of several grain crops will be made available at adjusted prices to countries needing them during the winter (D_3); reciprocations left open-ended.

(Russia proposes that, beginning January 1, the conquest of space be made a joint human enterprise on the model of the International Geophysical Year [IGY] and invites international co-operation through the UN [we interpret this as reciprocation for A_3]; C_2 and D_2 still not reciprocated by Russia; Nehru urges that she do so.)

November 20: We announce that, as of the next meeting of the UN (December 1), we will move the substitution of Communist China for Nationalist China on the Security Council—reciprocation in the form of recognition of Taiwan as a sovereign country with representation in the General Assembly requested (B_4); we announce that, as of February 1, we will open this country unilaterally to inspection and monitoring by authorized UN teams, as further evidence that we have no intention of surprise attack—reciprocation in kind is invited from all countries (C_4).

(The demilitarization and evacuation of Quemoy and Matsu accomplished without major incident [Chiang Kai-shek's threats of retaliation countered by large non-military spending program in Taiwan]; Russia has reciprocated, in part, on C_2, but not D_2; under strong urging from Great

*Britain, plans for full-scale disarmament negotia-
tions under UN auspices are being prepared.)*

Does this read like something out of *Fantasy and Science Fiction?* It certainly must in detail. It is presented as
a purely hypothetical sequence of events—I have no crystal
ball! The time scale is obviously compressed for conven-
ience, and the many difficult and worrisome details of communication and countercommunication, misunderstanding
and clarification, probing and holding off are necessarily
short-circuited. However, a number of probable characteristics of the process are illustrated. For one thing, it is
apparent that much of the reciprocation obtained would
be made to appear as initiation by the opponent, inviting
our reciprocation. This is obviously desirable, as long as
the unilateral initiations are in the right direction, but it
means that we must be flexible and quick-witted in estimating the nature and magnitude of such steps and in
preparing our own reciprocations. For another thing, it is
suggested that differences in the perception of what is
equable would often mean that their reciprocations would
seem inadequate but their requests exorbitant (and vice
versa, of course). However, one of the advantages of unilateral and reciprocated action is that agreements on what
is equable are not required—each side merely monitors its
own subsequent unilateral action in terms of its perception
of prior reciprocation.

Assumptions Underlying This Policy

Graduated reciprocation in tension reduction is based on
the assumption that the problems we face are essentially
matters of human nature and human relationships, and
therefore that solutions must be found in how human beings think and how their judgments, attitudes, and beliefs
can be influenced. It assumes that the Russian people and
leaders are more like us than like the bogy men our

psycho-logic creates, and that they are as eager to reduce the chances of full-scale nuclear conflict as we are. It assumes that the men in the Kremlin are susceptible to pressures, both from within and from without, since such pressures are an index of the success or failure of their system; and particularly it assumes that the less dogmatic Communists, like Khrushchev, are concerned about the mounting pressures from China. It assumes that the Communists are as convinced that their way of life will win out in non-military competition for men's minds as we are (or should be) that ours will. And finally, therefore, it assumes that the Russians would accept an unambiguous opportunity to reduce world tensions for reasons of good sense *even* if not for reasons of good will. Let us look into some of these assumptions.

Are our policy problems essentially matters of human nature and human relationships? I do not believe anyone, no matter how technically oriented, would assert that nuclear science naturally produces bombs or that space science naturally produces missiles. As a matter of fact, many scientists rationalize their contributions to weaponry on precisely the ground that they are not personally responsible for the social utilization of their discoveries. Even casual perusal of the *Bulletin of the Atomic Scientists* reveals that most of the articles are concerned with questions of ethics, of politics, of psychology, of economics, and so on. Witness the following excerpt: "But 'accidental war' refers to a war that he may begin when he imputes intentions to us that make him too afraid to wait. (Or one that *we* begin when we think that he expects us to and will not wait to see.) . . . There is an enormous advantage, in the event that war occurs in starting it, and . . . each side will not only be conscious of this but conscious of the other's preoccupation with it . . . the urge to pre-empt can become a dominant motive (Schelling, 35)." How psychological can one get? It is interesting in this connection that many of the strategy implications of relations among nations can be demonstrated in n-person games played in laboratory settings, including some implications essential to reciprocal tension reduction (cf. particularly Deutsch, 6).

Are the Russian people more like us than bogy men? The social sciences have amassed considerable evidence for the essential similarities of peoples of different races and nationalities in many basic characteristics—for example, in intelligence, in ability to solve problems, in the variety of emotions and capacities for feeling and expressing them. In our own work (21, 22, 27) we have been able to show that groups as different as Americans, Greeks, Japanese, and Navajo Indians use essentially the same basic dimensions in making meaningful judgments and even share subtle synesthetic tendencies and metaphors to a surprisingly high degree. The relative ease with which novels and even poems can be translated and appreciated across languages also testifies to the extent of shared habits and traits.

But what about the Russians? There is certainly no reason to believe them deviant from the rest of humanity. In fact, according to Nehru (New York *Times*, October 10, 1960), the Soviet Union and the United States are more alike than any two countries in the world and will become more similar in the future. Erich Fromm (9) has warned that we must not be deceived by the slogans of Communist ideology: "Soviet Russia in its Khrushchevist stage is a state which in no way represents Marxist Socialism. . . . It is a new form of state capitalism, economically effective, humanly impoverishing. . . . The Soviet Union . . . is today one of the most reactionary, conservative powers."

I realize that one can point to what seems to be contrary evidence about the Communists: there were blood baths during the early days of their revolution and some violent purges since then; there was the ruthless stamping down of resistance in Hungary; there are salt mines in Siberia and there have been executions of men like Nagy. It is to be regretted that men can be inhumanly cruel to other men, but this is a potentiality in all of us. The Russians would point to the sadism and cruelty of the Germans whom we are now rearming; they would ask us about the "beam" in our own eye—about our massacres of whole Indian villages, about our use of atomic bombs against Japanese civilian centers, and about the racial violence going on right now in our southern cities. True, we have explanations for these things, but the Russians are just as blind to our justifications as we are to theirs.

What, then, may we conclude about the Russian Bogy? I am sure it would be unrealistic to discount completely the real differences between the Russians and ourselves—particularly those concerning the value of the individual human being which stem from our ideological conflict. These real differences—in mode of thought, in culture, in personality—need to be carefully and objectively studied. But I am also sure that the Russian Bogy has been grossly overdrawn in the workings of our own mental dynamics—particularly by those intellectuals who are emotionally incapable of distinguishing between Russian communism and German nazism. In other words, *the Russian Bogy can be cut down to more realistic size and shape.* By doing so, we will free ourselves for more rational and flexible dealings with this opponent; by not doing so, we keep ourselves in a mental strait jacket in which we can only be stubborn.

Are the Russians as eager to reduce the chances of nuclear war as we are? Recent travelers to Russia, including some scholars whom I know personally, have been impressed by the "mirror image" of our own attitudes that they find among both the people and the leaders there. "Why do you Americans want war?" our informal ambassadors are asked. And when they answer that we most certainly do not want war, the Russians ask, "Then why do your leaders prepare for it? Why do they ring us about with missile bases?" When our travelers ask them why *they* are maintaining a great army and building up nuclear weapons for long-range attack, they reply, of course, that we leave them no choice. This "mirror image" phenomenon is confirmed in reports of our own USIA (United States Information Agency).

I believe that we must accept these protestations of good faith as genuine. They blame their warlike behavior on us, just as we blame ours on them. As a matter of fact, since men who have experienced a disaster are more wary about it than men who have only heard about it, I would expect the Russians to be even more deeply worried about a "hot war" than we are—their cities were subjected to bombing and they lost some five million people in the last war. My colleague, George Gerbner, who specializes in studies of the mass media as a means of understanding popular culture, visited Russia and several other countries in East Europe recently and reported being impressed with the emphasis on peace themes in the media there as compared with our own emphasis on more aggressive themes. According to the Twelfth Report of the Commission to Study the Organization of Peace (5), Chairman Khrushchev has definitely scrapped the Marxist-Leninist notion of the inevitability of war with the capitalist nations and is sensitive to the need to meet growing consumer demands, to the popular opposition to war, and to the uncertainty of what might happen in the satellite states in the case of hostilities.

Are the men in the Kremlin susceptible to pressure from within and from without? We are accustomed to contrasting the responsibility of our leaders to the will of the people with the irresponsibility of the Soviet government, and characteristically we exaggerate the difference. We are also accustomed to thinking about the average man in the Communist state as being kept completely ignorant of what is going on in the outside world, and this, too, we exaggerate. Ithiel Pool (in *Daedalus*, 14), who is certainly expert in such matters, points to the vital significance the

Soviet leaders attribute to public opinion (polls of a sort have recently been started in Russia); he also emphasizes the fact that Western ideas continually penetrate the Soviet wall, through highly effective word-of-mouth channels and through the monitoring operations of the elite. It is extremely doubtful if the Russian leaders could prevent awareness of a cumulative program of tension-reducing steps from reaching their people—even if they wanted to.

The Russians are also keenly aware of, and alert to, developments outside the Soviet Union. I do not think it can be denied that they have made more effective use of feedback than we have. If strong moral pressures developed in the neutralist nations, we could be sure the Russians would know about it and react to it in some fashion. It is also undeniable that the Russian Communists are aware of the growing power of the Chinese Communists and feel themselves to be in competition with China for leadership of the "have-not" countries (cf. Fromm, 9). The situations in the Congo and in Cuba (e.g., the recent sixty-million dollar loan agreement between China and Cuba) are cases in point. Without trying to make Communist China the scapegoat, the *real* bogy, it is nevertheless perfectly obvious that Russia is close to the explosive force of the New China and must be able to read certain writings on the Great Wall. The Soviets have not been notably eager to put nuclear weapons in Chinese hands, for example; if we, through our tension-increasing activities, force the Russians to take this step, we may well be making the most disastrously shortsighted blunder in our national history.

Are the Communists as convinced that their way of life will win out in non-military competition for men's minds as we are that ours will? Quite some time ago—and without obvious implementation, to be sure—Khrushchev announced the doctrine of "peaceful coexistence." By this was meant "peace" as far as military means are concerned but "war" as far as social, political, and economic means are concerned. President Eisenhower and his administration were then unwilling to take up this challenge—apparently on the ground that it is too far from the ideal of "peaceful co-operation." Khrushchev has stuck to this position, however, despite the summit debacle and despite strong pressures from both the Stalinists and the Chinese Communists. This is also testimony as to where Khrushchev himself stands and as to the state of public and elite opinion in much of Russia. It is naïve on our part, I think, to assume that every rebuff to Khrushchev that weakens his position internally is automatically to our advantage.

Do the Russian people have confidence in their way of life? Reports of our foreign observers and travelers again are almost unanimous on this matter. The Russian man in the street appears to be extraordinarily conscious of the material progress made in the past few decades, just as he is equally conscious and envious of the contrast in material wealth and well-being that still exists between himself and the average American. In a somewhat less flamboyant way, the Russian of today seems imbued with much the same spirit as the American of the period of westward expansion. It also seems to be the case that many peoples in "have-not" countries see in the Communist model a more rapid, if politically dangerous, means to modernization.

What about ourselves? Are we equally confident that our way of life would win out in peaceful competition for men's minds? In our rather recently acquired role and self-image as "Defenders of the Free World" (which, in practice, seems to have come down to defending the *status quo*), we have lost sight of the fact that our way of life is itself a major revolution in the relation between individual and state. One thing I find hard to understand about Americans is their apparent insecurity about their own principles—insecurity which fosters concern over exposing young people to "alien ideas," which is agitated by nonconformity, and which supports so-called "un-American activities" committees. I, for one, am convinced that the democratic way of life is the "natural" state toward which human beings tend as they acquire economic sufficiency, political security, and intellectual opportunity. But to convince others of this requires demonstration in deeds, not suffocation in words.

Would the Russians, therefore, accept an unambiguous opportunity to reduce world tensions? I believe all of the arguments above lead to this conclusion. The similarities between us are probably much greater than the differences we stress; their perceptions of the present situation and reactions to it may be much like our own, and they probably would welcome a way out of this mess as much as we would. We have seen that they are probably even more worried about a "hot war" than we are because of their national history. We can use this concern to justify a "get tough" policy—which, we should have learned from experience by now, merely drives them all the harder to outrace us in armaments—or we can use it to justify a gamble that they would reciprocate in an open, unambiguous policy of tension reduction.

It is precisely because our policy must be *unambiguous* that programs of graduated unilateral action are recommended. Although bilateral agreements, particularly mutual treaties formally signed and ratified, may be more explicit and binding *once attained*—it is the matter of attainment under present conditions of distrust and suspicion where's the rub. Graduated unilateral action would enable us to create conviction as to our intentions through deeds rather than words and would enable us to generate mounting moral pressure toward reciprocation. This policy is not to be construed as an alternative to mutual agreements through negotiation; quite to the contrary, it is designed as a "psychological primer," as a means of reversing the arms race and reducing world tensions to a level where serious negotiations can be entered into and significant agreements successfully concluded.

Some Likely Objections to This Policy

There are many deep-seated objections to any unilateral, non-aggressive policy of this sort, and it will be well to anticipate them. I have had the benefit of critical discussions of this proposal with colleagues in many fields, and I think they have helped press it into clearer form. Objections tend to fall into two general classes: those based on more emotional grounds and those based on more rational or practical grounds.

The most deep-seated objection to the policy I have outlined stems from what I have called the bogy-man conception of the enemy. Many people will argue that any unilateral act designed to reduce tensions would be interpreted by the Russians as a sign of weakness and, given their despotic drive toward world communism, would encourage them to encroach further on the free world. I cannot deny this as a possibility, even though I consider it remote. But, if this is their inherent nature, then we should make sure of it before the present balance of power has shifted to any significant degree. At least we would have made a sincere effort to test their intentions, and the risk involved should be more than offset by a gain in favorable world opinion. Surely it would be a tragedy, a cause of cosmic irony, if two of the most civilized nations on earth were to drive each other to their mutual destruction because of their mutually threatening conceptions of each other—without ever having tested the validity of these conceptions.

Some Americans will see this policy as a deliberate subversion, a Communist-inspired Trojan horse. My argument that it is actually a strategy designed to get us out of a serious dilemma, and in the long run to preserve our way of life, would be incomprehensible to them. Psycho-logic lubricates the groove along which we slide those who disagree with us into the Communist camp—particularly when the disagreement involves matters of basic security. However, everything that isn't blue doesn't have to be red, and similarly everyone who disagrees with our present policy doesn't have to be following the Communist line. The fact that this objection flows more from emotion than from reason does not minimize its effectiveness.

Many more people will probably see this policy as the coward's way. They would interpret it as a proposal that we surrender without a fight, a kind of "moral disarmament," and therefore entirely distasteful. For Americans, pacifism may be weak but good in time of peace, but in time of war ("cold" or "hot") it easily becomes weak and bad. This, too, is as illogical a criticism as it is potent. The man who relies on his brain rather than his brawn is not necessarily a coward—particularly when his brawn is peculiarly susceptible to the effects of radiation. And, in any case, it can hardly be called "surrender" if the unilateral acts designed to reduce tensions are made deliberately, on our own initiative, and as a means of applying pressure on an opponent to reciprocate.

Probably many people, however, will see this policy as an idealist's fantasy—certainly not one that faces up to the hard realities of the world we live in. They would say that to weaken one's own position in any way in the present situation is as softheaded as it is softhearted. However, what seems realistic within one's time-bound frame of reference may be highly unrealistic in the broader scheme of things. As I pointed out in an earlier section, what we call "realistic" usually depends upon what is habitual, what is familiar, and upon immediate goals. Thus it is "realistic" to concentrate on earning a living, getting one's children through school, and getting a little fun out of life, but it is "idealistic" to concentrate upon the world of the future. So, too, is it deemed realistic to demand more weapons when faced with external threat and idealistic to worry about where it is all leading. But novel situations demand new definitions of what is realistic, and now we are certainly in a novel situation. The real idealists today, as Marc

Raskin put it to me so well, are those who actually believe that the arms race can be continued indefinitely without something going wrong, who actually believe that the men behind the nuclear weapons are suprarational and will behave like so many computers.

More rational objections to this policy might come from those who agree with the logic of my general argument but nevertheless come to the conclusion that it is simply not feasible under present conditions. And they would probably be referring not so much to Russian reactions as to our ability to initiate such a policy here at home. Existing public attitudes, coupled with my own principle of psycho-logic, they would say, make it likely that even if such a policy were adopted and sponsored by thoughtful and courageous leaders, both it and they would be rejected by the vast majority of people in this country. My answer is that unpopular causes have been won before. It is not easy, and today it would require equal courage and dedication on the part of those who determine policy in the mass media. But attitudes and beliefs can be changed. During the period when Russia became our ally and defended Stalingrad, some of my own research at the time (37) showed that we came not only to think of RUSSIANS as much more *kind, noble,* and *fair,* but even as more *Christian!* And this happened in the brief span of a few months. Changes in public attitudes and beliefs depend particularly on events—if not those that occur inadvertently in the world, then those that are produced by men whose opinions count.

What about the objection that even graduated unilateral action involves too much risk? Although this policy does involve risk—indeed, the open and explicit assumption of risk is essential for its acceptance by an opponent—I believe that such risk must be taken in the interest of our long-term security. Our present policies, as I have tried to show, involve equal or even greater risk, but yet offer little hope in the long run of either preserving our way of life or guaranteeing our physical security. We must simply accept the fact that *there is no policy, no alternative we can choose, that entails no risk.* The best we can do is to weigh the risks involved in different policies against the ultimate security that might be achieved.

Another objection on the grounds of feasibility has been this: Is it possible to have acts that reduce tensions to any significant degree that do not at the same time endanger our heartland? In the first place I would argue that there is no perfect correlation between the military significance of events and their psychological impact, and this policy is concerned with maintaining psychological pressure. The Russians' first sputnik and their more recent shot at the moon did little to change the balance of military power, but they certainly had far-reaching psychological effects on the people of the United States. Recognition of Communist China on our own initiative likewise would have psychological impact far beyond its military significance. In devising programs of unilateral action it would be necessary to consider most carefully what does and what does not constitute actual military potential. Furthermore, the real "defense" of our heartland under present conditions lies only in deterrence, in our second-strike capacity. And here, as Milburn (24) has argued so cogently, I think, there is a certain minimum capacity for retaliation that has a near maximum deterrent effect upon an opponent—to be able to annihilate him ten or a hundred times over probably doesn't deter him much more than to be able to annihilate him just once! Properly appreciated, this fact should free us both economically and intellectually for more rational endeavors than the arms race.

This leads to another criticism—that this policy seems to amount to betrayal of our obligation to defend our allies. Although it is true that graduated reciprocation in tension reduction would mean reducing our military support in some areas where communism is in delicate balance with more liberal political views, does this necessarily imply defeat of our way of life in these areas—particularly if we were to succeed in reducing tensions between East and West generally? In the long run, the so-called "underdeveloped" countries will achieve greater security if we and the Russians stop using them as pawns in a global chess game. Most importantly, our own security in a nuclear age is coming to depend less and less upon allies or upon territorial control—particularly as intercontinental missiles with nuclear warheads become available. Just as we would not now risk starting a full-scale war for some remote foreign objective, so is our own liability to attack coming to be independent of geographic distance. The British are already well aware of this sobering fact, as evidenced by the Labour party's position on unilateral disarmament. And even if we were, against our own self-interest, to engage in continuous "brush-fire wars" about the perimeter of the free world, one can reasonably ask in just what sense this "defends" other nations. In the sparring of the two giants, it is the little countries on whose soils the skirmishes take place who suffer the most severe wounds.

This is a good place to point out the essential difference between the Kissinger Plan and graduated reciprocation in tension reduction. Both rely on our massive retaliatory capacity for ultimate security of the heartland, but also use it as the basis for other stratagems of foreign policy. The crucial difference is this: where Kissinger would use nuclear deterrence as the psychological support for further tension-*increasing* acts ("war as usual"), I would see us use nuclear deterrence as the psychological support for further tension-*reducing* acts. My proposal views the United States and Russia as gradually and carefully disengaging themselves along the far-flung border between Communist and non-Communist worlds, rather than as gradually and dangerously engaging themselves more and more inextricably. Where a policy of graduated tension reduction holds out at least the hope of ultimately eliminating the massive nuclear deterrents themselves (and the threat to survival they represent), the Kissinger Plan offers no such hope.

Finally, there are some questions of practicality. Even assuming we were to undertake such a policy, would the Russians accept our unilateral acts and we their reciprocations, as bona fide? Applying the same arguments I brought to bear against achieving mutual agreements through negotiation under conditions of stress, wouldn't the Russians perceive our acts as cold-war deceptions? And wouldn't we be even more distrustful of their apparent reciprocations without any hard and fast agreements about inspection and the like? I would argue, first, that our real protection against being "tricked" or "taken advantage of" lies in our undiminished capacity for second-strike retaliation, and exactly the same thing is true for the opponent. Second, and perhaps most important, unilateral acts, unlike mutual discussions, have the status of *fait accompli*, just like the satellites circling our globe. It is difficult to deny the fact of their commission (particularly if they are announced in advance and can be publicly observed), and argument over the motivation of the first tends to be resolved by execution of the second. Third, not only would it be difficult for the Russians to practice deception over the long run but we have good reason to believe (cf. arguments under "assumptions" above) that they are as eager to ease tensions as we are. Finally, as to our distrust of Russian reciprocations, there is a principle of human behavior that is relevant here: Man A's interpretation of Man B's reaction to him depends heavily upon A's own prior behavior toward B. If American Man has already made an intentional conciliatory act toward Russian Man, he is much more likely to perceive the Russian's reciprocation as bona fide than if it came unsolicited.

But what if one side tried to take advantage of the other's unilateral actions? Wouldn't this have the "boomerang effect" of even further intensifying mutual bogy-man conceptions? Here would be the self-fulfilling prophecy with a vengeance! This, of course, is the risk we take, but with graduated unilateral action the initial risks are small. Actually, I think the real danger would not lie so much in deliberate encroachments by either side on the other as in failures to appraise correctly the risks and benefits in particular unilateral acts or reciprocations as seen by the other side. Thus what might be perceived by the Soviets as a big concession in the area of inspection, we might consider piddling—and once again we are back in the problem of biased perceptions of the equable. As Fisher (8) has put it, "unless there is a good deal of negotiation and communication between the two sides they will not know what is bothering each other, what steps each side thinks it can undertake, and what steps it considers equivalent." This obviously puts a premium on preparation of our policy makers in depth and breadth; it also means that such a policy should be accompanied by a high level of informal communication designed to modulate the reciprocative acts. In practice, the graduated and unilateral characteristics of the process should provide ample room for mutual adjustments.

I believe that, even granting the atmosphere of mutual distrust in which such a process must be begun, both internal and external pressures of public opinion would force the opponents into at least token reciprocations at the low-risk level at which this policy would be initiated. And here another principle of human behavior becomes relevant: when people are made to keep on behaving in ways that are inconsistent with their actual attitudes (e.g., as if they really trusted each other), their attitudes tend to shift into line with their behavior. In other words, I think that if we could initiate a series of reciprocated, tension-reducing acts and maintain them over a sufficiently long period, the basic attitudinal conditions that now prevent us from taking larger, more significant steps toward world peace would be eliminated.

Reciprocal Initiative

Competent authorities assure us that both Russia and the United States will soon have nuclear, biological, and chemical weapons capable of annihilating each other many times over. Right now submarines are slipping into the depths from both sides of the Atlantic armed with destructive power equal to all that was delivered on Germany and Japan during the last World War. This presents mankind with a completely novel situation. Never before in the history of this planet have so few actually had the power to destroy so many.

But in the last analysis we are merely human, nothing more and nothing less. We are creatures of habit, servants of our emotions, victims of our own mental dynamics. This completely novel problem posed by the advent of the nuclear age hits us precisely at a time when competitive nationalism as a form of intergroup relations is near its crest. Mature nations have reached their positions of eminence through the exercise of power politics and young nations are busily trying to emulate these models of success. So we find nations trying to solve this novel problem along traditional lines—by responding to each power threat with a still greater threat of their own—firmly believing this course to be "realistic."

Rational, objective analysis of our present policy of deterrence through threat of nuclear retaliation reveals its flat inadequacy in terms of even the minimal criteria. It clearly does not eliminate the threat to our biological survival— indeed, the arms race reaches toward ever more fantastic means of destruction. It does not tend to preserve our way of life—indeed, it promotes conditions which support totalitarianism both at home and abroad. It is not even feasible over the long haul—only the most optimistic idealists among us, the soldiers for whom men are automata and the strategists for whom policy is just another game of chess, really believe that humans are suprarational and can go on indefinitely handling such power without making a fatal mistake.

Sober appraisal of what is really going on in the world about us shows that mutual deterrence is slowly but surely producing a "great freeze" on initiative in foreign policy. No one dares move too suddenly or freely for fear of upsetting the atom cart—for then, truly, would all hell break loose! So, for all our terrible power, we stand chained by it rather than set free.

In what direction, then, lies a course of initiative, of positive, consistent policy? Traditional unilateral action of a tension-increasing nature has become prohibitively dangerous. Traditional bilateral action of a tension-reducing nature (e.g., negotiated disarmament agreement) seems foredoomed by the very international tension which promotes it. And so, bit by bit, we are forced toward a highly untraditional course—unilateral action of a tension-reducing nature.

But here we run headlong into the full-flowing tide of nationalism, and it soon becomes perfectly obvious that abrupt and complete unilateral disarmament—no matter how logical and humanly appealing it may be—will never be accomplished in our time. Is there any other alternative? I believe there is, and it lies in another, more subtle and more flexible, form of unilateral action designed to reduce tensions. I have called this policy graduated reciprocation in tension reduction, and I propose it as a key to initiative in foreign policy in this nuclear age.

This policy can be viewed as an attempt "to have our cake and eat it, too." It asks the opponents in the present conflict to use their capacities for nuclear retaliation (second-strike forces) as the security base from which to initiate carefully graduated unilateral acts designed to reduce tensions. These acts would, as far as possible, be publicly announced as part of a consistent policy, publicly observed, and would invite reciprocation. This policy is

designed to permit freedom of action, to induce reciprocative behavior from an opponent, and yet operate within
acceptable limits of security.

Such a policy seeks its justification in the sciences of
human nature and human interrelationships—and this is
fitting because this is where our difficulties lie. It assumes
that the opponent is sufficiently like us to accept an unambiguous opportunity to get out of this mess. It assumes
that running the arms race in reverse—which is what this
policy amounts to—is fundamentally feasible. It aims for
ultimate elimination of the nuclear deterrents themselves
and the threat to humanity which they represent.

Resistances to such a policy of non-aggressive unilateral
action are also to be found in the dynamics of human
thinking and behavior. Psycho-logic creates a world inhabited by angels and devils; everything must become
channeled into this one evaluative polarity; and it becomes
more and more difficult to conceive of anything other than
stubborn resistance—you can't do business with a devil!
The relativity of our social judgments to our own experience bemuddles our attempts to see things from the other
fellow's point of view. The deep-lying anxieties created by
the arms race reduce our awareness of alternatives, stereo-
type our thinking, and restrict our perspective—and, like
the normally intelligent raccoon, we keep banging our nose
against a door that used to be open. All of these things
together produce a deep and fatalistic sense of the inevitability of eventual military conflict.

So much for the road behind. What about the task
ahead? What are the prospects for the future? No one as
impressed as I am with the complexity of our problem
and the magnitude of the contrary forces could be very
sanguine about our chances of escaping from this dilemma
unscathed. But I have convinced myself, and I hope the
reader as well, that it can be done. To mount such a "peace
offensive" as I have described will require truly extraordinary understanding, flexibility, and self-restraint on all

sides. But, fortunately, the policy of graduated reciprocation in tension reduction includes mechanisms for developing, in course, such understanding, such flexibility, and such self-restraint. It will require courage and dedication not only on the part of governments but also on the part of the mass media and thereby the publics which support them. The hopeful side of the picture is the remarkable adaptability of the human species. The democratic system, too, is adaptable; it includes mechanism for the discovery of fresh ways of solving novel problems—if they are allowed to operate.

It sometimes proves helpful to back off from a problem and try to view it within a larger chunk of space and time. Taking the long view in space, as from a planetary system many light-years away, the events which today are shaking the very fabric of our lives are all transpiring on the knife-thin edge of a little pebble in the sky, and they won't cause the slightest perturbation in the cosmos. Taking the long view through time, one can envisage the interlacing, ever expanding tree of human life, bearing its generations of ephemeral blooms, yet but little affected by the changing national climates in its course. The organizations among men we call "nations" come and go—a name may persist and the human content change, or the reverse—and this is as true for what we now call "Russia" and "the United States" as it was for Rome and Babylon. Viewed in sufficiently wide perspective, these are relatively minor themes in the tapestry of civilization, important though they may be to the individual human threads.

The real question, I suppose, is whether—like the dinosaur before us—the human species has moved into a situation where its own peculiar specialization renders it unfit for continued survival. Our monkey facility in technology has far outstripped our capacity to understand and control ourselves, and the present generation is faced with the consequence of this imbalance. We are, in truth, little monkey fellows running around with awesome weapons in our clever hands, but directed by minds that run in primitive channels. Is this our Achilles' heel? With his giant foresight, Albert Einstein many years ago put it in words that could have been written today: "Our world is threatened by a crisis whose extent seems to escape those within whose power it is to make major decisions for good or evil. The unleashed power of the atom has changed everything except our ways of thinking. Thus we are drifting toward a catastrophe beyond comparison. We shall require a substantially *new manner of thinking* if mankind is to survive."

REFERENCES

1. Abelson, R. P., and Rosenberg, M. J. "Symbolic Psycho-logic: A Model of Attitudinal Cognition," *Behavioral Science*, III, 1958, pp. 1–13.

2. Brown, H., and Real, J. *Community of Fear*. Center for the Study of Democratic Institutions, 1960.

3. Burke, D. "Effects of Motivation upon Word-association Hierarchies." Unpublished master's thesis, University of Illinois, 1960.

4. Colborn, R. "Silence: and After." Unpublished paper, 1960.

5. Commission to Study the Organization of Peace, Twelfth Report. *Peaceful Coexistence: A New Challenge to the United Nations*, 1960.

6. Deutsch, M. "Trust and Suspicion," *Conflict Resolution*, 1958, 2, pp. 265–79.

7. Festinger, L. *A Theory of Cognitive Dissonance*. Evanston, Illinois: Row, Peterson and Co., 1957.

8. Fisher, R. "Arms Control and Self-restraint." Unpublished paper.

9. Fromm, E. "Russia, Germany, China: Remarks on Foreign Policy." Unpublished paper.

10. Hebb, D. O. "Drives and the C. N. S. (Conceptual

Nervous System)," *Psychol. Review*, 1955, 62, pp. 243–54.

11. Heider, F. *The Psychology of Interpersonal Relations.* New York: John Wiley and Sons, Inc., 1958.

12. Heider, F., and Simmel, M. "An Experimental Study of Apparent Behavior," *American Journal of Psychol.*, LVII (1944), pp. 243–59.

13. Helson, H. "Adaption-level as a Basis for a Quantitative Theory of Frames of Reference," *Psychol. Review*, 1948, 55, pp. 297–313.

14. Holton, G. (ed.) *Arms Control*, special issue of *Daedalus*, Fall 1960.

15. Hook, S. "A Free Man's Choice," *New Leader*, May 26, 1958, pp. 9–12; "Bertrand Russell Retreats," *New Leader*, July 7, 1958, pp. 23–28.

16. Hovland, C. I., Harvey, O. J., and Sherif, M. "Assimilation and Contrast Effects in Reactions to Communications and Attitude Change," *J. Abnorm. Soc. Psychol.*, 1957, 55, pp. 244–52.

17. Hull, C. L. *Principles of Behavior.* New York: Appleton-Century, 1943.

18. Johnson, D. M. *The Psychology of Thought and Judgment.* New York: Harper & Brothers, 1955.

19. King-Hall, S. *Defensive in the Nuclear Age.* London: Gollancz, 1958.

20. Kissinger, H. A. *Nuclear Weapons and Foreign Policy.* New York: Harper & Brothers, 1957.

21. Kumata, H. "A Factor Analytic Investigation of the Generality of Semantic Structure Across Two Selected Cultures." Unpublished doctoral thesis, University of Illinois, 1957.

22. Kumata, H., and Schramm, W. "A Pilot Study of Cross-cultural Methodology," *Public Opinion Quarterly*, XX, 1956, pp. 229–37.

23. Malmo, R. B. "Activation: A Neuropsychological Dimension," *Psychol. Review*, 1959, 66, pp. 367–86.

24. Milburn, T. W. "What Constitutes Effective Deter-

rence?" U. S. Naval Ordnance Station. Unpublished paper.

25. *1970 Without Arms Control; Implication of Modern Weapons Technology*. National Planning Association Special Project Committee on Security Through Arms Control (#104), Washington, 1958.

26. Osgood, C. E. "Motivational Dynamics of Language Behavior," *Nebraska Symposium on Motivation*, University of Nebraska Press, 1957.

27. Osgood, C. E. "The Cross-cultural Generality of Visual-verbal Synesthetic Tendencies," *Behavioral Science*, 1960, 5, pp. 146–69.

28. Osgood, C. E. "Cognitive Dynamics in Human Affairs," *Public Opinion Quarterly*, 1960, 24, pp. 341–65.

29. Osgood, C. E., Suci, G. J., and Tannenbaum, P. H. *The Measurement of Meaning*. Urbana, Illinois: University of Illinois Press, 1957.

30. Osgood, C. E., and Walker, E. G. "Motivation and Language Behavior: A Content Analysis of Suicide Notes," *J. Abnorm. Soc. Psychol.*, 1959, 59, pp. 58–67.

31. Peak, H. "Psychological Structure and Psychological Activity," *Psychol. Review*, 1958, 65, pp. 325–47.

32. Reusch, H. *Top of the World*. New York: Pocket Books, Inc., 1951.

33. Russell, B. "World Communism and Nuclear War," *New Leader*, May 26, 1958, pp. 9–12; "Freedom to Survive," *New Leader*, July 7, 1958, pp. 23–28.

34. Schelling, T. C. *The Strategy of Conflict*. Cambridge: Harvard University Press, 1960.

35. Schelling, T. C. "Meteors, Mischief, and War," *Bull. Atom. Scientists*, 1960, 16, pp. 292–97.

36. Spence, K. "Theory of Emotionally Based Drive (D) and Its Relation to Performance in Simple Learning Situations," *Amer. Psychologist*, 1958, 13, pp. 131–41.

37. Stagner, R., and Osgood, C. E. "Impact of War on a Nationalistic Frame of Reference: I. Changes in Gen-

eral Approval and Qualitative Patterning of Certain Stereotypes," *Journal of Social Psychology*, XXIV, 1946, pp. 187–215.

38. White, R. K. "The Cold War and the Modal Philosophy," *Conflict Resolution*, II, 1958, pp. 43–50.

December 1960

SIX

Economic Adjustments
to Disarmament: Research and Policy

BY EMILE BENOIT

Professor in the Graduate School of Business, Columbia University; Director of the Program of Research on Economic Adjustments to Disarmament

Recent political events have stirred new public interest in disarmament, including interest in the question of what will happen to the United States economy and to the world economy if general disarmament ever comes about. This leads to the question of how we can best meet the economic changes that can then be expected.

The present paper is concerned with the research needed if we are to go beyond the offhand answers we commonly hear. It seeks to outline what ought to be investigated, rather than to supply the answers in advance. Research on disarmament can be valuable even though the defense program at the present time is expanding and undergoing various changes.

"Disarmament" is here envisaged not as the immediate and total abolition of military forces, but as a staged and balanced reduction of forces which would take at least several years to complete, and which would probably leave, at the end, a solid core of international deterrent and police forces plus significant lightly armed national forces of a purely defensive character. This might follow some such pattern as a reduction of six billion dollars a year in U.S. defense costs—a reduction starting from a substantially higher level of defense expenditure than we have now, and bringing the annual security budget down to about twenty to twenty-five billion dollars. These are sample assumptions to provide a starting point; they might be considerably changed on further investigation.

FEAR OF DISARMAMENT

A widespread fear, which the people holding it rarely admit outright, is that disarmament might result in a major economic upset. This was dramatized by the sharp decline in values on the New York Stock Exchange on August 10, 1959, which the New York *Times* attributed to "peace jitters."

The reason why such fears are not more openly expressed may be that up to now there has seemed little danger that disarmament was about to "break out." If there were any reason to think that negotiations were really on the point of succeeding, alarm about the economic results might become more vocal and clamorous.

The shaping-up of sound public and private plans for adjustment to disarmament could serve not only to allay unfounded fears at home but also, perhaps, to help convince other nations of our sincerity in negotiation. This is particularly in order because of our insistence on certain technical safeguards, which may delay the conclusion of an agreement and be misconstrued as indicating that we don't really want to reach agreement. An adjustment program could also help to cope with those radical shifts in the defense economy which arise not from disarmament but from new weapons developments and the like.

Government, in the past, has seemed reluctant to set up such plans, or even to make thoroughgoing studies to pave the way for realistic plans. This may have been due partly to fear of weakening the nation's morale, its willingness to bear the heavy burden of armaments, before making sure that a disarmament agreement is possible.

IS THERE A REAL PROBLEM?

At the other extreme from those who are fearful of disarmament impacts are the people who argue that there is no real problem and therefore no need to worry. They point out that there are plenty of good uses for the savings which might come from disarmament and that the cutbacks would be no worse than those to which we rather easily adjusted after the Second World War and after Korea.

As we shall see, the full relevance of these earlier examples is now questionable; it would therefore seem unwise to dismiss entirely the lingering foreboding which so many practical people—in government as in labor and management—still feel about the possible impact of disarmament. Such fears, even if unfounded in theory, may turn out to have considerable basis in fact. Certain public attitudes and governmental arrangements can prevent or delay those economic adjustments which, if properly planned and carried out, would make, in theory, for a smooth and rather painless transition.

It may, in fact, prove quite difficult to mobilize *in time* the available public or private projects which would quickly take up the slack in defense expenditures. Indeed, this may be the heart of the problem. The required measures may not have nearly enough acceptance by politicians, lawmakers, and administrators to insure adoption and timely carrying out of the needed steps.

Further, there is a real question whether conditions in 1945–47, or even in 1953–54, were enough like those of today and tomorrow to form a reliable guide as to how we can best meet a future cutback in arms spending.

WHY ADJUSTMENTS MIGHT BE MORE DIFFICULT NOW
THAN IN THE PAST

In 1946–48, the early postwar years, there was an exceptional supply of liquid funds in the hands of consumers, along with an abnormal demand for goods which people had gone without during the war. The federal government had accumulated budget deficits of around 255 billion dollars, while individual savings had grown by 160 billion. Between 1944 and 1947, as more supplies of refrigerators, automobiles, and other "durables" appeared in the market, and construction of homes went briskly forward, the rate of personal savings sharply declined, while purchases of durable goods tripled and the construction of urban dwellings rose more than tenfold. In this kind of situation the resources and manpower which were freed from military production were easily and quickly caught up into the business of supplying the active civilian demands.

No such rapid pace of expansion of spending out of abundant personal savings could be expected today. From 1945–59 the outstanding money supply (cash plus demand deposits) went down from about *one half* of the total national expenditure to about *one fourth*, while consumer debt rose from less than six billion dollars to fifty-two billion—about one sixth of all disposable income (personal income after taxes). Under today's less liquid conditions, consumer spending would presumably be more quickly and adversely affected by any interruption in the flow of individual income.

After the Korean War defense cuts of over eight billion dollars were accompanied by a recession involving a decline of between one and two per cent in the national product (GNP). Its impact was softened by the fact that the economy had then been operating at a very high level; there had been full employment (average unemployment of about only three per cent) from 1951 to 1953, and virtually full utilization of productive capacity. Consumer debt was still, in 1954, only about ten per cent of disposable income, leaving room for the credit-financed auto and housing boom of 1955. By contrast, we have now been operating with over five per cent average unemployment for several years, and with substantial underutilization of capacity and an unprecedented level of consumer debt. In this kind of social climate, another such rapid expansion of consumer debt would seem unlikely and, if it did take place, dangerous.

The experience of 1957–58 suggests the sort of difficulties we might now encounter. In 1957 Congress approved a four billion-dollar defense cut and, though this was never actually carried out, even the threat of such a cut, coming at a time of already high unemployment rates and slow growth momentum (less than two per cent gain in 1957 GNP), was enough to trigger the 1958 recession. The government refused at that time to provide tax cuts which might have cushioned the decline, and the 1959 revival, though vigorous, proved to be a brief one. Though such historical precedents are far from conclusive, they do suggest that we badly need a more rigorous study of prior experiences before drawing reassuring conclusions about the actual situation which might confront us in the event of a future disarmament agreement.

A MODEL FOR MEASURING THE IMPACT OF DISARMANENT

An understanding of what disarmament would mean requires first of all an understanding of what is now involved, for the economy of the nation and the world, in military production and financing.

Beyond this we must consider the rapid changes already taking place within the defense program and the nature and timing of the disarmament program by which it might be superseded. Much of the required information is not yet collected or is "classified," but informed guesses will often be good enough to give us the broad orders of magnitude which determine the appropriate policy responses. What are the main elements to be considered?

First, they are the plants, scattered over the country but highly concentrated in certain areas, which produce most of the goods and services entering into the defense budget. Directly or indirectly, these affect production, investment, imports, exports, patterns of land use, growth or decline of communities, and so on.

Second, there is the labor force employed in these plants, in the armed forces, and in military installations and departments both at home and abroad. This employment affects payroll distribution, levels and types of skills, wage rates, standards of living, and community relations.

Third, we have the *regional* distribution of military contracts and subcontracts and of military installations and activities. There are communities that now depend in varying degrees on defense contracts, with varying potentialities for alternative industrial activities if and when military production ceases to absorb available resources.

Fourth, there is the direct and indirect contribution of defense funds to education and research, and to the development of new civilian products.

Fifth, we must re-examine the extent to which the economies of certain other countries are dependent on, or built around U.S. military expenditures and military aid, as well as their own military budgets.

Sixth, in the light of the continuing rapid development of technology, there are the likely upcoming changes in all of these parts of the structure, between the present time and the time when disarmament agreements are made and carried out.

A *seventh* factor is the *timing* and pace of any disarmament measures in so far as they can be foreseen on the basis of present or past negotiations, proposals, and plans.

The eighth and final factor to be considered is the kind

of minimum security establishment that might be left after substantial disarmament were carried out, and the make-up and costs of such a reduced establishment—including the U.S. contribution to international inspection, policing, and deterrent forces.

A study model built around all these factors can show the estimated funds, manpower, and physical resources being used by the military establishment at the start of disarmament and the amounts of these which might be released to civilian use year by year, on various assumptions about the pace and pattern of disarmament. Specialized techniques of economic analysis can then be applied to such a model: input-output analysis which can measure the impacts of cutbacks of defense orders upon the output and employment of the various industries that directly or indirectly supply the defense economy; national income multiplier analysis which can estimate the over-all depressing effect (both initially and in its secondary ramifications) of the cutbacks in demand for defense goods and services; and flow of funds and other financial analyses tracing the effects on savings, liquidity, ownership, and price of assets, etc.

THE PROBLEM OF MAINTAINING DEMAND

The most obvious and challenging problem in the economic adjustment to disarmament is, of course, the danger of provoking a depression. There are other dangers, generally ignored, to which a balanced examination must also pay attention, but the stabilization aspect of the problem— keeping the whole economy going at a normal rate—rightly demands a major share of attention.

The stabilization problem is often mistakenly thought of as involving the physical shifting of employment and output from the armed services and from defense production to non-defense activity. This *is* a problem, to be sure. We call it the *transfer*, or reconversion problem, and discuss

235

this in a later section. While it is true that the sudden overnight cancellation of the whole defense program would create a tremendous reconversion problem, this is entirely unlikely to happen. The need to set up adequate inspection and enforcement measures makes it inevitable that the reduction will be staged, and over a period of several years as a minimum. Our hypothetical model, which itself assumes a much more rapid pace than is probably achievable in practice, implies annual shifts of less than two per cent of the gross national product. This is roughly of the same order as the changes already occurring in the economy from technological improvements and better working methods. Reconversion, at this tempo, could probably be accomplished without creating any significant decline at all—*if adequate over-all demand were maintained.*

This "if" is the very heart of the stabilization problem. A shrinkage in total demand would imply a decline in activity even aside from reconversion problems and would make those problems much harder to solve.

There is no built-in reason why demand should *have* to fall off after defense cuts. In spite of Marxian fantasies, a capitalist economy does *not* require military expenditures to keep going, and it is by no means impossible to substitute demand for other goods and services as military production is cut back. Even in the relatively "affluent" United States there are many unmet needs and desires, not to mention the less economically developed countries; and human beings have a seemingly limitless capacity for developing new wants. To be effective, however, demand must be backed up by purchasing power, and the danger of inadequate total demand in this sense is real. It comes from two main sources. First, Congress is not well organized for making prompt decisions about *which* new demand should replace the old. Military demand is supplied by the national budget, and adequate offsets to defense cuts will probably not come automatically, but will require legislative action. Such action could be by way of appropriations, loans, or guarantees for public civilian projects—housing, public health, education, research, parks, roads, etc.—or by tax cuts to encourage more private spending (including business spending on capital goods) or both. Choices would have to be made not only between public and private spending but among different types of one or the other—*which* public works or *what* pattern of tax cuts.

Such choices are not easy for Congress to make; they involve serious clashes among interest groups and power and status struggles among some congressmen and congressional committees. Congress still finds it very difficult to approach these matters from the point of view of short-term national interest in stabilization; it is geared to debating such issues with regard for long-term accommodations and balancing of conflicting interest groups or regions. Furthermore, a number of the public services most requiring expansion are, under the federal system, the responsibility of state and local governments, whose capacity to spend on new projects will not necessarily improve when federal defense spending is cut back. (Indeed, in some cases their revenues will be sharply reduced as a result!) Also, some vital programs, such as the support of pure research, higher education, public health, and resource development, have not yet been fully accepted by public and congressional opinion as appropriate responsibilities of government except when they are connected with defense.

A second and even more fundamental difficulty arises out of congressional and public attitudes toward *national debt*. These attitudes are somewhat vague but can be summed up roughly thus: "We have an obligation to reduce and pay off the national debt, since it is morally irresponsible to saddle future generations with debts which this generation has accumulated. Defense expenditures have a special importance which can sometimes justify deficit financing and *increases* in the national debt, or postponement in paying it off; however, *no other types of expenditure,* public or private, have this special overriding importance, and therefore any savings from reduction of the arms budget should be applied, at least in part, to debt reduction." This sentiment seems to be widespread both in Congress and among the general public and calls for some detailed examination of the way in which national debt operates and the effects which the use of defense savings for debt reduction may be expected to have.

THE PROPENSITY TO REDUCE THE NATIONAL DEBT

The role of debt in economic growth has been much misunderstood. As a matter of fact there has been, historically, a close relation between changes in debt and changes in production—a tendency to rise or fall together, except during the great depression when debt could not be liquidated as fast as production declined.

Business activity depends on debt formation in our economy because a large part of our savings are and must be invested in debts. Banks, insurance companies, and trust funds and pension funds of all sorts, which are the repositories of a large part of our savings, are debarred by law and custom from investing more than a fraction of these savings in equities—such as common stock. (Their equity holdings are increasing, but only gradually and not enough to change the essential situation.) The greater part they can invest only in other people's debts: bank loans, mortgages, and bonds. Unless there is a sufficiently rapid formation of debt, it is difficult to find investment outlets for the full amount of savings which people wish to make, and there will be a slower growth in activity than would otherwise be possible.

The existence at the present time of a large public debt (a product mainly of wartime financing) is an important part of the problem. About a third of total debt is now public debt. Attempts to reduce this part of the debt structure throw an additional burden on private debt formation. As we have seen, production and income can generally increase no faster than total debt, and since the public debt is now such an important part of the total, attempts to remove it could have a profoundly unsettling effect.

In order to take up the slack from a reduction in the public debt, private debt would have to increase faster than normally, and—indeed—faster than private income. If such a trend began, borrowers would before long become "overextended" and would begin to reduce their rate of new borrowing and to concentrate for a while on repayment. This is clearly the right and prudent course for *individuals*, but the effect on the growth of total debt— and presumably on production—for the country as a whole might be severely restrictive.

Even if the retirement of public debt might increase bank reserves and make it easier for banks to lend, it would probably make it more difficult (or dangerous) for borrowers to borrow. In running a budget surplus, the government takes from taxpayers more purchasing power than it uses for its own expenditures on goods and services, or for transfer payments to other spending units. The initial effect is a smaller total expenditure by both government and private spenders than would otherwise occur, with a depressive effect on economic activity unless the economy has been at or above full employment. With restricted markets and surplus capacity, the *incentive* to borrow is reduced, even if the supply of loanable funds has been raised by retirement of national debt. These depressive effects, which may follow from a budget surplus, are in fact recognized by a majority of economists.

THE GROWTH PROBLEM

In its concern with the economic effects of disarmament, public opinion has mainly emphasized the immediate danger of depression. It is possible, however, that a loss of impetus to growth might be an even more serious danger in the long run. This would be especially important in a period when, owing to the reduced likelihood of military conflict, there would be increased emphasis on economic, technological, and other aspects of "competitive coexistence." Defense cuts which depressed growth to a rate below that of our rivals could then have serious consequences. Perhaps the fear of such a development is one motive for resisting disarmament. At any rate, if disarmament is to occur, it clearly behooves those who value the survival of democratic and liberal institutions to face up to the growth difficulties which may follow and to canvass the ways in which such difficulties may be avoided.

The record is not reassuring for the United States in recent years. After the 1920s the periods of rapid growth have been those of rising defense outlays—1940–44 and 1950–53. Indeed, the only years of even moderate growth (substantially above two per cent, let us say) outside these periods have been based on either (a) recovery from a low recession base (as in 1955 and 1959), or (b) filling war-created backlogs of demand (1948). The reasons for the correlation in the United States between defense spending and growth should be analyzed. The contrary experience noted in the last few years in Western Europe should also be examined.

A survey of the relation of defense to long-term growth in the United States brings into view four points which are discussed below.

(1) Defense spending in recent years has made extraordinary contributions to education, science, research, and product development. This accounts for a substantial part of the total current U.S. research effort, especially in the physical sciences. Among the fruits of this research are most of the important new products appearing in the last decade.

(2) The large amounts of defense expenditure go-

ing into construction (roads, barracks, air bases, and similar developments), or into heavy or durable equipment, vehicles, etc., all of which are, or resemble, capital goods, and many of which have collateral civilian uses or will ultimately be turned over as surplus equipment to the civilian economy, thereby strengthen, for the most part, its productive capacity, physical plant, and economic infrastructure. Such expenditures have, moreover, by sharply raising the output of certain key industries, stimulated cost saving, introduction of labor-saving machinery, and productivity improvement generally.

(3) Some reasons why defense spending has contributed to industrial progress are: (a) more rigorous demand for continually improved performance under field conditions, and (b) the trend to standardization and the setting-up of formal specifications, which are imposed by military needs and tend gradually to be adopted in non-defense plants as well.

(4) The ability to experiment and bring in new products without regard to profit makes possible some long shots in radical new developments. Lavish spending on pilot plants and models and the use of improved models without regard to possible capital losses may pay off in terms of growth.

RESEARCH ON FISCAL AND MONETARY POLICY

Success of the transition to a postdefense economy will be crucially affected by the monetary-fiscal policies adopted. Among the factors to be considered in understanding the impact of these policies, and in arriving at policies suitable for such a period, the following need particularly to be examined.

1. The proportion of defense savings which will be devoted to debt reduction.

2. The extent to which offsetting price and wage ad-

justments can be counted on to generate new demand, without deliberate compensating action.

3. The effects of built-in stabilizers—unemployment compensation, farm price-support payments, etc.—in cushioning the deflationary effect of the cuts and the question of their adequacy over a period of several years, with cuts of rather large size.

4. The "negative multiplier" effect of the cuts to the extent not offset by automatic stabilizers.

5. The extent to which defense savings not used for debt reduction are used to finance tax cuts on the one hand or expanded public services on the other.

6. Ways in which particular patterns of tax cuts that might be adopted, or particular programs of public services, would tone down or build up the inflationary impact.

One further question is how far the substitute bill of goods, private or public, is *comparable* with the defense bill of goods it is to replace. If the new bill of goods draws upon *different* industries and *different* regions from those which formerly supplied the defense demands, this may cause temporary but important structural problems. There might even be substantial deflation in one part of the economy while an inflationary trend developed in another.

There are some basic questions also on *timing.* How long does it take to translate the decision to discontinue a certain program into actual contract termination, notices of termination, and shutdowns and layoffs at the plant level —both with prime contractors and subcontractors? How quickly would the impact filter down to non-specialized producers of raw materials and intermediate-stage products? During a period of cutbacks, would the prime contractors retain more defense work for themselves at the expense of subcontractors, or would they hasten to reconvert so as not to fall behind their competitors? What might be the influence of political pressures from particular areas on the decision makers? What degree of flexibility and discretion in making adjustments could be maintained by public agencies?

On the timing and use of public works programs, studies should be made of the backlog of established "needs" in health, education, research, resource development, transportation, urban renewal, and the like. The state of readiness of programs in these fields should be examined and realistic estimates made of their possible timing. Evidence should be assembled, on the basis both of questionnaires and surveys of previous congressional action, as to how congressmen feel about the importance of these programs and how likely they are to approve projects of the required size. There should also be study of the *amounts* and *kinds* of labor and materials needed for such projects, compared with the resources to be released by the defense cuts. Beyond this, a fundamental question is how speedily Congress could be expected to get through the needed legislation to make such public projects effective as "fill-in."

Special attention might be given to the capital and technical-assistance needs of underdeveloped countries, the willingness of Congress to expand these programs rapidly, and the rate at which underdeveloped countries could absorb such assistance without needless waste. Here again we meet the question as to how far these needs would call for the same types of materials and skills as those released by defense cuts.

If tax cuts are favored as a substitute channel for demand, we need to examine the extent to which existing tax-withholding and social-security systems can work to expand consumer buying power. In the light of historical tendencies to save or to consume, what increases in private spending might we expect from various kinds of tax cuts? What would be the outlook for streamlining congressional action to carry out a tax-cut policy? For example, could a stand-by tax cut be voted in advance, providing for proportional reductions "across the board," which would come into effect upon a presidential proclamation (perhaps on a joint basis with a key congressional committee, such as the Joint Economic Committee) that defense cuts of specific size had been ordered? What constitutional or other difficulties might prevent the use of such a device, and how deep-seated and widespread would congressional opposition be?

The use of special money measures to help smooth the change-over should be studied in the light of experience and of the powers already available to the Federal Reserve System and the Treasury. The points below might call for particular attention.

1. The extent to which the additional free banking reserves resulting from rapid reduction in the national debt would be translated into a rapid increase in bank loans and other forms of private debt, and the extent to which this might discourage new borrowing in the next time period.

2. The expansion which might follow from a relaxation of credit terms in the housing field (and with respect to state and local public works), and the time lag between the easing of credit and the increase in actual construction.

3. The hesitation about providing more liberal credit which might be felt if prices were rising, due either to structural bottlenecks or other factors.

4. The use of selective credit controls to cope with excessive demand in special areas at a time of low over-all demand and the question of imposing such selective controls in a period of general credit relaxation.

ECONOMIC GROWTH WITHOUT DEFENSE

To preserve or replace the more dynamic effects of the defense program is a challenge to initiative, imagination, and the spirit of adventure. A few possible steps are set down here.

We should by all means keep up and even expand the educational and research parts of the defense program despite any cutbacks in other parts, with a shifting of these functions to non-defense uses. Here a serious question arises as to whether Congress would support these activities on anything like present levels in the absence of a defense motive.

A solid part of any defense savings should be earmarked for expanding higher education and research, especially in the training of scientists and engineers and for subsidies to teaching and research in these fields. This might even lead to the creation of a new "Department of Higher Education and Research"!

A further portion of the savings should be earmarked for the rapid development of promising new processes and products, including the building of pilot plants—possibly by endowing public "Research and Development Institutes." These should be permitted to finance ventures of private companies for such purposes, for example by purchase of convertible bonds along the lines of a "Small Business Investment Company."

Some needed revisions in our patent and anti-trust laws might stimulate more research and more rapid application of research results to product development and improvement.

The government might well take more initiative in the establishment of uniform specifications, for product testing and grading, and for making the results of these known.

Another promising move would be to earmark a part of defense savings to set up productivity centers in this country such as the United States has successfully promoted and underwritten in Europe, and for area and regional development plans for our own underdeveloped or permanently depressed areas.

We could afford to experiment with reducing the tax burdens on innovation, risk-bearing, and extra work, for instance, by permitting longer carry-forward of losses on new companies, reducing taxation on overtime work, and permitting larger deductions for women workers with family responsibilities. A non-tax measure tending in the same direction would be revision of social-security legislation to encourage older persons to work rather than curtailing their pension rights if they do.

THE TRANSFER OR RECONVERSION PROBLEM

Defense production, as we know, has been heavily concentrated in certain areas and industries. The personnel employed in the permanent defense establishment have specialized skills not always readily transferable to other work. It would be highly desirable to get a sharper picture of exactly what and where these problems are, to take their measure so that the people best suited to work on them could be setting up suggestions for their solution. It may now be possible to use certain specialized statistical methods, especially "input-output" analysis, to get some clues as to the industries, the communities, and the types of workers most likely to be heavily affected by disarmament cutbacks.

To be sure, most of the complex shifts in a society such as ours can and will take place automatically, through the market and in response to the attempts of individuals to find new jobs and of managements to maintain profits. The reassuring thing about the Second World War reconversion experience is the demonstration of how well this process works if only adequate over-all demand is maintained.

The urgent hard-core reconversion problems are more easily and directly identifiable and are probably confined for the most part to these five categories:

1. Heavily defense-centered communities, with little alternative employment opportunity as yet.
2. Companies like General Dynamics, with a large percentage of sales in defense contracts.
3. Other companies with large specialized facilities or identifiable divisions for defense work.

4. Production or research facilities owned by the Defense Department.

5. Armed services personnel lacking educational or professional training required for civilian employment at comparable pay and prestige levels.[1]

In order to avoid the danger of bogging down in a welter of unmanageable detail, research on this kind of adjustment might well give major emphasis to the following objectives:

1. Surveying the broad dimensions of the hard-core adjustment problem and its major types.

2. Analyzing a few illustrative examples of particular defense commodities or defense-contract-centered companies, to show in some detail the kinds of problems they face, the kinds of alternatives they have, and their resources for coping with the situation.

3. Surveying the plans which the "hard-core" companies and communities are developing for the change-over, with detailed examination and evaluation of a few specific cases to examine the realism of their assumptions and their adequacy to the problem; where no planning is under way, examining the attitudes and expectations by which the lack is justified.

4. Sampling the plans and attitudes of individuals who seem likely to face serious readjustments.

5. Summarizing adjustment studies already made on non-hard-core areas—e.g., Professor Walter Isard's study of the impact of disarmament on Philadelphia.

6. Compiling a few case histories of community and industry adjustments to prior defense cuts—or to other major changes in demand or technology—with a view to discovering factors in these experiences which un-

[1] Problems of how best to dispose of defense-owned surplus plant, stocks, and real estate, while important, need not be urgent. Absorption into the civilian economy can take place gradually and as needed.

derlie satisfactory or unsatisfactory performance in making adjustment.

7. Examining and evaluating various recommendations made in the past for facilitating transfers—such as, retraining and relocation assistance, reconversion and developmental loans, etc. (Note in this connection that in many cases it now becomes more expensive to replace the basic community facilities—homes, roads, public utilities, schools than actual plants and equipment—with a trend therefore toward bringing new factories to established communities rather than vice versa!).

8. Finding out what is relevant in various congressional hearings and technical studies on depressed communities in the United States.

THE PROBLEM OF EQUITY

This is perhaps more an aspect of some of the other adjustment problems, particularly that of transfer or reconversion, than a problem in its own right. It involves an examination of the adjustment problems previously considered, but this time on the question of whether the costs of making the necessary adjustments are fairly distributed. In particular, it raises the question whether the individuals and companies who are, so to speak, at the focal point of a major change in government policies should have to shoulder all or the major part of the cost of the change.

Recognition of public responsibility in this area, and of the desirability of widespread sharing of the burden, might point in the direction of some such devices as:

1. Liberal termination pay provisions as a deductible cost in cancelled defense-contract settlements.

2. Institution of supplementary or extended unemployment-compensation payments for former workers

on defense contracts, or for workers generally during the reconversion period.

3. Liberal government-financed education, retraining, or relocation grants or loans, and possibly small business and mortgage loans, to disemployed personnel from the armed services and defense production.

4. Generous terms of settlement and prompt payment on prematurely cancelled defense contracts; special tax concessions, such as extended carry-forward or carry-back of losses, or rapid depreciation provisions on new and reconverted plant and equipment, or other financial aids to defense contractors, especially small ones.

Research under this heading might be mainly confined to examination of the likelihood of serious hardship to certain workers or companies, case studies of the financial impact on individuals and companies in previous cutbacks, and the probable effects and costs of such devices as mentioned above for equitably sharing the financial burden.

The experience of the Social Fund of the European Economic Community (and the past experience of the European Coal and Steel Community) might also be worth examining from this point of view, in light of the somewhat analogous purpose served. Comparisons could also be established with studies made in support of legislation in the United States to provide adjustment assistance to industries, workers, and communities injured by competition from imports resulting from tariff concessions.

THE INTERNATIONAL IMPACT OF DISARMAMENT

This discussion has centered almost exclusively on the United States economy and the problems it might encounter in adjusting to disarmament. However, these basic problems would present themselves to other countries as well. They would affect world trade and international financial transactions. Of course the details would vary from country to country. The fact that interest in such problems is growing throughout the world is shown by the adoption of a resolution (introduced by Pakistan) by the United Nations Assembly providing for a study of international economic impacts of disarmament.

In earlier postwar years many countries were having difficulty in accumulating enough *dollar* credits for their needs, and it looked as if any cutting off of U.S. overseas military spending would compound this difficulty. In recent time the trend has been reversed, and the United States has begun worrying about the "gold drain" arising from the fact that large dollar balances have been accumulated abroad. This might make adjustment to a cut-off of U.S. military spending easier, except in those countries which are heavily dependent on exports of strategic materials. In fact, we cannot be sure that the effect would stop with restoring a balance; it might again result in troublesome dollar shortages unless *international adjustments* were planned as well as internal ones. Certainly a better system of international reserves could be set up than the one we have drifted into since the Second World War.

Besides the over-all payments balance, there are important regional problems. The balance of payments of some of the less developed countries might be seriously affected by United States or world disarmament. A number of these countries now receive substantial amounts of defense-support aid which, besides permitting them to support larger armed forces than they otherwise could, also contribute to their general economic progress. In some countries even the strengthening of the armed forces may make an economic contribution through educational and training functions and the better preservation of law and order.

Among the regional problems there is the dilemma of the country which depends upon one crop or mineral product and has to export that in order to pay for its necessary imports of other necessities. If this one product is a strategic item entering into U.S. defense production and stockpiles, a sudden cut in such imports would be a serious matter. This would be made worse if stockpiles of such products now held by importing nations were to be thrown onto the international market.

Clearly many of these problems could be offset if a sizable part of the savings on armaments were diverted into international development. Two kinds of questions arise at this point, however. First, to what extent is there genuine willingness in this country, on a politically effective (congressional) level, to follow this course? Second, to what extent could the pattern of goods and services released from military preparation be really used for international development purposes? Clearly there is room here for careful study.

CONCLUDING COMMENT

A clear examination of the economic problems that disarmament might raise, and hence of the kind of research which their solution calls for, naturally puts a great deal of emphasis upon such problems. This should not be taken as indicating that the present defense program is an economic boon or that the economic problems of transition are a fearful enough bogy to halt the nation's effort toward disarmament. In order to keep a balanced picture, we need to remember some homely and obvious facts.

First, the defense program holds a large area of waste, not only through inefficient organization but most of all in its claim to resources which could be used for positive human betterment.

Second, while disarmament readjustments *may* be painful, they *need* not be, if we use forethought and adopt wise policies.

Third, even if the transition were to prove painful in some ways, it would still be worth making. One need only think of what twenty to twenty-five billion dollars a year could mean to the nation and the world if invested in public health, research, education, foreign aid, and tax cuts, especially in a world where tensions had been eased through disarmament agreements and actual disarmament.

Fourth, disarmament is and must remain fundamentally a political and not an economic issue. Economic analysis of defense can be helpful by showing us how the decisions which we have to make on non-economic grounds can be implemented most effectively and with the least cost and trouble. But these decisions themselves should, normally, be made entirely independently of economic considerations. Within broad limits we can always "afford" to purchase all the defense we really need and to eliminate all the defense we don't need—the criterion of "need" remaining throughout a technical, political, and moral problem, not an economic one.

In the long run, a world disarmed and freed from the threat of war would not only be a more secure, a happier, and an ethically sounder world to live in but it could also be a world with substantially greater resources to enrich human existence. One contribution economists might make to help create such a peaceful world is to assess the difficulties of the transition and plan in advance how they can be met, thereby dispelling economic fears of the transition. It is for this purpose that the program of research presented here has been conceived.

SEVEN

Southeast Asia and Japan

BY VERA MICHELES DEAN

Director, Non-Western Civilizations Program, the University of Rochester; editorial consultant to the Foreign Policy Association; author of many books on international affairs, among them *The Nature of the Non-Western World*

INTRODUCTION

In projecting future United States foreign policy toward any area of the world, it is essential, first of all, to define the assumptions on which this policy is expected to be based.

The suggestions presented in this paper on policy toward Southeast Asia and Japan are developed on the assumption that in the years ahead the cold-war struggle between the United States, as leader of the non-Communist coalition, and the U.S.S.R., as leader of the Communist bloc, will henceforth be focused not on preparations for a military showdown but on plans for economic and ideological competition. If this assumption is correct, then United States policy in Southeast Asia and Japan should have as its principal objective not the military build-up of the countries in this area but the strengthening of their political stability, their economic development, the improvement of their social welfare, and the expansion of their educational facilities.

Such a program of non-military, peaceful reconstruction of non-Western areas, designed to prepare them as rapidly as possible for effective participation in the world commu-

253

nity of the twentieth century, should be carried out irrespective of whether these countries have strong Communist elements or, of their own free choice, political and economic relations with members of the Communist bloc.

ATTITUDE TOWARD DEMOCRACY

In dealing with the countries of Southeast Asia we must recognize that the peoples of this area (like those of Russia, sections of Eastern Europe, the Middle East, Africa, and Latin America) have not shared the experience of Western Europe and the United States. These peoples have been little or not at all affected by the main forces which have shaped Western civilization, such as the Greek city-state, the legal and administrative ideas and practices of the Roman Empire, the concepts of the Roman Catholic Church, the Reformation and the Renaissance, the English, French, and American revolutions, and the Industrial Revolution. They have long and glorious histories of their own; they have forged great civilizations based on Hinduism, Buddhism, Islam; they have made distinguished contributions to the cultural heritage of the world through their religions, philosophies, architecture, art, literature, music. But their political, economic, and social development, for a variety of historical reasons, has been profoundly different from that of the Western peoples.

It is therefore unrealistic to expect that, merely because in the last decade the peoples of Southeast Asia have achieved independence from the colonial rule of Western powers—Britain, France, the Netherlands—they will simultaneously bridge the gap of centuries which separates them from Western Europe and the United States and establish political institutions familiar to the Western democracies. These institutions, it should be recalled, took hundreds of years to develop in the West—a fact little understood in the United States, which had the good fortune to inherit ideas and practices for which the peoples of England and

France had fought and died in many a bloody struggle. If we take the Magna Charta as the point of departure for democracy, we can see that it took Britain 700 years to develop its modern democratic institutions. We must therefore show understanding of the myriad difficulties faced by the technologically underdeveloped peoples of Southeast Asia in achieving what we call democracy. Nor should we urge them to set up democratic institutions which, unless rooted in their own traditions, may prove merely a façade for continued authoritarianism, as proved to be the case in Japan before Pearl Harbor.

Instead, we should face the fact that the peoples of Southeast Asia, who are wrestling with tremendous problems of population growth, demand for land reform, shortages of food, tensions and maladjustments resulting from the early stages of industrialization, and internal stresses between various political, racial, and linguistic groups, need today and probably for many years to come strong governments capable of maintaining the unity of newly independent nations, of modernizing their economies, of carrying out necessary but often harsh reforms, and of protecting their territories against encroachments by their neighbors.

This means that we shall have to accept the existence in Southeast Asia of authoritarian governments of one kind or another—whether the military rule under martial law of Marshal Ayub Khan in Pakistan or the recently terminated military rule of General Ne Win in Burma, or the "guided democracy" of Sukarno in Indonesia, or the military dictatorship of Thailand. The best we can hope for in this area is authoritarianism without totalitarianism—that is, governments which have authority to take whatever measures they regard as desirable, but are willing to assure civil liberties and do not seek to brainwash or indoctrinate their citizens, as has been done by Communists in China and Russia.

In our relations with these authoritarian governments we should avoid criticizing them for not being democratic in the Western sense of the term. Instead, we should commend them for all steps they take to improve the welfare and protect the personal freedoms of their citizens. The governments of Southeast Asia, whatever their political label, find themselves forced to adopt measures which many Americans may criticize as tantamount to "socialism," if not to "communism," for the simple reason that they must control and direct, more or less strictly, the economic and social development of their peoples if stagnation and hence continued misery, which produce rising discontent threatening internal upheavals, are not to be the fate of the nations they rule. We must therefore rid ourselves of fear about "socialism" in Southeast Asia and accept the fact that even governments we would regard as "conservative" cannot escape intervening in the operation of their countries' economies. At the same time, we should not hesitate to point out the features of our own democratic institutions of which we are particularly proud —and at the same time should do everything in our power to correct failings in our society, notably with respect to our Negro fellow citizens, that mar the image of democracy which we offer as an example to be followed by other peoples.

In this over-all picture of non-totalitarian authoritarianism, two countries appear as exceptions: India and Japan.

India, like other countries of Southeast Asia, lacks the elements which the West usually regards as prerequisites of democracy: a homogeneous population of manageable size; natural resources sufficient for a viable economy, with a balanced ratio of resources to population; a strong middle class; large-scale industrialization; and universal literacy. In spite of this, India, through an exceptional combination of its own religious and philosophical traditions, its political and administrative experience under enlightened rulers such as the Hindu Emperor Asoka and the Muslim ruler Akbar, and the comprehension of the basic concepts of Western democracy, which it absorbed from the British during the period of colonial rule, has developed new patterns of democracy in which Western ideas and practices have been adapted to Indian traditions. The success of the Indian form of democracy, as contrasted with the totalitarian system of Communist China, may determine whether other countries of Asia will, in the future, choose the Indian model in preference to that of China. But even in India the stupendous task of transforming a premedieval village society into a modern state capable of making use of atomic energy for peace-time purposes has been carried out under the direction of an outstanding "charismatic" leader, Jawaharlal Nehru, who, however, in contrast to the leaders of other Southeast Asian nations, has respected and made effective use of democratic institutions. And the experience of some Western nations—notably France under President Charles de Gaulle—would indicate that even experienced democracies, when faced with grave problems, resort to authoritarian rulers.

It would be hazardous to predict the political situation that might develop in India after Nehru has left the scene. No leader of comparable stature and influence has yet emerged, and it is possible that India might experience a period of transition during which a "caretaker" government headed by one of Nehru's present associates, such as Finance Minister Morarji Desai, might prepare the ground for a new governing team, which might be strongly staffed with technicians. It is probable, however, that if India succeeds in making its economic "take-off" and in providing its people with at least modest improvement of their living conditions, it will thereby succeed in preventing the growth of communism and maintain a political system based on parliamentary institutions, respect for law, protection of the rights of the individual, and nonviolence at home and abroad. But if India is to achieve this objective, it will require, according to 1960 estimates, at least five billion dollars in outside assistance, which would have to come largely from the United States in loans, credits, and commodities such as wheat and rice.

By contrast to India, Japan, having made an early start on modernization a century ago, has succeeded in creating an efficient and diversified industrialized economy, has achieved a high degree of literacy, and has developed a significant and influential middle class, although it has not yet succeeded in solving the many problems created by its large population which, although now subject to various forms of regulation, continues to press dangerously on its resources. The Japanese have established the institutions of a parliamentary democracy and, following their military defeat in the Second World War, have reduced the role of the once dominant emperor to that of a ceremonial head of state.

It is not yet clear, however, whether the Japanese people have absorbed the ideas of democracy, either in their political life or in their relations with each other. Experts fear that, in the foreseeable future, Japan, while outwardly a two-party state, will continue to be ruled by one party, the conservatives Liberal-Democrats—much as West Germany, although a two-party country, continues to be ruled by the conservative party of Chancellor Konrad Adenauer. Should the possibility of political change continue to be blocked, it is not impossible that communism may make greater gains in Japan than in India, where a more flexible political system and a greater degree of self-criticism permit the existence of a variety of smaller parties which can, and do, challenge the ruling Congress party. The riots staged in Japan by opponents of the United States-Japanese security treaty in the spring of 1960, which prevented the visit of President Eisenhower to Japan, revealed the strength of resistance to rearmament and the fear of the Japanese, not limited to the leftists, that military co-operation with the United States might draw the country into a nuclear war, whose dangers are most keenly felt by a people who experienced the consequences of Nagasaki and Hiroshima.

The resounding victory of the ruling Liberal-Democratic party under Premier Hayato Ikeda in the November 1960 elections, which won 300 out of 467 seats in the House of Representatives, was due not to popular approval of the United States-Japanese treaty, as claimed by some editorial writers in the United States, but to economic considerations, notably Premier Ikeda's promise that his government would double the national income in ten years. The future military relationship of the United States with Japan remains subject to question by the opposition; and the need to expand the country's economy may lead Japan to develop economic ties with Communist China. Given these circumstances, it is particularly important that the United States should be acquainted and maintain contacts with the non-conservative groups in Japan and not give the impression that it is committed solely and irrevocably to the conservatives as the bastion of our security in Asia.

ATTITUDE TOWARD ECONOMIC DEVELOPMENT

The countries of Southeast Asia now, and for years to come, require substantial aid both in terms of money and of technical know-how of all kinds. This aid can come from several sources: the United States; the industrial nations of Western Europe—primarily Britain and West Germany; Japan; the U.S.S.R. and the industrial nations of Eastern Europe, notably Czechoslovakia; the Colombo Plan; international financial agencies such as the World Bank, the International Monetary Fund, and the newly created International Development Loan Association; specialized international agencies such as the Food and Agriculture Organization and the World Health Organization; and the technical-assistance program of the United Nations.

In planning future aid to Southeast Asia, the United States should bear the following considerations in mind:

1. It is estimated that aid will be required for some fifty years if the countries of Southeast Asia are to reach

the point of "take-off" for modern economic development. Of all the countries in this area, India alone is regarded as being at the take-off stage—but, just because of this, India is in particularly urgent need of expanded aid, so that it will not lose the momentum already achieved. Thus the United States should make long-term plans for aid to this area.

Long-term planning is essential for effective planning by the Southeast Asian governments, which are trying to map out their economic needs and set their targets over periods, usually, of five years. The practice followed by the United States of voting foreign-aid appropriations on an annual basis—with uncertainty every year both on the part of the Executive and of the nations requesting aid as to what will be the final outcome of congressional debates—should be replaced by a system under which long-term (preferably five-year) appropriations would be voted, subject to congressional review at the end of every fiscal year.

2. Aid is needed for several purposes: for the modernization and diversification of agriculture; for the building of each country's infrastructure—roads, dams, transportation facilities, irrigation projects, and so on, which are essential to create a base for industrialization; for the construction of industrial enterprises, whether light or heavy industries, depending on each country's available raw materials; for the training of personnel in modern science and technology; for the creation of educational facilities; for the expansion of community development projects, which have the triple purpose of accelerating the transformation of village life, of increasing agricultural productivity, and of encouraging grass-roots self-government.

Private investors and philanthropic foundations can and do make a valuable and welcome contribution to some of these tasks. At the present stage of development, however, the bulk of aid will have to come from governments or international agencies, either because the projects to be undertaken cannot bring the financial returns which private investors legitimately expect, or because the size of the funds required is beyond the resources of private investors and private philanthropies—or both. Thus American political leaders should endeavor to explain to voters in the United States that contributions by our government cannot be effectively replaced by private investment or by private charity, although both should be encouraged to the utmost. And while private investors can legitimately seek guarantees for compensation in case of nationalization and for repatriation of their gains, the United States government needs to weigh carefully the question whether it should take any actions that could be regarded as underwriting and special protection of private investments and thus, conceivably, as intervention in the internal economic affairs of the underdeveloped country where investments are made.

3. The scope and variety of aid required by Southeast Asia are so vast that there will be plenty of room for every country and every agency which can be enlisted in this task. The United States should not oppose aid by the U.S.S.R. and the countries of Eastern Europe; on the contrary, it should welcome such aid. For if our objective is to speed up the technological development and the welfare improvement of Southeast Asia, then aid from any quarter can prove useful. We should not fear competition by the Communist countries. On the contrary, we should invite it by challenging them to outdo us in generosity, efficiency, and quality of performance. Unless the United States economy suffers grave retrogression, this country should be able to succeed in such a competition by increasing its own rate of economic growth.

Nor should we refuse aid to Communist countries, if aid is requested. We are already giving aid to Communist countries in Eastern Europe—Poland and Yugoslavia. The eventuality of undiluted Communist regimes is not at present anticipated in Southeast Asia. However, the United States might make a powerful impression on countries in this area by declaring that it would be ready to give aid to Communist China, which now relies almost exclusively on financial and technological aid from the Soviet bloc, once Peiping has been admitted to represent China in the United Nations.

4. Over the long run, however, national aid, whether by individual nations or by nations grouped in some new agency like the agency for aid to underdeveloped countries proposed by now Secretary of the Treasury C. Douglas Dillon for Western Europe, Canada, and the United States, may prove less desirable and less effective than the channeling of aid through international agencies, and particularly through the technical-assistance program of the United Nations. Competition in aid to underdeveloped countries by the West and the Soviet bloc has many advantages for the recipient countries, which are now in a position to bid one side off against the other—but such competition, although clearly preferable to the cold-war struggle, continues to have political overtones. If all the technologically advanced nations (and this group now includes the U.S.S.R. and Czechoslovakia, in addition to the United States, Canada, the Western European nations, and Japan) could be persuaded to pool their resources, and to place them under the administrative supervision of the United Nations, three gains would be achieved:

(a) The pooled aid could be allocated to the nations requiring aid at periodic meetings attended by both givers and recipients, as is now done under the highly successful Colombo Plan. The psychological tensions created by the recurring need of each country to go, hat in hand, to Moscow or Washington, London or Bonn, for one kind of aid or another would be eliminated, and a genuine partnership between the "have" countries and the "have-nots" could be created.

(b) The pooling of aid would permit long-term planning on a regional basis, thereby eliminating the dangers of duplication between requests for aid, individual projects, and nationalistic demands for developments which may contribute to a country's prestige but not enhance its over-all development. The success achieved by Western Europe in pooling its resources to develop Euratom is an example of what might be done in Southeast Asia.

(c) The administration of aid by the United Nations would permit strict supervision of the use made by each recipient country of the funds allocated for its develop-ment, without the danger that such supervision—which is essential to the honest and efficient operation of all aid programs—will be denounced by the recipient as an act of "imperialism," or "intervention," or "strings attached" by the contributing nation. Then distressing episodes such as the alleged mismanagement of United States aid to Laos and Vietnam could be avoided.

It must therefore be hoped that the United States will overcome its present reluctance to channel the bulk of its aid funds through the United Nations and instead take the leadership in urging primacy for this method of admin-istering aid for underdeveloped countries.

The economic position of Japan is in sharp contrast to that of the countries of Southeast Asia. Japan is a highly industrialized and technologically competent nation. In spite of its population problem, it is a "have" nation, with a standard of living infinitely superior to that of any of its Asian neighbors. And because of its financial and tech-nological resources it is in a position to give aid to less developed countries. However, those of the Southeast Asian countries which suffered from Japanese conquest during the Second World War—particularly the Philippines and Indonesia—do not share the enthusiasm of the United States for Japan and, while eager to obtain reparations for war damages inflicted by the Japanese, are not always eager for aid or trade with Japan if other sources of assistance and other markets are available. In this respect, too, channeling of aid through the United Nations would make it possible to use contributions by Japan, a member of the UN, without the stigma of the national label.

Meanwhile, Japan itself needs aid—but of another kind than the countries of Southeast Asia. If Japan is to maintain its present standard of living and, hopefully, to improve it, the Japanese will need to find expanding markets overseas for their varied manufactured goods. Unless the United States can enlarge its purchases of Japanese products such as textiles, cameras, stainless-steel cutlery, and so on, Japan will need to look elsewhere for customers. While the countries of Southeast Asia need many of the consumer goods as well as the heavy-industry products of Japan, they usually do not have the foreign currency to make purchases there; and meanwhile India and Communist China now compete with Japan in the export of various goods—India particularly in textiles, Communist China in a wide range of products, from textiles to bicycles and flashlights. The presence in several Southeast Asian countries (Thailand, Indonesia, the Philippines) of large Chinese communities facilitates Peiping's export drive in the area. The one important exception to this situation is India, which was not invaded by Japan in the Second World War, finds there is a market in Japan for some of its raw materials, notably iron ore, and is importing machinery and other goods, as well as technical assistance, from Japan. In the long run, however, the Japanese may have to seek markets in Communist China—and they can be expected to do so if and when Peiping is admitted to the United Nations.

A new and highly controversial question about foreign aid has been raised in connection with the problem of population growth in the underdeveloped countries, including some of the Southeast Asian countries, notably India. The population explosion, as is well known, results from the sharp decline in the death rate due to medical improvement and public health measures, with no corresponding decline in the birth rate. The 1959 report of the Draper

Committee, entrusted by President Eisenhower with the task of reviewing military and economic aid, stated that "no realistic discussion of economic development can fail to note that development efforts in many areas of the world are being offset by increasingly rapid population growth." The committee recommended that, in order to meet more effectively the problems of economic development, the United States should, among other things, "assist those countries with which it is cooperating in economic aid programs, on request, in the formulation of their plans designed to deal with the problem of rapid population growth."

The Draper report, it will be recalled, brought a strong statement on November 25, 1959, by the Roman Catholic bishops of the United States, opposing birth-control aid by government agencies. So far as can be ascertained, no country has asked the United States for information about birth control, which is now a matter of common knowledge throughout the world. What several underdeveloped countries, notably India, seek are two things: increased economic aid, so that they can allocate more of their own resources to population-regulation measures they have chosen to undertake (in India, as well as in Japan, the government supports programs of birth control and sterilization, and abortion is widely practiced in Japan); and intensification of research in the United States for the discovery of a contraceptive which would be both inexpensive and easily usable under the living conditions of underdeveloped countries (an experiment with oral contraceptives which might be useful under such conditions is being conducted in Puerto Rico). In any case, it would be wise that any measures which may be undertaken to further planned parenthood in underdeveloped countries should be effected through the United Nations and other international agencies, on a multilateral basis, rather than initiated by individual nations.

The views of all religious groups are entitled to respectful consideration. The question must be faced, however, whether the United States can continue to assist death control through aid to public health and improved welfare in the Southeast Asian countries, without taking some responsibility for the resulting population pressures which arise in the absence of birth control. If the United States government is precluded from taking the measures proposed by the Draper Committee, then American political leaders have a responsibility to urge increased efforts by private organizations and individuals in this country, through research and other means, to bring nearer the day when underdeveloped countries can, of their own free choice, and with the support of leaders of their own religious faiths, deal as they choose with population growth within their borders.

ATTITUDE TOWARD ARMS AND NEUTRALISM

In Southeast Asia, as in other non-Western areas of the world, the United States, since the onset of the cold war, has been confronted with two categories of nations: those which, like India, Burma, and Indonesia, have chosen not to become aligned with either of the two blocs—the non-Communist bloc led by the United States and the Soviet bloc led by the U.S.S.R.; and those which, like Pakistan, Thailand, the Philippines, South Korea, South Vietnam, have chosen to take a strong stand against the Communist bloc and to accept military aid from the United States.

For many years after the Korean War the United States was highly critical of what it first called "neutrality," and later "neutralism," although official statements on this point did not always harmonize (thus in 1956 Secretary of State John Foster Dulles, referring to India, said "neutralism is immoral," while approximately at the same time President Eisenhower declared that he understood the policy of India, which made him think of the no foreign-commitment policy of the United States under George Washington). Many American spokesmen kept on asking Mr. Nehru: Are you with us or against us?—although if they meant that India had to decide for or against democracy this was a futile question, since India had answered it immediately after accepting independence, when it voluntarily joined democratic Britain in the Commonwealth. Meanwhile, in the Southeast Asia Treaty Organization (SEATO) the United States backed the countries which had pledged themselves to oppose Communist aggression and gave each anti-Communist country military aid.

During 1959 this policy underwent a noticeable, although not yet explicitly formulated, change. The United States appears to have accepted non-alignment as a position worthy of respect and no longer subject, as in the past, to criticism and derision. President Eisenhower, during and after his spectacular 1959 visit to India, indicated that he was deeply impressed by that country and by its leader, Mr. Nehru, and subsequently urged increased aid to India. Neutralism appears to have become respectable. In fact, the United States may find that, with the decrease in emphasis on military aspects of the East-West struggle, military commitments in Southeast Asia need to be deemphasized.

Three facts are coming to be generally recognized:

1. Military aid given by the United States may prove a burden, rather than a boon, for underdeveloped countries. These countries need every ounce of their resources, in terms of money, trained manpower, and raw materials, to develop their economies as rapidly as possible. Yet in order to utilize United States military aid they have to expend a considerable portion of their own limited resources—for example, Pakistan allocates seventy per cent of its budget for defense. The question therefore needs to be raised whether it would not be wiser for the United States to increase its economic aid and to decrease its military aid, in the hope that the recipient country will then strengthen

itself through internal development and resulting political stability, both of which may have to be held in abeyance if attention continues to be focused on defense.

2. Assuming that both power blocs agree to impose a permanent nuclear test ban and to initiate phased disarmament, the United States may find that it will no longer need bases around the periphery of the U.S.S.R. and Communist China, and that instead, pending effective arms reduction, it should place its chief reliance on long-range missiles to be delivered from its own territory. Should such a decision ultimately emerge from the current debate about defense policy, this would sharply reduce the value of military installations in Southeast Asia. It might then be advisable to give only minimum military aid, in the form of experts and a limited range of non-nuclear weapons, to the governments of this area for the training of local troops, which would be used primarily for the maintenance of law and order.

3. If such a decision is reached, it would reduce the tensions between some of the countries of Southeast Asia which have hitherto feared that United Nations military aid given to one of them would be used eventually not against the U.S.S.R. or Communist China, but against a neighbor—as in the case of India and Pakistan. Such reduction of tensions would, in turn, lead to political stabilization in the area and encourage long-term economic development.

4. Once the military aspects of the East-West struggle are de-emphasized, non-alignment, instead of being a threat to the United States, might come to be regarded as a distinct advantage, for while the non-aligned countries would not be committed to the United States side, neither would they be committed to the side of the Soviet bloc. Thus the non-aligned countries would in effect form a demilitarized, denuclearized zone between the two blocs hitherto arraigned against each other.

Such a change in our policy about military pacts and

military aid would involve a review of our attitude toward Japan, which is now regarded as our principal ally in Asia. Many Japanese have had reservations about their country's military alliance with the United States, even after we had accepted in 1959 a number of modifications of the United States-Japanese security treaty favorable to Japan. Nor are the Japanese eager to rearm. The question would then arise whether the security of Japan would be more effectively safeguarded by the use of United States long-range missiles in case of an emergency than by the presence of American troops and/or weapons on Japanese territory.

SUMMARY

To sum up: Assuming that both political parties agree on the need to negotiate now with the U.S.S.R., and eventually with Communist China, rather than to seek a military showdown with one or both of the great Communist powers, and expect that the post-Second World War struggle between the two power blocs will henceforth be waged on economic and ideological, rather than military, battlegrounds, United States policy toward Southeast Asia and Japan should be focused on the following three objectives:

1. To foster, so far as possible, political stability and civil liberties, without expecting the emergence in the near future of democratic governments on the Western pattern, in full realization that the United States cannot intervene in the internal affairs of other countries, however worthy our motives may seem to us, without incurring their resentment.

2. To expand governmental economic aid on a long-term basis, preferably through the United Nations and other international agencies, rather than on a bilateral or multi-Western-nation basis.

3. To respect the position of non-aligned nations and to reassess our over-all defense policy, with a view to

269

determining whether it would be in our interests, as well as in the interests of our allies in the area, to de-emphasize military aid and to provide protection by long-range missiles rather than by the continued build-up of local forces which may not necessarily be friendly to the United States, as in Laos and South Vietnam.

EIGHT

Considerations for the Latin American Policy

BY FRANK TANNENBAUM

Director of University Seminars and Professor Emeritus of Latin American History, Columbia University

The democratically oriented countries in Latin America are few, even though some believe themselves to be democratically minded. The distance that separates the poor or the peasant on the plantation and the rancho from the cultured and wealthy that govern the country is so wide that it is difficult to think of how it can be bridged or, even narrowed. For unless the favored of fortune and the poor, who in most countries are very poor, achieve some broader basis of identity, democratic government must remain an aspiration or an illusion. This separation between rich and poor, between the university graduate and the illiterate, is so traditional, so taken for granted by the indigent as well as by the opulent that neither side would know how to reduce the distance even if the idea occurred to them. This is especially true in the rural districts. The difficulty is not merely one of difference in wealth but in the total attitude toward life. There is an almost overwhelming acceptance of authoritarian attitudes and not merely in government. The acceptance of absolute authority and complete submission is not just a matter of political arrangements. It is an ingrained habit, an expectancy, a way of life. The poor are treated with dignity and respect, their personality as human beings is neither denied nor intruded upon (except if they are Indians), but all of this in its proper place. The leader is an aristocrat by training and tradition and he expects obedience that is unquestioned. The attitude toward the *Amo* is one of submission and acceptance. This feeling of obeisance and lordship survives political revolution and social change.

In countries where the Indian element in the population is large the distance between the self-conscious elite and the common folk is even greater. All of this is important to keep in mind when one is talking about democracy in Latin America. For all of this is the basis of the caudillo, the temporary strong man, the unremitting partisanship between the followers of one political leader and the followers of another and ultimately the grounds upon which the dictator may be accepted and tolerated.

I have said all of this in the beginning so as to make it clear that there is no easy path to the encouragement of democratic government or to its certain emergence. For democracy and social reform are not identical. However, in Latin America I am certain that social reform must precede the effort to develop democratic ways. And the social reform that stands at the top of the list is the breakup of the old hacienda system. It is at this point that the leadership, even the democratic leadership, is most likely to stumble because all of the leadership, conservative or liberal, has its roots in the agrarian family with the large plantation in the background. There are other sources of wealth and prestige, of course, especially in modern times. There are mines, urban property, banking, commerce, and international trade. But the number of families involved in these enterprises, other than urban property, who are native rather than foreign are few, and even these probably found their entrée into non-agricultural activities through family connections based upon large-scale landholding. The only other means to leadership and influence are the army, law, medicine, and government office. But for these the surest route is through connection with a landholding family.

If democracy in an agricultural country requires, as it did in the United States, the previous existence of the family farm, then it really means that Latin America needs a profound agrarian revolution. And the present leadership does not come from the family farm, does not derive from parents who tilled their own lands, and is really not prepared to carry through a land program that would convert its present hacienda system into self-sufficient family units. If the proposal to support democratic growth in Latin America is taken seriously, then we would have to support an agrarian program. For without it no prospect of democratic development can be looked for. The only cases of the liquidation of the hacienda system that we have are in Mexico and Bolivia, and in both these cases it was the result of violence and revolution. What will happen in Cuba remains to be seen. An example of what might have been good American policy would have been to offer to lend Madero, in 1911, twenty-five or fifty million dollars at a low interest rate to expropriate and break up those properties in areas where the land question was most pressing. Had such a policy been carried through, then we might have escaped thirty years of strife in Mexico, the growth of strong anti-American feeling, and even the ultimate expropriation of the oil industry. Obviously we were not prepared to adopt such a policy in 1911, and it remains to be seen whether we are now. For it may not be too late—if the policy is widely publicized and promptly put into practice—to save such countries as Peru, Ecuador, and Chile, to mention only the most obvious, from facing the social violence that swept over Mexico, Bolivia, and is now existent in Cuba. It might still be possible if the money were at hand in the form of a long-term loan—say fifty years—to the governments as an agricultural development proposal to buy up the properties that come on the market, or in some cases to expropriate them, or to use the money for credit and aid in the breaking up of the haciendas held by the government itself. In Ecuador a very large number of haciendas are leased out at a low rent to neighboring hacendados and worked on a basis of peonage (Huasi-pongo) as they have always been. As money goes these days it would not require great amounts. But this money is not to be considered an investment except in political stability and good will. It should be a credit to be repaid when conditions permit it to be repaid. It should not be a banker's loan. If encouragement of democratic governments is to be more than lip service, this is the first item in the program—and one to be pursued over many years and in most, if not all, places. I know all the arguments that can be raised against the proposal, but what we are talking about are the conditions under which democratic institutions and, in the end, democratic leadership may develop. For these are still primarily agricultural countries, and in agricultural countries small independent landholding is the prerequisite to democratic development. Our own Homestead Act is a case in point. That such a program will in addition call for small amounts for credit to "homesteaders," technical aid, agricultural education, county agents, etc., is taken for granted. But most of this could be locally financed. With this ought to go a "point four" program imbued with "a philosophy of little things," a small fish pond, a small dam, a windmill, a thousand little things rather than a few big ones.

In the urban centers, small and large, the best thing we could do would be to support the growth of voluntary autonomous groups, not only trade unions but parent and teacher associations, athletic associations, leagues of women voters, etc., etc. Some way has to be found in Latin America to lay the basis for effective local government and one way of doing it is to build up as many local groups accustomed to take part in public life as possible. But all of this does not really meet the question posed in "How can American policy in Latin America encourage democratically oriented governments?".

The simplest answer to this is by encouraging them. I mean by making it perfectly clear that we will do so—by saying so publicly, by announcing it from the White House, the State Department, the Congress—that we will support democratically oriented governments, and especially that we will support their democratically oriented projects. The way to do this is to do it. To have a policy known to the wide world, including our diplomatic representatives, that the United States stands for democratic governments. That a democratic government will receive support in the shape of loans, technical aid, diplomatic and military support, whilst a dictatorial government will be cold-shouldered, discriminated against, and, as far as possible, diplomatically isolated. I know, of course, that the argument of non-intervention will be brought up. But the argument is specious and weighted with malice. It was used to justify support for Batista in Cuba, for Perez Jimenez in Venezuela, for Rojas Pinilla in Colombia, and for Trujillo in Santo Domingo. The difficulty is not the doctrine of non-intervention. For anyone can recognize a dictator like Trujillo and a democrat like Lleros Camargo. The difficulty lies in the fact that we are committed to the *status quo,* by which I mean the government and American businessmen. This is natural enough and I am not suggesting malice of forethought or any unholy and hidden intent. What I am suggesting is that the *status quo* in Latin America is fragile, unstable, and incongruous in a world of jet planes, atomic energy, universal communication, and the cold war. The *status quo* in Latin America is incompatible with democracy, industrialism, the safety of foreign investments, and even with our campaign against communism. The *status quo* in Latin America is explosive, and not because of Communist influence. It is explosive primarily because of our influence. We are the great revolutionary influence in fact and the conservative influence in policy. We stir up the conflagration by our mere presence, by our innate egalitarianism, by our backslapping, good-fellow attitudes, by treating everyone we meet the same way, by having none of the attributes associated with a stratified social structure, by really not recognizing the difference between a "big" man and a "little" man. We also set the conflagration going by the incredible emphasis upon consumer goods through every medium available to us. We announce to the world that everyone ought to have a "Cadillac," a "television set," the best of furniture and modern plumbing and ten thousand other things as well. We do our best to stir the appetite for the ease, comfort, luxury, and material possessions which are unattainable in the mass among the people in Latin America without a complete social upheaval and may not be obtainable after it while, at the same time, we do our best to sit on the lid or help the present governments sit on the lid; and when the explosion occurs, we find ourselves completely surprised as to what happened and blame it on the Communists, who, I am certain, are glad to get the credit for being the "friends" of the people who are merely trying to change the situation which makes all that we offer unattainable. The present situation was graphically described by a French anthropologist when he took a good look at the present hacienda system in Peru: "Not since the thirteenth century has anything like this existed in France or in Western Europe." The serfdom in which people are sold with the land is not only a Peruvian institution. This is the reality which makes it easy for dictators and difficult for "democracies." And our problem is to help the democratic governments make the transition from the thirteenth to the twentieth century without too much convulsion. The transition we cannot stop. We are, in fact, more responsible for setting it in motion than anyone else, and we cannot help continuing the agitation and making the "hunger" almost unbearable. For we cannot as a culture and as individuals stop being what we are or stop having the influence that we have. We will either help the Latin American governments make the transition from serfdom and poverty to the modern essentially American twentieth century or have to accept the alternative of a series of convulsive and bloody revolutions in which we will be the chief sufferers and in which we will be cast as the culprits who stand in the way of "progress" and in the path of the legitimate aspirations of the common people—aspirations that we will have been responsible for stirring up, but the credit for which will accrue to the Communists because we will identify with the *status quo* and try to hold back the flood with a teaspoon or a diplomatic note.

Unless we are prepared to support the democratic governments and to help them in their efforts to bring their backward countries up to the modern world, we must resign ourselves to a whole series of violent revolutions in the next twenty-five to fifty years in which we will be cast in the role of the devil. We actually run the risk of losing, for a period crucial in its timing, the good will of the people of Latin America and the support of the new governments they will raise to power—not all at one time but in all probability in the next generation, or at most two. This will happen not because anyone advocates or agitates these changes deliberately, but simply because the twentieth century, which we represent and project across the globe with such incredible force and persuasiveness, cannot tolerate or abide the thirteenth. That is the dilemma we face in our relations with Latin America and which we cannot escape. And that is the real meaning of "democracy" versus "dictatorship" in Latin America. And, as we said in the beginning, the democratic process even for the "democratic" governments is made the most difficult by the centuries of authoritarian and "seignorial" tradition. The phenomenon is so complex and difficult in some countries such as Guatemala and Peru, for instance, as to seem almost baffling because even our friends there would like to be able to live in both worlds—the thirteenth and the twentieth centuries. The question, therefore, of whether we ought to support the "dictators" or the "democrats" is one that reaches far beyond the specific individuals and far beyond the present moment.

This is clearly seen in our position toward Cuba. So far as most Latin Americans are concerned—I am not speaking about their governments, for they speak with tongue in cheek—they sympathize with Castro and certainly with the revolution he stands for, and we cannot say an effective word about the matter because we have tolerated and, until recently, supported Trujillo in Santo Domingo. He, after all, was one of the worst and most heartless of tyrants in the modern world; the things we stand for—the sacredness of life, liberty, human dignity, private property, privacy, or even personal self-respect and respect for the members of one's family mean absolutely nothing to him or his henchmen. And yet he has been one of the supporters we accepted in defense of western "democracy." If we had a clean record about Trujillo, our case against Castro would be much more convincing. If now we were to condemn Trujillo, it would be too late, too deliberate to be effective. It is hard to live by a double standard and expect to be respected in either. If we want the good will and support of the next generation of Latin Americans, then we must make it clear by word and deed that we will have no further truck with dictators even if they play the anti-Communist game, in public, so that we can be gulled into believing them.

The anti-Communist campaign in Latin America has for the United States been a poor investment. It has aligned the dictators on our side and permitted them to persecute good, decent democrats who opposed tyranny on the grounds that these democrats were Communists. In this connection the Walter-McCarran Act as applied to visas for entrée to and passage through the United States has made us more enemies in Latin America than almost any other single policy. It has made enemies for us of those who were naturally our friends because they were being persecuted for believing in democracy and were opposed to dictators. We have found it difficult to draw the line between dictators and others because businessmen whose interests are in the present and whose commitments are to the *status quo* have been able to beguile our policy makers into believing that all was for the best and that any change would be for the worse. And our policy makers, harassed on all sides and having no clear mandate from Congress or the President and no clear conviction that it is to our interest to defend and support democratic governments not only behind the Iron Curtain but in Santo Domingo and Venezuela as well, have permitted themselves the painfully expensive luxury of clamoring for democratic movements in Poland and Hungary while supporting some of the world's worst tyrannies in this hemisphere and then wonder why we are suspected, disliked, and considered hypocritical by the intellectuals who shape public opinion in Latin America.

One thing is clear. We must, if we wish to retain the good will of Latin America, do what can be done to help them industrialize their economies. We must do this even if we recognize that it will hasten social change, and perhaps precipitate the convulsion we would avoid. And this will involve us in large-scale financing of public utilities, transport facilities, building of dams for the harnessing of water power, and extensive sanitation projects for which private capital is difficult to get. These outlays are, however, preliminary to private investment for industrialization. Industrialization is no panacea, but if the gap that divides the well-to-do and the poor in Latin America is to be narrowed, some industrial development is an essential means and if the gap between the United States, with an average annual income per person of $2200, and that of Latin America, with $200, is to be narrowed, then some industrialization is seemingly indispensable. And it might be added that as long as this disparity exists be-

tween the average income in the United States and our
neighbors to the south, it will be impossible to charm them
into identifying their destiny with our own, or making
them as concerned as we are about the ideas inherent in
our philosophy of politics. It is not the differences in income that are so important, but the change in world outlook that follows the effort to increase the real income of
the people which makes the difference. In the present
world these efforts at acquiring and distributing an income
that would be remotely comparable with that of the United
States would so change the outlook and preoccupation of
the mass of the people as to give them and us something
like a basis of common discourse and common ends.

This brings us to the question of a common market with
Latin America. The disparities in the income, education,
effective resources, skills, and capital between the two are
so great that a common market with the free flow of capital and, by implication, labor would, from the Latin American point of view, seem like a new conquest—or coloni-
zation. That it would in the end result in the material
improvement of the Latin American economies there can
be little doubt. But there can also be little doubt that with
nationalism on the march it would not be acceptable at
the present and for a considerable time to come. Conceivably a greatly improved standard of living and much
more fully industrialized economy when that has come
about will make it easier to bring this idea into acceptance.
This should, however, not prevent us from encouraging
the common-market plan which Latin Americans are now
adopting. It should be recognized that it will be a long
time before this program will make any noticeable change
in the economic relations between these nations.

Certainly our aid to Latin America does not require additional military assistance and we have overplayed our
hand in this matter. No one in Latin America assumes that
any of the armies we have equipped would be available
to us in case of a war in which we were engaged or that

in an atomic war they would be of any consequence even if available. It was often pointed out by the liberals that we were arming the dictators, saddling the soldiery upon the government, and alienating the thinking elements in the area. For what we accomplished in fact was what we had not intended. We upset the political process traditional in Latin America—resort to a revolution by some local leader when the central government became intolerable. When the local militia was as well armed as the central-government troops, a kind of rough democratic process could be enforced and the dictator kept in check by the fear of a "popular" uprising. The arming of the central government's forces upset this traditional bridling of tyranny at the center and made it impossible for anyone to overthrow the government except the army, which means that no one can be elected or keep office unless he is acceptable to the army. All of civilian government (or nearly all) is at the mercy of the army. And it will be most difficult to change our policy because the army can force the heads of government to insist on a continuing supply of arms as a condition of good relations with us, or force the government to purchase arms in other places. It also means that countries with a budget insufficient for their real needs will have to maintain an army larger than they require and at a cost greater than they can afford. We have really contributed to the formation of a new ruling class—the armed military. Not that it did not exist before, but it could be defeated. We have made it omnipotent.

NINE

Communist China

BY ALLEN S. WHITING

Taught courses in the Far East at Northwestern, Michigan State, and Columbia; author of *Sinkiang, Pawn or Pivot?* and *China Crosses the Yalu*

Harold Isaacs coined a felicitous phrase when he described American beliefs about China as "scratches on our minds." Like scratches, these beliefs seem to appear suddenly, leaving a crosshatch of surface disfiguration with little or no penetration of our thinking. Over the past century we have accumulated a lore of contradictory but coexisting "scratches," or impressions about Chinese and China, replete with such adjectives as "thrifty, industrious, patient, passive, and inscrutable," on the one hand, as against "cunning, fanatic, secretive, and scheming" on the other.

At the turn of mid-century, however, two events in swift succession cut so deep a scar on the American mind as to transfigure sharply our image of China. In October 1949, Mao Tse-tung established the People's Republic of China, an avowed Communist regime with its main enemy defined as "world capitalism led by American imperialism." In October 1950, Mao's armies swarmed across the Yalu River to give U.S. troops one of the most stunning defeats this nation has suffered in modern times.

Not since the anti-foreign violence of the Boxer uprising had the American people experienced so rude a rebuff from a China which seemed in need of our missionary help, our political guidance, and hopefully our economic wares.

Our reaction far outlived the Korean War. In contrast to our relations with Red China's guardian ally, Soviet Russia, we froze into a posture of non-recognition and, with rare exception, non-contact. We prohibited Americans from entering China and took legal action against those who did. We banned the importing of publications from China, except to academic and governmental institutions. We fostered an image of a fragmented China, with ten million persons in Taiwan administered by Chiang Kai-shek, supposedly united in spirit with their 600 million fellow countrymen on the mainland. Somehow the fragments would unite to overthrow the "non-Chinese" or "Soviet-imposed" regime in Peking.

It would be a travesty of history to present this as a unilateral reaction, unprovoked by the other side. From the jailing of American consular officials in Mukden in 1949 to the most recent editorial attacks against "U.S. aggression in Asia," Peking has maintained a relentless drumfire of hate-America propaganda, unequaled in duration and intensity even by the efforts of its Soviet ally. American citizens have been imprisoned under false charges and submitted to prolonged mental torture, and America's allies and friends, from Japan to India, have suffered Chinese economic and political pressures obviously designed to alienate them from the United States.

It is not my purpose to assess blame or to strike a balance sheet for the behavior of each side. Rather I recall the past record for its effect upon our thinking about Communist China. Our limited access to information and the necessarily subjective view we have as Peking's chief enemy combine to impair our analysis. This is particularly true, concerned as we are with the many points of Chinese pressure, such as Japan, Taiwan, Laos, Burma, and India. The overseas Chinese in Singapore, Thailand, and Malaya provide Peking with further leverage. Finally, the indigenous Communist parties of Southeast Asia offer a prospective extension of Mao's empire. Thus, short-run crises consequent from Peking's policies have impeded longer-range appraisal of Communist China's strategy and tactics.

Such an appraisal should not be undertaken in the hope it will make the problem disappear. The Chinese Communist challenge to United States interests in Asia is real, it is dangerous, and it is going to dominate our thinking in that area throughout the foreseeable future. Having said this, however, perhaps reappraisal will provide a better understanding of that challenge. This should enable us to assess alternative responses more rationally than in the crisis-ridden, emotion-laden atmosphere of the past decade.

Space precludes retelling the story of Chinese Communist foreign policy. Fortunately a superb survey of this subject is afforded by A. Doak Barnett's study, *Communist China and Asia*, published by the Council on Foreign Relations. Mr. Barnett's careful and comprehensive examination of Peking's policies at home and abroad is required reading for anyone concerned with Communist China.

Instead, I would like to highlight three characteristics of Peking's foreign policy, as exemplified by major moves in its first decade of power. These might be termed the "three C's" of Mao's strategy—its Chinese element, its Communist element, and its element of caution. All three elements may not be equally operative in every situation. But to ignore any one factor is to miscalculate the ends and means of the regime.

It would seem banal in the extreme even to suggest, much less examine, the Chinese and Communist elements, so obvious are these in our very term Communist China. Yet the frequency with which one encounters the word "irrational" as characterizing Peking's behavior compels us to question the degree to which these two elements are properly comprehended. Irrational may mean a subjective ordering of reality in violation of the objective or "true" world. In so far as this is a criticism of assumptions underlying Chinese Communist behavior, it may well be valid. But on an *a priori* basis it is no more apparent that Peking's assumptions are in this context irrational than the assumptions held in Delhi, Paris, or even Washington.

However, in everyday usage, irrational implies an absence of logic in thought and deed. Actions are taken in violation of values and with jeopardy to goals. If this is the meaning when applied to Chinese Communist behavior, then I would question its validity and argue that a selective but rational blending of Chinese and Communist elements underlies the choice of ends and means in foreign policy. By Chinese I mean those aspects of interpreting the world, and reacting to it, which are common to both Mao Tse-tung and Chiang Kai-shek, inheritors of a cultural heritage which goes back more than a millennium. By Communist I mean those aspects which distinguish Mao from his Nationalist rivals and his imperial predecessors, and which are derived from the lineage of Marx-Engels-Lenin-Stalin. The Chinese element is characterized chiefly by ethnocentrism, by limited expansionism, and by xenophobia. The Communist element is characterized by exclusive reliance upon the Soviet Union, as an exception to xenophobia, by extension of a single social order throughout the world, as an extension of expansionism, and by its assumption of omnipresent struggle or conflict—the celebrated "contradictions"—in opposition to traditional Chinese assumptions of harmony.

The third element, caution, is self-explanatory. A recurrent theme in Mao's writings on strategy over the past twenty years, it is exemplified by his formula of "strategically despise the enemy, tactically take them seriously." In an extended metaphor he wrote, "Strategically we take the eating of a meal lightly: we know we can finish it. But when actually eating, we do it a mouthful at a time. It would be impossible to swallow the entire feast in a single mouthful. This is called a piecemeal solution. And in military literature, it is called smashing the enemy bit by bit."

[Speech to meeting of representatives of the Communist and Workers' Parties of the Socialist Countries, Moscow, November 18, 1957.]

Admittedly, caution is found in both the Chinese and Communist characteristics. Christopher Rand, at the time of the 1955 Bandung Conference, described Chou En-lai's strategy in terms of Chinese boxing. Unlike the Western style with its emphasis upon swift movement and an early knockout, Chinese boxing stresses slow motion, prolonged tension, and a final small but upsetting blow. So, too, does Communist literature abound with admonitions against "adventurism," against what Lenin scornfully called "left-wing Communism, an infantile disorder."

Yet the element of caution merits separate attention because of its specific denial by Western analyses which characterize Chinese Communist behavior as fanatical. A sophisticated variant of this approach introduces a psychological *motif*. If aggression is derived from frustration, then Peking's failure to realize its external goals prompts it to violence. According to this analysis, when violence fails to attain its objective, the frustration-aggression syndrome takes another turn, with obvious hazards for international relations. Still a third variation on this theme attributes such fanaticism to the youth or early stage of revolution in China, implying that this will moderate in time.

However, the past decade suggests that neither fanaticism nor frustration-aggression cycles characterize Chinese Communist foreign policy. Whatever the verbal level of violence in Peking's propaganda, its actions reflect a cautious approach, accepting the risks of war but limiting so far as possible the consequences of such risk-taking.

Three notable instances of Sino-American tension offer insight on Chinese Communist strategy and tactics: the Korean War of 1950, and the so-called offshore-islands crises of 1954 and 1958. These are not only of historic interest but provide guide lines for anticipating future moves by Peking. The present leadership of Communist China is, with few exceptions, identical with that of 1950. At top levels and immediately below there has been none of the high turnover which has characterized the Soviet bureaucracy. This is a cohesive elite with a self-conscious ideological discipline. Thus its behavior of the 1950s should offer clues for interpreting its actions in the 1960s.

Of these three crises, the Korean War presented the most serious risks to Communist China. We do not have records of the secret deliberations which preceded the Chinese intervention, but other evidence provides a framework within which we can trace the outlines of decision-making in the summer of 1950. Our inferences are derived from the controlled Chinese Communist press and radio broadcasts, from troop movements detected at the time and reconstructed from later interrogation of war prisoners, and from secret archives captured when UN armies swept into North Korea. Finally we have the benefit of hindsight to buttress our inferences.

Two phenomena demand explanation: first, the slowness with which Peking moved to identify itself with Pyongyang, in domestic propaganda, in international political communications, and in military assistance; and second, the fact that Red China *did* intervene when the North Korean cause seemed lost, risking Peking's precarious hold on a nation already ravaged by fifteen years of foreign invasion and civil war.

To refresh our memory, a brief chronology is in order. On June 25, 1950, North Korean armies crossed the thirty-eighth parallel. Two days later President Truman ordered U.S. air and sea units, later supplemented by land forces, into action against the invaders. For one month bitter fighting slowed but did not stop Communist invaders. Throughout this time, domestic Chinese Communist propaganda repeatedly stressed, "The North Korean people have their struggle, and we have ours"—"ours" being the so-called "liberation of Taiwan and Tibet." No material support was demanded for Korea nor was any material assistance given. Indeed, it was not until mid-August that Peking's first ambassador arrived in Pyongyang, seven months after the exchange of recognition.

Yet Sino-Soviet calculations were not sanguine. Despite the map-marking advances of North Korean armies, Peking's accounts of the war took on a curiously pessimistic tone. In late July an authoritative journal conceded that "prolonged war" faced the North Korean people. Still no alarm was sounded, and no Chinese help was given. Instead, Jacob Malik returned to the Security Council, where, as president, he made a display of stonewalling that dismayed those who hoped for a change of heart and an end to the struggle.

All was not what it seemed, however. Malik's moves, both in public and in private, explored United States–UN interest in a compromise settlement. Failing this, Red China's initial involvement emerged. On August 20, Chou En-lai cabled Lake Success, protesting the mid-June resolutions long since passed, and warning that China, as an interested party, must participate in settlement of the Korean War. Two days later, Malik warned, "Any continuation of the Korean War will lead inevitably to a widening of the conflict." The two moves obviously followed from earlier joint decisions which aimed at forcing negotiations through the combined power of Peking and Moscow, should Moscow's maneuvers alone fail to win a satisfactory response.

The timing and nature of this initial Chinese Communist move is significant. It came almost a month after "prolonged war" was forecast for Korea, but fully two months before Chinese Communist "volunteers" locked battle with UN troops. No explicit action was threatened, nor did any military moves accompany the political ones. Hints of Chinese involvement were hoped sufficient to deter the UN from pursuing its apparent objective of unifying Korea by force.

The maneuvers failed, whereupon the hints became explicit. In late September and early October Peking informally and formally notified the Indian ambassador that U.S. crossing of the thirty-eighth parallel would bring China into the war. Simultaneous troop movements into Manchuria strengthened the threat. Time passed. On October 7, U.S. forces crossed the parallel. Two weeks later they captured Pyongyang. Nowhere did they encounter Chinese troops. The drive to the Yalu seemed certain of success. Peking failed to deter Washington through political moves.

Then, without publicity at home or fanfare abroad, Chinese Communist "volunteers" began crossing the Yalu River in mid-October. By October 26 they had sufficient strength to decimate advance South Korean units near the Yalu and to maul U.S. forces farther back. Then, just as suddenly, they broke off action in the first week of November. No contact occurred along the front for three weeks. Then MacArthur's "home by Christmas" offensive of November 26 triggered a Communist counterattack which sent the United States–UN forces reeling back to the thirty-eighth parallel.

The over-all pattern of propaganda emphasis, political maneuver, and military deployment indicates that Peking was unwilling to assist in Pyongyang's victory, or even to prepare a defense in depth which would safeguard the North Korean capital. Although the *casus belli* was specified as the thirty-eighth parallel, the sequence of Chinese Communist calculations and movements indicates that North Korean territory as such was not the issue. Rather it was the survival of a *de jure* North Korean regime which motivated Chinese Communist entry into the war. It was one thing to negotiate reorganization of that regime through merger with South Korea, as hinted in the Malik proposals. It was quite different to acquiesce passively in its liquidation by force.

The Communist element was paramount in these deliberations. American assurances of peaceful intent toward China were rejected as Machiavellian maneuvers of imperialism, bent on destruction of communism and domination of Asia. Victory in Korea would only whet the imperialistic appetite for further "adventures," perhaps in East Europe, perhaps in China itself. America had already reversed its policy on Chiang Kai-shek, suddenly thrusting its Seventh Fleet between Communist and Nationalist armies. With General MacArthur's visit to Taiwan in August, and his expressed admiration for the Generalissimo, Mao Tse-tung had surface evidence reinforcing his assumptions concerning the imperialist threat.

By comparison, the Chinese element, although present, was subsidiary. Certainly no Chinese identity of interest linked Peking with Pyongyang any more than with Seoul. It has been argued that intervention sprang from a traditional Chinese desire to dominate the Korean peninsula. Yet up to mid-1950, North Korea had been an exclusive Soviet satellite with a leadership systematically maneuvering against rival Korean factions of a pro-Chinese orientation. Intervention did not remove this leadership, nor is there evidence that intervention initially aimed at wresting the entire peninsula from UN control.

Nevertheless, the Chinese calculus did reinforce its Communist counterpart at significant points. Peking's expressed concern over a United States-Japanese hegemony in Northeast Asia was not entirely fantastic, given the *rapprochement* between Tokyo and Washington already evident in 1949–50. The historic invasion path up the peninsula through Manchuria made such a *rapprochement* of genuine concern, should it be accompanied by an anti-Communist, MacArthur-Rhee conquest of North Korea. Furthermore, a century of maltreatment at the hands of foreign powers, even when on the victors' side in two world wars, had sensitized Chinese to decisions by others at China's expense. If "new China" could not affect the course of events on its very doorstep, how could it ever recover its leadership of Asia? Especially when the U.S. Seventh Fleet shielded Taiwan, such Chinese considerations appear to have reinforced the Communist element of policy.

Neither of these elements went unobserved at the time, but their role has been forgotten with the passing years. By comparison, our third element, caution, won little attention then or later. Indeed, it has been argued that Peking entered the war in a militant spirit, cocksure after its victory in China, and confident that it was riding a Communist crest in Asia. If this is so, it is not reflected in the evidence, while there is evidence to the contrary. Both the delayed entry into Korea and the three-week suspension of operations after that entry seem designed to test the United States–UN response. This permitted flexibility, since Peking did not commit itself publicly to the form, degree, or goals of intervention. It also afforded opportunity for the enemy to reconsider goals and to clarify intentions, thereby permitting more confident calculation in Peking on the next phase of strategy.

As a parallel phenomenon of caution, Peking cancelled its projected invasion of Taiwan, following the Seventh Fleet interposition order of June 27, 1950. This reversal of plans involved obvious political risks in the deferred elimination of Mao's hated rival, the postponement of entry into the United Nations, and the humiliating admission of impotence before the so-called American "paper tiger." It also involved strategic risks, providing the shattered Nationalist armies on Taiwan a breathing spell and perhaps a fresh source of military advice and supply. Yet anathema as such a move must have been from both the Communist and the Chinese considerations of policy, caution dictated postponement of action against Taiwan under the existing circumstances.

This is not to condone the Chinese Communist entry into the Korean War, much less excuse its subsequent flouting of United Nations resolutions and armistice terms. Rather it is to derive some analytical lessons from a move which is commonly labeled aggression. Proper as this term may be descriptively, it misdirects our attention and, by oversimplifying the complex motivation of the move, causes us to misinterpret the nature of the challenge posed by Red China.

This becomes evident if we consider the two crises surrounding the offshore islands. The first, in 1954, consisted of brief but intensive bombardments of the Nationalist garrisons on Quemoy and Matsu. The second, in 1958, featured a concerted blockade and bombardment, principally against Quemoy, accompanied by an intensive buildup of nearby air bases. In neither case were invasion fleets massed nor were heavy troop concentrations evident in the immediate area. In neither instance was an attack launched against Taiwan itself. Indeed, no offensive action of any sort has hit Taiwan since the Nationalist flight to the island in 1949.

Much was obscure at the time, both from the belligerency of Chinese Communist statements and from the inadequate information on Chinese Communist intentions. Now, hindsight plus examination of the evidence provide clues to Peking's strategy and tactics. Unlike the Korean War, neither offshore-island crisis grew from external threats to Peking in terms of the Chinese or the Communist element of policy. Despite the minor prickings of Chinese Nationalist operations against the mainland, both in 1954 and in 1958 the pattern of statements and actions showed the initiative to be with Peking, and not with its opponents.

With this difference in mind, two similarities with the Korean situation emerge: first, the slowness with which Chinese Communist moves evolved; second, especially in 1958, the fact that they occurred at all, given the limited gains and the apparent risks involved. Once again, a brief reconstruction will place the events in proper perspective.

In January 1950, President Truman publicly refused further military assistance to Chiang Kai-shek, declaring, "The United States Government will not pursue a course which will lead to involvement in the civil conflict in China." In June he reversed this policy, ordering the Seventh Fleet to neutralize the Taiwan Strait. This reversal was modified by subsequent statements which linked the move with North Korean aggression. Thus a satisfactory truce in Korea might restore the *status quo ante* on Taiwan. Peking's entry into the war vitiated this policy, although it was not officially scrapped until February 1953. At that time, President Eisenhower removed the Seventh Fleet "shield" from Red China, implicitly leaving it to protect the Nationalist government. In the space of three years the United States had moved from non-involvement, through neutralization, to open support for one side in the prolonged Chinese civil war.

Throughout these shifts the position of numerous small islands remained ambiguous. Occupied by Nationalist garrisons often within a few miles of the China coast, they served as bases for harassment raids against the mainland. Peking had little opportunity to explore the problem so long as fighting continued in Korea. With the truce agreement of July 1953, however, Mao could turn once more to his Nationalist opponent. Fresh railroad and airfield construction laid the logistical foundation for invasion of the two main points of Quemoy and Matsu, and eventually of Taiwan itself.

To the surprise of most observers, no such invasion occurred. Instead, prolonged artillery attacks tested Chinese Nationalist and U.S. response in the area. In 1954, Peking bombarded the offshore islands and unleashed intensive anti-American propaganda for the "liberation of Taiwan." A "war scare" in Tokyo and Washington had a twofold result. In December, Secretary Dulles signed a Mutual Defense Treaty with the Chiang government. In January,

Congress hurriedly endorsed a so-called "Formosa Resolution" authorizing the President to deploy U.S. troops as he deemed necessary for the defense of Taiwan. By implication, the offshore islands could be included in such a move, although they were explicitly outside the provisions of the Mutual Defense Treaty.

If Peking's bombardment and propaganda were designed to unnerve Nationalist circles, the U.S. response checked any such reaction. In the absence of any serious military buildup accompanying the campaign, it is difficult to credit it with more ambitious goals. In any event, it foundered, changing the United States–Taiwan commitment from that of presidential statements, of no permanent importance, to treaty obligations, with all the sanctity of international contract. In April 1955, the crisis suddenly subsided when Chou En-lai, at Bandung, offered to discuss "relaxation of tension in the Taiwan Strait" with U.S. diplomatic representatives. Although this initiated Sino-American ambassadorial exchanges at Geneva, such *de facto* recognition was a small gain for Peking, compared with the qualitative change in United States–Nationalist relations effected by the Communist bombardment.

For the next three years relative quiet reigned in the Taiwan Strait. Then in August 1958 the crisis returned, this time in more serious proportions. Completion of the Communist rail- and air-network facilitated an impressive concentration of heavy artillery and jet aircraft. After weeks of preparation, Communist batteries unleashed an unprecedented barrage while local broadcasts demanded surrender of Quemoy. Jet fighters strafed Nationalist shipping in a concerted effort to strangle supply lines to the beleaguered garrisons. Once again a massive domestic propaganda campaign pledged Peking to "smash the American paper tiger and liberate Taiwan." This time the American response came through politically ambiguous statements, hinting support for the offshore islands, without specifically committing U.S. forces. In the area ingenious measures for breaking the blockade together with stunning victories by Nationalist pilots combined to lift the military pressures. Even before this point was reached, however, Peking proposed resumption of the suspended ambassadorial exchanges and shortly thereafter reduced its artillery attacks to sporadic firing on alternate days. Tension abated as suddenly as it had erupted.

Of the two crises, that of 1958 is the more revealing. Unlike 1954, it came in the face of explicit U.S. treaty commitments to Chiang Kai-shek. Furthermore, it followed greater Chinese Communist interest in and awareness of nuclear weapons. Yet despite the increased American commitment on the one hand, and the increased Chinese Communist strategic sophistication on the other, the attack did occur, although still without invasion.

Again, a blending of our three factors would seem to underlie Peking's strategy, only here the Chinese element merits prior attention. From time immemorial, claimants to the Chinese throne were measured by their ability to defend the frontiers and to pacify the country. This so-called "Mandate of Heaven" may not be a living concept today. But there is vigorous unanimity between Nationalist and Communist in asserting sovereignty over Tibet, in marking territorial boundaries around the South China Sea, and in asserting prerogatives of overseas Chinese. There is similar unanimity on the question of "two Chinas," both sides insisting that Taiwan and all its accompanying islands are inalienably Chinese and not subject to international negotiation or supervision. Actually, Taiwan remains in legal limbo as former Japanese territory. Its status remains to be defined by the participants in the war against Japan. However, there is no question as to Chinese title over the offshore islands. Small wonder, therefore, that Peking feels both politically compelled and legally justified in asserting its claim by force.

Indeed, the Chinese component may dictate the use of force against the offshore islands, to the exclusion of other means. Mao may have gambled on linking Quemoy with Taiwan so as to frustrate any American move toward a "two China" policy. The 1955 "Formosa Resolution" permitted U.S. defense of the islands *only* if the President felt that their fall would jeopardize Taiwan. In August 1958, Peking publicly proclaimed seizure of Quemoy as one step in the "liberation of Taiwan." The reaction from Taipei and Washington seemed to include the islands in a joint Nationalist-American defense commitment. This made their abandonment practically impossible.

Such abandonment would place 100 miles of ocean between the "two Chinas," thereby strengthening Taiwan's international position as a separate entity, worthy of protection. If this was not Peking's concern, it was certainly affected by the crisis. The U.S. inability, or unwillingness, to dissociate these rocky outposts from Taiwan's defense poses a major obstacle to any tacit or explicit "two-China" policy.

The Communist element reinforces the Chinese compulsion toward pressure in the Taiwan Strait. Mao Tsetung's belief in "the continuing revolutionary process," his hailing of Soviet sputnik achievements as "East Wind prevailing over West Wind," and his claim that "imperialists are paper tigers" combine to produce inherent and compelling pressures in Peking's foreign policy. These pressures constantly test the half-moon of countries facing China, probing for points of weakness. In the Marxist-Leninist credo, passivity is worse than a vice; it is a cardinal sin. The prize which was unobtainable yesterday is worth trying for tomorrow. The means may vary and the target area may shift, but the pressure should be unremitting. The alternation of political, economic, and military probing, and the transfer of attention from Japan to Taiwan, to Laos, or to India, all manifest the Communist component of policy. Thus the offshore islands are certain to plague the world again in the 1960s.

Yet pressure does not preclude caution. On the contrary,

the flexibility of means and the ability to change targets
permit testing of enemy responses. In 1958 such testing
paralleled the three-week suspension of hostilities in 1950,
during the Chinese Communist intervention in Korea. In
the Quemoy crisis, Communist batteries fell silent when
the first American convoy accompanied Nationalist supply
ships. The U.S. vessels approached the three-mile territorial
limit surrounding Quemoy and stopped. Only then did
Communist commanders resume their fire, sinking the Nationalist ships. Similar precaution was observed in the air.
MiG pilots, despite very fast speeds, never brushed with
American planes protecting Nationalist air-drop missions.

In short, Peking appears to have observed strict rules
designed to minimize the risks of war with the United
States. When the objective proved unattainable within
these rules, the Communists, as in Korea, turned to political
means of warfare. This prevented the further spiraling of
tension without, however, openly abandoning the military
means or the political goals of action.

I have dealt at length with Peking's military behavior
for two reasons. First, recent events along China's borders
have focused Western attention upon Peking's aggressive
intentions. In 1960 the Indian and Burmese border problems seemed to foreshadow the shape of things to come,
with Chinese armies inexorably pressing upon weak neighbors to the south. Yet neither situation is wholly analogous
to the Korean and offshore-islands crises. True, Chinese
Communist troops killed Indian border guards and occupied portions of the Burmese frontier. But, qualitatively as
well as quantitatively, these deserve the classical term of
"incidents." In both cases the location of the frontier was in
historic dispute. In both cases local threats to Chinese
Communist security were not susceptible to control by the
neighboring regime. Had Tibet not erupted in revolt, no
shooting might have occurred between Indians and Chinese. Instead, Peking probably would have continued to
press quietly for its interpretation of the frontier.

The Burmese problem was complicated by the presence of several thousand Chinese Nationalist troops in Burma, supplied from Taiwan. They justified Peking's attention to the boundary question. Finally, in neither case was military pressure mitigated by concern over the risk of war with the United States, as in Korea and Quemoy. Instead, military means, having attained limited objectives, gave way to political avenues of action.

However transient may be these border disputes, a second and more troublesome development justifies examination of the military component in China's foreign policy. I refer to the prospect of Communist China acquiring nuclear weapons. So far, this prospect has not materialized. This does not mean, however, that Red China is not striving to acquire such weapons at the earliest opportunity. In 1958 Liu Ya-lou, commander of Red China's powerful Air Force, declared, "China's working class and scientists will certainly be able to make . . . atomic bombs in the not distant future." In 1961 Foreign Minister Ch'en Yi spoke of China's nuclear capability as "only a matter of time."

These words cannot be dismissed as hollow boasts, similar to Peking's exaggerated harvest claims in the "great leap forward." We know of at least one nuclear-research reactor, built with Soviet assistance, in Peking. More may be under construction, if not already in operation. We know, too, of extensive past Soviet technical assistance and training for China's atomic-research program. In view of the statements and the evidence, it seems reasonable to assume that in the absence of a comprehensive international control agreement, Peking will detonate a nuclear device by 1963, perhaps in 1962.

Is this the door to Doomsday? Peking's propaganda repeatedly hails the turning points in history whereby the First World War spawned the Soviet Revolution and the Second World War brought Communist victory to China.

Will its surplus population and its agrarian economy encourage Red China to trigger the Third World War?

If such were the prospect, Russia should be as anxious as America. Indeed, some Western observers sensed precisely this concern in Moscow and Geneva. They felt that Soviet-American agreement on nuclear weapons and test controls was certain, given the mutual desire to close the Pandora's box opened at Almagordo in 1945. So far, however, the Russians have shown no haste to conclude an arms-control pact. Even should an eventual agreement be reached on nuclear tests, the problem of detection stations in China is certain to arise. Nothing in its past or present behavior suggests that Peking would quietly sign such an agreement without tangible political and perhaps strategic concessions from our side. Nor does a test ban preclude weapons production. And if we were to agree to exclude all nuclear weapons from Asia, where would this leave the balance of conventional forces, given China's manpower and air power?

But we need not hypothesize this far ahead to assess the validity of American speculation on Sino-Soviet nuclear relations. It is clear that without the past level of Russian assistance, minimal as it may appear, a Chinese nuclear-test explosion could not occur for at least another decade. One does not give matches to a pyromaniac. So, too, Moscow would not lay the foundation for Peking's nuclear capability if its fear of the capability were so deep-seated as is widely assumed.

Perhaps one explanation for Russia's nuclear assistance to China, however grudging, lies in Peking's past policies. In Korea and in Quemoy-Taiwan, the Chinese Communists carefully controlled their use of force. Their methods and their targets have varied according to their estimates on the balance of forces, the risks of war, and the need for action. Miscalculations have occurred; plans have gone awry. But over the past decade the regime has shown remarkable balance in its use of both traditional and revolutionary means of policy.

Projecting into the future is admittedly hazardous. We do not know how much of this balance resulted from Soviet advice. Such advice may play a smaller role as China becomes increasingly independent of Russian economic and military assistance. Nor do we know the role of past uncertainty in Peking when China's only nuclear strength lay in the Soviet commitment. Chinese possession of such strength may encourage accepting greater risks of an American nuclear attack.

Certainly Mao's repeated boast about the "superiority of men over weapons" portends greater belligerence when he possesses both men and weapons. Yet Mao's strategy does not make military power the exclusive or even the primary means of policy. True, he once remarked, "Power grows out of the barrel of a gun." But this does not mean that the gun must be field fired to achieve one's ends. Instead, Mao employs military power in a political way, to threaten, to cajole, to harry, and to isolate his enemies. Only in the final instance, where other means have failed and when victory is certain, does he launch a frontal assault.

Here again the past decade is instructive. In the Indian and Burmese border disputes, Peking's military superiority was only marginally employed. Its mere presence was sufficient to advance the desired objectives. Thus we may expect Peking to use its nuclear capability primarily in a political, rather than a military way. Indeed, this is precisely what its much stronger ally has done so far. This does not simplify the problem for the United States. On the contrary, it complicates it. But it is not so terrifying a prospect as if we were to assume an irrational, irresponsible, or fanatical enemy in control of such immense powers of destruction.

This may seem of small comfort, given Peking's persistent pressure along the periphery from Japan to India. Nuclear power will undoubtedly increase such pressure. But whether it will trigger the Third World War is highly doubtful. Much depends on the calculations of the Chinese Communists which, in turn, are affected by their interpretation of United States moves. In Korea we misread Peking's willingness to risk war, and near-disaster followed. In Quemoy both sides moved to the brink, but avoided the final misstep. In the absence of regular diplomatic relations between the two powers, in direct confrontation throughout Asia, it is reassuring that no more serious miscalculations have occurred.

This reassurance is meaningful, however light it may weigh in the scales of hope and despair. Its significance lies in the justification it provides for careful, constant, and constructive study of Communist China as a major opponent of United States policy. Such study would be of no political worth were this regime wholly enigmatic, or genuinely fanatic. Its first decade of policy, however, proves just the opposite. It is a rational, calculating regime, pursuing ends and adopting means within a clearly defined framework embracing both Chinese and Communist components. Its actions are not predictable. For that matter, neither are those of other governments, perhaps least of all the United States. However, they are susceptible to analysis and, with time and experience, to projections of probability.

The need for such analysis and projection is compelling. We have fought two wars in Asia within the past two decades. The next one may be the last. Its avoidance, or its outcome, may well depend on our ability to assess Communist China's power and objectives, and to weigh these against our own priority of interests. We must expect losses as well as gains. To the degree that we anticipate these losses, their impact can be softened, at least psychologically. To the degree that we deny their possibility and refuse to review policy in the light of changes in China and Asia, their impact will be heightened. But whatever we do, we must expect to remain in constant struggle with the People's Republic of China over the destiny of Asia.

TEN

Disengagement and NATO

BY H. STUART HUGHES

Professor of History, Harvard University; author of
Consciousness and Society and *Contemporary Europe*

The problems of "disengagement" and military alliances
in Europe cannot be discussed independently of the political and economic situation in that area. American policy
is currently based on assumptions that have long outlived
their usefulness and that have acquired a false air of per-
manence through the power and prestige of three elderly
statesmen—Konrad Adenauer, Charles de Gaulle, and Harold Macmillan.

All three of these men at present exert an unshakable
authority over their countrymen. But no one of them can
go on forever—and in the case of Adenauer the moment
of retirement cannot be long postponed. Should one or
another leave the scene, there would almost immediately
come to the surface a strong current of opposition and
criticism that until very recently has been restricted to a
small minority. It is significant that the last year has seen
widespread questioning of De Gaulle's position and the
swelling to a mass movement of the British opposition to
Macmillan's military policy.

Should a change of leadership occur in the major Western European powers, the underlying ambiguity of the
present situation would be revealed—that is, it would become clear that the current popularity of Adenauer, Macmillan, and De Gaulle is based much more on domestic

than on foreign considerations, Adenauer's and Macmillan's on their association with economic prosperity, De Gaulle's on his pacification of civil strife and his promise of solving the Algerian problem. Because these statesmen have been successful on the domestic scene, their countrymen have also trusted their judgment in foreign affairs. Thus they have been able to sustain foreign and military policies that might otherwise have aroused the gravest fears. Their successors would probably be unable to repeat such a performance.

In brief, De Gaulle and Adenauer and Macmillan have perpetuated into the age of nuclear stalemate an outmoded concept of foreign and military policy, a concept of armed resistance to the Soviet Union based on a coalition of national military forces. At NATO's inception, thirteen years ago, this policy made sense, and both partners in the coalition—the Truman administration and the European governments, which shared a "left-center" ideology—believed in it. Today this is no longer true. From the military standpoint, NATO has become something quite different from what it was at the start. It is no longer a military coalition in the familiar European tradition, provided with sufficient *conventional* ground forces to act as a deterrent to Soviet expansion. It has become little more than a trip wire for "massive retaliation." The United States' decision to supply its European allies with nuclear warheads has robbed NATO of its military *raison d'être*. It has destroyed the earlier concept of an old-fashioned ground army that would make the Soviet Union hesitate to incur the losses and the international opprobrium which overrunning Central and Western Europe would entail, and it has substituted for it a new theory which reduces Europe to the status of an advanced outpost of the United States in the planning for general nuclear war.

Thus the NATO powers are currently trying to carry out a policy in which they have no real trust. In Britain the campaign for unilateral disarmament has split the

Labour party, with a majority of the delegates to the national conference urging abandonment of nuclear weapons. It is true that in Parliament two thirds of the Labour M.P.s remain faithful to the American alliance as currently defined; but even the right wing of the party is committed to advocating universal disarmament, a position which is hard to reconcile with the present theory of NATO. Moreover, the anti-nuclear campaign extends far beyond the adherents of Labour; it is attracting young people of the most varied political allegiances and activating those who have previously been apolitical. In Scandinavia, too, neutralism is a force to be reckoned with, and both government and opposition would like to redefine the alliance in terms that would make it more compatible with the idea of disengagement.

In Italy, Germany, and the Low Countries, loyalty to NATO runs deeper, but here also there are strong crosscurrents of dissent. In Italy the left-wing Socialist party opposes American missile bases. Beyond that, the reliability of France itself within the alliance is far from clear. By keeping most of his ground troops in Algeria and by withdrawing his strategic air force and a good part of his navy from NATO control, De Gaulle has struck at the whole concept of the alliance, making no secret of his belief that the proper organization for Europe should be a loose league of sovereign states under the leadership of his own country.

The logical consequence of such an idea—joined to the prospect that in the near future all the larger powers will be able to manufacture their own nuclear weapons—would be a competition in weaponry *within* the NATO alliance. If each major nation possessed its own bombs and missiles, in addition to those provided by the United States, the distinction between the two types would tend to disappear. As the proud possessor of ultimate weapons, each nation would be a law to itself, and the concept of the alliance would become less and less meaningful.

If one adds to these political and military considerations the current economic split within the NATO powers between the "inner six" and the "outer seven," one can only conclude that the alliance as originally devised a decade ago is falling apart at the seams. In this crisis of NATO, nationalism and neutralism reinforce each other. The first is largely a conservative tendency, the second is characteristic of the democratic left, but they both in effect work against the NATO alliance. For when a nationalist like De Gaulle exploits his countrymen's nostalgia for past grandeur and concentrates his attention on France's African "mission" and on restoring great power status through an independent atomic capability—when France, which was to have been the key pin of NATO, goes off on a nationalist tangent, then internationally minded Europeans are far less likely to seek their salvation in a military alliance, and far more inclined to trust to disarmament, disengagement, and even neutrality for their future preservation.

Since NATO can scarcely be preserved in its present form, the real question is: Should it be transformed by some new principle or should it be abolished? The first would seem the more prudent—although a change of name might well be in order—since the sudden abolition of NATO might entail a crisis of European confidence. In either case, however, the prime goal should be to keep Europe out of the nuclear race by progressively enlarging a Central European area of military disengagement. The idea of disengagement—of removing the hostile forces of East and of West from direct contact with each other—can be formulated in two different ways. In its more cautious form it proposes merely to forbid the deployment of nuclear weapons in a specified area. In its more thoroughgoing form it suggests that the area in question be neutralized and hence removed from the East-West struggle. The proposal of the latter sort advanced by George F. Kennan in his Reith Lectures over the BBC in 1957 occasioned widespread discussion both in Europe and in this country, where it first familiarized the public at large with disengagement possibilities.

This goal can be fully realized only as part of a wider settlement with the Soviet Union. But there are certain things that can be negotiated right away. Among them the most important are the establishment of an initial zone of disengagement and the denial of nuclear weapons to further powers.

The logical place to start negotiation on disengagement is some version of the Rapacki Plan—which has gone through various modifications, but which has usually had as its central feature the nuclear demilitarization of East and West Germany, Poland, and Czechoslovakia. It is far from sure that Khrushchev is currently ready to accept this plan, and it is quite certain that both De Gaulle and Adenauer are against it, but it has great appeal both for Britain and for the Soviet satellites. Above all, the fact that it has been under informal discussion for so long a time has made it appear less threatening than any alternative proposal to both sides in the power struggle. At the very least, an announcement by the American government that it was ready to begin negotiations on this basis would offer two important advantages—it would give evidence that we had serious intentions of reducing military tension in Europe, and it would quite clearly suggest that our policy was no longer tied to the views of our conservative allies.

Moreover, the Rapacki Plan presents a realistic alternative to the "liberation" of East Central Europe about which Republican politicians have talked so much and done so little—witness the failure to give aid to the Hungarian revolution of 1956. On the one hand, its adoption by the United States would offer assurance to the Communist rulers of the Soviet Union and the satellite states that we had abandoned any intention of overthrowing their regimes by subversion or force of arms. At the same time, it would clearly convey to the peoples of East Central Europe that we had not lost interest in their fate—rather, that

307

we were substituting for a purely rhetorical notion of "liberation" a more workable policy for relieving direct military pressure on them and thereby for strengthening the liberal tendencies within their borders.

The Rapacki Plan has the final advantage—as the person of its author, the Polish foreign minister, implies—of "disengaging" two of the Soviet satellites with the strongest Western ties. Thus it offers the most coherent proposal that has appeared to date for bridging the gap between the Western and the Soviet spheres. Currently this is no more than a faint hope. But some partial version of the Rapacki Plan might at least run a chance of acceptance on a trial basis. If, for example, the United States and the Soviet Union were to agree on demilitarizing a relatively small but contiguous area including one province of each of the four states in question—say, Bavaria, Saxony, Bohemia, and Silesia—it could be the beginning of a disengagement by stages that would finally include the whole four-nation zone.

The denial of nuclear weapons to fifth or sixth powers —which means preventing Western Germany and Communist China from joining the present "nuclear club"—is absolutely crucial and grows more urgent with each passing month. Since the French bomb test in the Sahara, there have been reports that the Germans have similar plans afoot, and no one knows exactly what nuclear capabilities exist in the Communist camp. One authoritative estimate —that of a committee of the American Academy of Arts and Sciences, published in 1959—suggests that nineteen nations have the technical capability of producing nuclear weapons in the foreseeable future. It should be obvious, then, that on this single matter at least the United States and the Soviet Union have a common interest in closing the nuclear club while there is yet time.

An obvious corollary to such a recommendation is strong opposition to any German plans for nuclear armament. I have already drawn attention to the fact that Adenauer's retirement will unquestionably entail changes in his country's foreign policy. These changes might go in either the neutralist or the nationalist direction—with the latter almost certainly including a drive for an independent nuclear capability on the French model. The two policy recommendations I have made both suggest that a neutralist Germany would be far preferable to a nationalist one.

The rearmament of Germany has aroused fears in Eastern Europe that are justified and that extend far beyond Communist opinion. The revival of German nationalist feeling and the return to positions of influence of many of the same individuals and groups that supported Nazi expansion represent a real danger to the peace. A Germany under conservative leadership—once Adenauer's moderating influence was gone—would give rise to widespread anxiety beyond the country's borders. A neutralist or partially demilitarized Germany under Social Democratic leadership would be much more reassuring.

If the United States should advance a serious proposal for disengagement, it would immediately relax tensions aroused by the Berlin issue. More specifically, the Western powers might even go as far as offering diplomatic recognition to East Germany and proposing a United Nations guarantee for Berlin's future status. The guiding principle in these concessions should be a frank recognition of the fact that West Berlin in its present situation is both untenable and an international anomaly. The problem it presents for us is far more human than it is military—that is, we should not be primarily concerned with maintaining an advanced outpost in power politics, but rather with honoring our pledges to two million West Berliners by seeing to it that their lives, their livelihood, and their liberties remain secure.

The final aim, then, in the case of Germany, would be equality of international status for the two German states, which would both eventually be disengaged from military alliances and left free to form some sort of loose federation.

At the start at least, within this federation two contrasting political and economic systems would continue to exist—communism in the East, capitalism in the West. But in the end it would almost certainly be the institutions and practices of West Germany—which would have behind them the bulk of the population and resources of the whole country—that would come to predominate.

So much for immediate goals. How do these proposals leave the long-range situation of NATO and of Europe in general? Here it is important to distinguish between NATO in its strictly military aspect, and the integration of Western Europe on the economic and cultural planes.

From the military standpoint, the logic of the above proposals is a drastic reduction in NATO's scope. A "disengaged" West Germany would cease to be a member. At a subsequent date Italy and Scandinavia might also prefer neutrality. Similarly France might be left to follow its own nationalist course: the policy recommendations I have made obviously imply a loosening of American ties with De Gaulle. Indeed, the logic of such a position might lead to an eventual neutralization of the whole six-nation area. This would leave NATO a truly Atlantic alliance based on the United States, Canada, and Great Britain.

Even within the reduced NATO area a change in armaments policy would be advisable. Should Labour, for example, ever win an election in Britain, the new government might well request the dismantlement of NATO missile or Polaris bases. The United States should be psychologically prepared for this and should begin right now to close down these bases throughout Europe. Currently they are not contributing to the *defense* of the West in any realistic sense; they are simply increasing tension and the danger of an accidental explosion that might bring on general nuclear warfare. Ultimately the defense of Western Europe should be reduced to conventional weapons alone. Kennan's Reith Lectures offer an imaginative suggestion for recasting the Western continental armed forces as strictly defensive units of a paramilitary or territorial-militia type.

From the wider standpoint, the former NATO powers could still form an economic and cultural unit. Indeed the release of military pressure might enable them to discuss more amicably their economic disagreements. Here the tactful mediation of the United States could be of crucial influence in reconciling the "six" and the "seven." Similarly American cultural interchange with Europe would become more fruitful once its military concomitants were removed. The progressive dismantling of NATO's present overexpanded structure need not suggest a loss of American interest in Western and Central Europe. On the contrary, as with the substitution of disengagement for "liberation" in our policy toward the Soviet satellites, the new American attitude toward the West would mean putting realism in place of arrangements which no longer correspond with the facts. And this change would further suggest that by abandoning a sterile and nearly exclusive emphasis on military measures our country was attempting to re-establish a hierarchy of values closer to the Europeans' own conception of their contemporary role.

Nor would the economic and cultural integration of Western Europe necessarily intensify the current cleavage between East and West. Indeed, it might do the very opposite by helping to convince the Soviet Union and its satellites that the Western nations were shifting from military to economic concerns. In this context a disengaged and federated Germany would be transformed from the constant source of contention that it is today into an economic and cultural bridge between East and West—as Poland and Czechoslovakia would be serving in a similar capacity on the other side of the ideological divide. And should this sort of economic and cultural interchange prove rewarding, the Soviet Union might be willing to take further steps toward relaxing its grip on its satellite states.

The basic contention in the above proposals is that it is

to the interest of the United States to decrease cold-war tension by drastically reducing the military emphasis of its European policy, by curtailing the nuclear aspirations of its allies, and by encouraging the constitution of a disengaged zone or zones. If we should take the initiative in such proposals, then there would be a good chance that the Soviet Union would respond in similar fashion by recognizing that disengagement and a nuclear truce are in its interest also.

ELEVEN

Policies for Strengthening the United Nations

BY QUINCY WRIGHT

Professor Emeritus of International Law, University of Chicago and University of Virginia

A program for strengthening the United Nations, which will commend itself to American liberals, requires consideration of (I) the meaning of liberalism, (II) the kind of world that liberals should work for, (III) the role of the United Nations in developing and maintaining such a world, and (IV) the contribution which United States policy can make toward strengthening the United Nations so that it can play that role effectively.

Experience since the Second World War should have made it clear that a liberal foreign policy must assume that liberalism and democracy can only flourish or indeed survive in a suitable environment, that such an environment under present conditions can be no less extensive than the entire world, and that, therefore, liberal foreign policy must look at the world as a whole. Any form of isolationism or regionalism is obsolete. The nation that would save itself must subordinate its immediate interests to the maintenance of a peaceful, stable, and just world. That is the assumption that the United States and other nations made in establishing the United Nations.

Failure to understand these assumptions and their implications has led to a combination of boredom, apathy, and fear among Americans, especially among liberals, resulting in a government policy of drift, platitude, opportunism, and wide disagreement, even among liberals who take an active interest in foreign policy. Such differences are especially notable on such issues as military appropriations, outer-space programs, summit conferences, development of NATO, attitude toward self-determination of peoples, economic aid to underdeveloped countries, prosecution of the cold war, the United Nations and collective security, world rule of law and the Connolly Reservation to the World Court statute. There are also differences in regard to the atoms-for-peace program, the recognition of *de facto* governments, and the policies to be pursued in relation to particular governments and particular groups, such as the Communist states, the NATO states, the non-allied states, and the Latin American states.

This almost total confusion among liberals indicates that liberals do not know their values, the kind of world suitable for the realization of those values, the contribution which the United Nations might make toward establishing such a world, and what specific policies or programs the United States government should pursue to these ends, both within and outside the United Nations. A new policy was initiated by President Eisenhower in the spring of 1959 and continued in the Camp David meetings with Premier Khrushchev in the following autumn. Its apparent object was to reduce international tensions, to end the arms race with the Soviet Union, and to establish relations of peaceful coexistence or even active co-operation with the Communist countries. This policy seems to have been widely approved by the people of the United States, but it was wrecked by the unfortunate U-2 incident, and the resulting collapse of the proposed summit conference, in the spring of 1960. Khrushchev's performance at the United Nations General Assembly meeting in the autumn and the debate during the presidential campaign did little to clarify thinking in the field of foreign policy. It seems clear, however, that the American people want a peace policy if they believe they can get it with national security. Militant voices from the armed services and among some political leaders confused many Americans and convinced others that their government was insufficiently aware of changing conditions and wanted to continue the cold war at the risk of hot war. The new administration which took office in January 1961 is committed to establishing "new frontiers" in both domestic and foreign affairs. American liberals should straighten out their thinking so that their influence will build toward a foreign policy that will support their values. These values seem to imply a frontier embracing the whole of the shrinking world.

I. AMERICAN LIBERALISM

American liberalism seeks to combine the historical liberal attitude, which attributes primary value to individual freedom, with the progressive attitude, which is aware of imperfections in any *status quo* and is always ready to initiate reforms. In its first aspect, liberalism is opposed to governmentalization—as Jefferson said, "The less government the better"—in its second aspect, liberalism is opposed to conservatism and committed to progress in the spirit of Franklin D. Roosevelt's "new deal." The American liberal wants to protect the individual from government impositions, thus looking critically at proposals for government intervention in business, religion, opinion, and association; but he also wants to improve the situation of the underprivileged, to increase the opportunities for self-realization by all, and to advance social justice and the achievement of social values, thus looking critically at opponents of all social and economic legislation, national or international. The liberal is ready to consider government action designed to regulate business in the public interest and to open resources to promote public welfare; to provide security for the sick, aged, and unemployed; and to promote equality of opportunity for all by programs of edu-

315

cation, economic development, and employment. The liberal appreciates that this "agenda of liberalism," if pushed too far, may result in excessive governmentalization, which will defeat the first aspect of liberalism. On the other hand, excessive regard for freedom of enterprise, freedom of contract, freedom from taxation, even freedom of speech and association may result in the delay of necessary reforms, and in the failure of society to adapt itself to new conditions, to utilize the opportunities presented by technological progress, and to prevent the subversion of liberal values by the propaganda or infiltration of minority agencies. Liberalism must, therefore, continually seek a balance between the protection of individual freedom from the government and the need of reform requiring action and appropriation by the government.

II. THE KIND OF WORLD SUITABLE FOR LIBERALISM

In the field of foreign policy the liberal is beset by particular difficulties because he believes, on the one hand, in the independence of nations and the self-determination of peoples, and, on the other hand, in respect for human rights based upon the values of individual freedom, democracy, constitutionalism, and social progress. He is, therefore, at the same time, an advocate of peaceful coexistence and mutual toleration among the nations and peoples of the world, with their vast differences in value systems, religions, ideologies, and forms of government, economy, and society; and a militant crusader for the American interpretation of freedom, democracy, constitutionalism, and progress. Emphasis upon the first would seem to tolerate tyranny, regimentation, and oppression, contrary to democratic values, but persisting in many nations, while the second would seem to require non-recognitions, propagandas, and interventions maintaining high international tensions and cold war, threatening hot war likely to destroy mankind. The dilemma is not unlike that faced by Lincoln.

Should he stand firmly for freedom from slavery, at the risk of civil war, or should he put preservation of the Union first, confident that within federal constitutionalism human rights would eventually be respected?

Throughout history, mankind has been faced by conflicting policies for establishing peace, order, and justice in the world, on the one hand, through institutions to maintain the coexistence of differences, and, on the other, through the universal acceptance and maintenance of a common ideology and government. The Pax Romana of the Antonine Caesars in the second century A.D. and the Pax Ecclesiastica of the Holy Roman Empire and the Holy Catholic Church in the thirteenth century exhibited moderate success of the latter method, for almost a century in each case. The failure of this method, however, was exhibited in the sixteenth century when the discoveries initiated continuous contact among peoples of vastly different civilizations, the advance of science shattered the foundations of supernatural religions, the reformation split Europe into hostile ideologies, and the concept of territorial sovereignty, supported by ambitious princes, utilizing the newly invented gunpowder and printing press, destroyed the political authority of universal institutions. The failure of the imperial power to re-establish the unity of Europe in the Thirty Years' War, the intolerable destructiveness of that war, and the opportunity it gave to Islam under Turkish leadership to reassert its ideological war on Christendom convinced statesmen that peace, order, and justice could be maintained in the world, or even in Europe, only on the basis of peaceful coexistence among territorial states, each dealing with problems of religion, ideology, government, and economy as a domestic matter. *Cuius Regia Eius Religio.* Whoever is the prince, that is the religion. This was the basis of the Peace of Westphalia (1648), which ended the Thirty Years' War, and it has been the basis of international law and international organization since, with a considerable measure of success during the Pax

317

Britannica from 1815 to 1914. During this century Europe enjoyed a high degree of peace stabilized by international law, the balance of power, and British sea power supporting a liberal economic policy. The situation was different outside of Europe, where peoples resisted the colonialism of the great European powers. The effort to achieve ideological and political unification by the French Revolution and Napoleon, by the Fascist revolution and the Axis, and by the Communist revolution and Stalin failed and again indicated that coexistence and co-operation among independent nations is the only basis for peace, order, and justice in the world of varied nationalities and ideologies.

By recognizing the equal sovereignty of states and non-intervention in the domestic jurisdiction of each, the United Nations Charter accepts the peaceful coexistence of sovereign states as the basis of its activity. It is true that the United Nations Charter accepts the principles of self-determination of peoples and respect for the human rights of individuals, qualifying the territorial integrity and political independence of states. But these principles are to be achieved by the peaceful processes of diplomacy, United Nations resolution, and the development of international law through general treaties and custom. The Charter assumes that states are sovereign, each within its territory, and free to make law, binding individuals and groups within that territory. The "new international law," qualifying this basic conception of traditional international law, in the interest of peace, nationalism, and humanism, does not permit intervention by a government or by the United Nations unless a state has abused its sovereign right by threat or use of force in international relations or by violation of obligations which it has accepted in special or general treaties, for the benefit of individuals or peoples in its territory.

It is believed that liberals must in the present state of the world accept this reconciliation. Liberals and democrats, no less than Communists, Christians, Moslems, Hindus, and

Buddhists, must subordinate their hope for a world united under their particular ideology to a world composed of territorial states each of which is free to deal with its ideological problems as a domestic question, subject only to concrete international obligations which it may have undertaken. Each must be content to abandon efforts to expand its ideology, religion, or economic system by military force or subversive intervention. Each must be content to let the subtle forces of communication and imitation operate in the market place of opinion, with the conviction that eventually the system best adapted to each people and nation will be voluntarily accepted, if peace and order can be maintained.

To those who believe in liberalism, this program should be particularly attractive because there is ample evidence that ideological crusading creates conditions of high international tension, insecurity, war, and poverty, under which liberalism is at a disadvantage. Democracy and liberalism have developed only within states which have enjoyed moderate prosperity and education and which have been secure from external attack because of geographical isolation, a stable balance of power, or a rule of law. When these conditions have existed, as they did in eighteenth-century England, in the United States through most of its history, in nineteenth-century Europe, and in twentieth-century Latin America, freedom and democracy have grown. People like to be free, and they accept regimentation and tyranny only when they think it necessary to protect them from foreign attack or to relieve them from starvation. Freedom from fear and freedom from want are the prerequisites to freedom of religion and freedom of opinion.

By attempting to use American power and influence directly to promote freedom and democracy in other countries, American liberals defeat themselves. Such crusading efforts tend to create conditions under which freedom and democracy perish. International peace and security, the reduction of international tension, the peaceful coexistence of all nations are conditions under which liberalism and democracy can grow. Liberalism cannot be imposed, men cannot be forced to be free, but if international peace and security are established and if economy and education progress, they will grow spontaneously from the spirit of man.

III.   THE ROLE OF THE UNITED NATIONS

The United Nations can play a major role in creating such a world, but only if the conditions for its functioning are established by the policies of the great states supported by the understanding and opinions of their peoples.

The United Nations did not function adequately in its early years because the governments at San Francisco hoped (contrary to all rational expectations) that the unity of the great powers, which had continued until the Axis was defeated, would persist in its institutions. The Security Council, designed to be the primary agent of political action to maintain peace and deal with political disputes, could not function in the absence of such unity. Fortunately this error can be, and has been to some extent, remedied by utilizing the powers of the General Assembly in accord with the procedures established by the Uniting for Peace Resolution of November 1950.

This political error of the Charter makers was accentuated by incorporation in the Charter of the concept that the United Nations should be composed only of "peace-loving states," defined at first as those states that had entered the war against the Axis, and later as those in ideological agreement with the majority of the General Assembly. Both of these definitions were abandoned when a "package deal" was made in December 1955 to admit many states from both sides of the Iron Curtain. In principle the United Nations has committed itself to the proposition that all sovereign states should be members. The   2 wisdom of this position has been increasingly recognized. It has become clear that the United Nations should not be a club, membership in which is a privilege, but a reflector of world public opinion as it actually is, an interpreter of the basic obligations of all states, set forth in the Charter, and a procedure for maintaining the responsibility and enforcing the obligation of its members. It has been recognized that inspections to assure observance of agreements concerning nuclear testing and disarmament cannot be carried out in the territory of non-members, and that states, like individuals, become socialized and law-abiding only through continuous and abundant contacts provided, in the international field, by diplomacy, international conferences, participation in international organization, and the exchange of persons. With this understanding, it appears that the worse is the behavior of a state the more important that it be a member of the United Nations. In spite of these understandings by most of the members of the United Nations, because of the tangle over the recognition of mainland China; the division of Germany, Korea, and Vietnam; the neutrality of Switzerland; and the relative isolation of Mongolia, nine *de facto* states, constituting nearly a tenth of the area, and more than a quarter of the population, of the world, are still outside the United Nations.

These errors in the Charter itself, fortunately capable of correction within its terms, were aggravated by the policy of the Western states, whetted by Soviet intransigence, in building the NATO alliance, inevitably countered by the policy of the Communist states in building the Warsaw alliance. These policies resulted in a polarization of the military power of the world and extreme instability of the balance of power. This situation of "cold war," a natural but not inevitable response to manifestations of Communist expansionism, created conditions in which "collective security" under the United Nations could not work when great power interests were directly involved. The military power of the world, being divided into relatively equal halves, the United Nations could not "collect" overwhelming power against a great power violating its obligation under the Charter not to threaten or use force in international relations. While these destructive alliances could theoretically be brought under the conception of "collective self-defense," recognized in the Charter, they were contrary to the spirit of the United Nations and frustrated its political effectiveness.

These errors of great power policy can be rectified by policies looking toward decentralization of power. Such decentralization is difficult to achieve so long as the arms race, and the high tensions it generates, continue, but it is probably inevitable if these tensions are reduced. Substantial differences of policy clearly exist between mainland China, the Soviet Union, and the Eastern European satellites, differences which would tend to undermine their unity once they cease to fear attack from the combination, led by the United States, which they call "the camp of capitalistic imperialism" pursuing a policy of "encirclement." Differences of policy have also been manifested among the leading powers of NATO, the United States, the United Kingdom, and France, especially in the Vietnam crisis of 1954, the Suez crisis of 1956, and the Algerian crisis since 1955. If the fear of attack from the Communist bloc were reduced, these differences would tend to moderate the unity of NATO, with the result that Communist fears would be further reduced, and the process of disintegration of the alliances would continue. If the world were divided into six or more major centers of power, and if a series of neutralist states of less, but considerable, power in Northern and Central Europe, the Balkans, the Middle East, South Asia, and East Asia separated the states of Communist and free-democracy ideology, the power equilibrium could be stabilized and collective security could work. The problem of limiting membership in the atomic club is important, but it seems unlikely that such a limitation can be agreed upon until France, and perhaps mainland China, as well as the United States, the Soviet Union, and the United Kingdom possess these weapons. With such a distribution, the prospects of any one destroying the launching bases of all the others would be reduced to the vanishing point, and the atomic stalemate would be strengthened, assuming that the atomic powers behaved rationally.

Finally, the makers of the Charter were insufficiently aware that an organization of independent states, without a central governing authority that can make effective decisions, must rest on clear rules of law which the members will be disposed to observe because each considers general observance in its national interest. Built on the illusion of a great power coalition, collectively controlling most of the military force of the world and able to make and enforce decisions, the United Nations was made primarily a political body. The basic concepts on which it rested, such as "aggression" and "domestic jurisdiction," were less clearly defined than they had been in the League of Nations Covenant. The organs of the United Nations, conceiving their functions as primarily political, have seldom asked for advisory opinions of the Court. That body has also been less utilized in litigated cases than it was during the League of Nations period. The "optional clause," which is the prime source of its jurisdiction, has been accepted by a smaller proportion of states, and the acceptances have been to a larger extent rendered illusory by reservations, than was the case during the League of Nations period. The United Nations, however, cannot function through recommendations of the General Assembly unless its members understand and accept its basic law and so are prepared voluntarily to implement such recommendations.

Rectification of these errors, creating conditions under which the United Nations can function and gradually achieve its purposes, is possible without amendment of the Charter, but such rectification involves a reversal of policies, particularly those of the United States, which have been followed by the great powers for a dozen years and which account for the progressive deterioration of world conditions.

Will American security permit such a reversal? It is believed that a careful analysis of the situation suggests not only that American security permits but that it demands such a reversal.

The world has witnessed an arms race in weapons of increasing destructiveness, rising international tensions, the bipolarization of power, and the incapacity of the United Nations to function politically. These are the consequences to be expected from Soviet expansiveness in the Stalin period which induced American policies, threatening massive retaliation against aggression, using non-recognition as a political instrument, treating NATO as the major instrument of defense, opposing clarification of the concept of aggression by the General Assembly, refusing to accept the jurisdiction of the International Court of Justice in legal cases, and encircling the Communist states with military bases and alliances in order to contain them or to "roll back" the iron curtain.

It is true that some military experts and some congressmen and commentators worry about the missile gap, which they think will presently give the Soviet Union capacity to wipe out the free world's retaliatory power, thus terminating the atomic stalemate, but these fears or hopes seem not to be shared by statesmen at either side of the Iron Curtain. There is no evidence that Premier Khrushchev would risk the vast economic construction and rising standard of living in his country by an aggression that would probably lead to atomic war. There is ample evidence that the Soviet people experienced all the war they want to experience from 1941 to 1945, an experience which it is estimated cost them twenty-five million lives and hundreds of billions in property destruction. While the direct influence of the people on Soviet policy may not be great, their indirect influence would weigh powerfully against such a policy. Furthermore, it seems unlikely that the Soviet government would wish to sacrifice the considerable degree of good will which it has established in the non-allied states by its proclaimed policy of "peaceful coexistence."

Similarly, while occasional American voices talk of "preventive war," there is no reason for thinking that an American government would be so irresponsible as to start such a war now that the Soviets have ample retaliatory power, particularly as no such war was considered while the United States had a monopoly of atomic weapons.

Whatever may have been the situation in the early stages of the "cold war," it appears that today tensions between the great political blocs exist, less because of expansionist or crusading policies than because of mutual fears which are not justified by anything known of the intentions of the governments at opposite sides of the Iron Curtain. While intentions and capabilities are different things and should not be confused, it seems obvious that estimates of intentions are the more important. If one wants to survive, it is more important to know the purposes and intentions of the man behind the gun than to know its caliber. The United States does not worry about increasing capabilities of the United Kingdom or France because their intentions are believed to be friendly. An equal conviction that the Soviets have no intention to embark upon nuclear war would reduce interest in the relative capability of the Soviet Union and the United States in missiles and other weapons.

But if there is little danger of *deliberate* atomic war from any present member of the nuclear club, there might be danger if nuclear weapons got into the hands of less responsible governments or if tensions rose to such a point that present nuclear powers became irresponsible and embarked upon *irrational* war. There is also danger that preparation for massive retaliation, huge civilian defense expenditures, and external air or missile bases may convince one side that the other is about to attack, inducing it to embark upon *pre-emptive* war. Furthermore, alertness for instant massive retaliation by airplanes on the wing in the Arctic, by submarines at sea with nuclear weapons, and by missiles able to go a quarter of the way around the world on the push of a button steadily augment the danger of *accidental* war. Finally there is the danger that *nibbling aggression,* border wars, perhaps initiated with conventional weapons by a small power as by Israel at Suez or by North Korea, perhaps initiated by a great power against a weak border state, could develop into a nuclear war if the losing party in such hostilities became convinced that there is "no substitute for victory."

The danger which the United States faces is not that of deliberate nuclear war but that of irrational, preemptive, or accidental war or that of nibbling aggression. The remedies for these dangers are reduction of tension, decentralization of power, and strengthening the United Nations to deal more effectively with nibbling aggression. That the United Nations can be effective in stopping minor hostilities has been illustrated in Greece, Palestine, Kashmir, Indonesia, Suez, and Lebanon. The success of its action in Laos and the Congo was uncertain in the winter of 1961. It failed in Hungary and succeeded only after heavy losses in Korea. A special conference stopped the fighting in Vietnam in 1954. The uncertainty of the United States whether it should leash or unleash Chiang Kai-shek, and the exclusion of Communist China from the United Nations, has prevented United Nations action to stop intermittent fighting between the two Chinese factions in the coastal islands of Matsu and Quemoy. The capacity of the United Nations to deal with nibbling aggression can be increased by admittance of all the *de facto* states to its membership; by agreeing that aggression means the illegal use of armed force in international relations, thus differentiating it from civil strife and from subversive utterances and infiltrations; by strengthening the procedures of the General Assembly under the Uniting for Peace Resolution; by the widespread earmarking of national military forces, especially of smaller states, for United Nations service; by establishment of a small permanent United Nations force; and by development of a United Nations program against "war mongering" and "subversive interventions" not involving the use of armed force. These problems are considered in the next section.

IV. A UNITED STATES POLICY FOR STRENGTHENING THE UNITED NATIONS

What can the United States do to strengthen the United Nations? This question may be considered under the heads: (a) general foreign policy; (b) the structure and procedure of the United Nations; (c) political action by the United Nations; (d) the rule of law; (e) economic and social welfare.

(a) General foreign policies to establish conditions under which the United Nations can function effectively have been discussed in the preceding section. The prime objects of such policies should be to reduce international tensions, to decentralize power in the world, to end the arms race, and to seek the settlement of outstanding political differences by negotiation. The high-level visits begun in 1959, the summit conference proposed in 1960, the voluntary maintenance of the nuclear-testing ban, and the public commitment by the principal powers to policies of peaceful coexistence might have contributed to a reduction of tensions had it not been for the U-2 incident and the events which followed. In proportion as tensions are reduced, a decentralization of the great power blocs should become possible and even probable, convincing both sides that defensive alliances, because of internal checks, as well as considerations of national interest and United Nations principles, cannot be used for aggression. Such progress should improve the prospects of disarmament discussions aimed especially at establishing inspection against sudden attacks and nuclear testing. Progress in disarmament should permit continuous negotiation looking toward the recognition of each half of the states, reunion of which now seems improbable in any immediate future. *De facto* existence of a government or a state for as long as ten years would seem adequate evidence to justify recognition. The idea that recognition implies moral approval should be abandoned. Recognition by the United States, and admission to the United Nations of Communist China, both Germanys, both Koreas, and both Vietnams would seem necessary for effective armament inspection and for stabilization of international relations in Central Europe and the Far East. Self-determination for Taiwan and Berlin and incorporation in mainland China of the offshore islands of Matsu and Quemoy should be provided for, and the way should be left open for eventual union of the now divided states by negotiation between their governments.

(b) Substantial amendment of the United Nations Charter will, for a long time, be impossible, because of the great power of veto, but the structure of the United Nations can be improved without such amendment. The United Nations should be made universal by admitting all *de facto* states, including the now divided states, and Mongolia and Switzerland, the latter, following the precedent of Austria, with understanding that its admittance will not affect its permanent neutrality. China should be represented by the Peking government which alone can meet the United Nations responsibilities of that vast state, and the people of Taiwan should be given the opportunity to vote under United Nations supervision, whether they wish to join China or to become an independent state.

It would also be desirable to enlarge the Security Council, so as to give permanent membership to India, next to China the most populous state in the world. With such a change in membership the Security Council could serve as a permanent conference of great powers at which foreign ministers and chiefs of state might occasionally attend, thus converting it into a summit conference. This would require Charter amendment but perhaps with the admission of mainland China the Soviet Union would consent to the admission of India.

The General Assembly should be strengthened as an agency for collective security by implementing the Uniting for Peace Resolution, already utilized effectively in later stages of the Korean hostilities and in the Suez and Hungarian hostilities. The Peace Observation Commission, the earmarking of collective-security forces by states, and the operation of a Collective Security Committee, provided for in that resolution, should be implemented. A small permanent United Nations force of the kind utilized in Suez might well be established for border patrols, tranquilization of disturbed areas, and supervision of plebiscites.

The Charter permits collective-defense alliances and regional arrangements which do not violate its principles, but it provides that such organizations shall report to the Security Council on their activities. These provisions of the Charter have been ignored and, as already noted, the activities of the great alliances have developed conditions of political, ideological, and military rivalry wholly inconsistent with the purposes set forth in the Charter. The United States might well take the initiative in implementing these Charter provisions. Report and debate in the United Nations organs of the activities of these organizations would manifest their subordination to the United Nations in principle and could exert a continuing influence to subordinate them in practice, thus greatly strengthening the United Nations and moderating a major cause of international conflict.

(c) These changes in the structure and procedure of the Security Council and the General Assembly should increase the capacity of the United Nations to achieve its political functions. If the atomic stalemate continues, and the organizations, commitments, and procedures recommended by the Uniting for Peace Resolution are implemented, the United Nations should be able to deal even more effectively than it has in the past with "nibbling aggression." Experience suggests that a United Nations cease-fire, whether issued by the Security Council or the General Assembly, will usually be observed and will stop fighting without the need to declare either party the aggressor. If one state declines to accept the cease-fire, it declares itself the aggressor and invites collective-security measures to frustrate its action.

The more difficult problem remains of settling the dispute which precipitated the fighting, and which continues to threaten the peace. Supposedly temporary armistice lines have existed in Palestine, Kashmir, Vietnam, Korea, and Germany for many years in spite of continuous efforts of the United Nations to persuade the parties to agree on a settlement or on a procedure which might lead to settlement. The authority of the United Nations is limited in this field to mediation and recommendation, and it seems unlikely that states will accept the competence of an international body to impose a settlement of political claims. They have even manifested reluctance to accept the jurisdiction of the International Court of Justice to deal with legal claims.

It would, therefore, appear that political controversies must be settled by agreement of the parties. But United Nations procedures of mediation, conciliation, fact-finding, and the use of advisory opinions to elucidate legal aspects can doubtless be improved to facilitate such agreement. The Charter itself provides that the parties should seek a solution by such methods before appealing to the United Nations, and the first step in United Nations action is usually to call upon the parties to utilize such methods of their own choice.

The Secretary-General himself, and mediators acting under his authority, have often contributed to settlements.

Secretary-General Dag Hammarskjold sought to avoid taking positions which would antagonize one of the great powers in order to maintain his capacity to serve as an impartial mediator, but in the Congo situation of 1960, in spite of such efforts, the Soviet Union, feeling balked in its hope to take over the Congo, launched a campaign against him. The problem of sending United Nations forces into disturbed areas to maintain order without interfering in the strife of local factions presents serious difficulties, and the original Security Council directives left room for divergent interpretations. The Soviet attack was, however, wholly unjustified and the Security Council resolution of February 22, 1961, on which the Soviet representative abstained, clarified the position.

It should be understood that the Secretary-General's functions under the Charter entitle him to draw the attention of the Security Council to conditions threatening the peace, to send temporary or permanent missions to the seat of government of any member whenever he deems it desirable for the purposes of discussion or mediation, and to utilize forces made available to him to implement resolutions of the Security Council and the General Assembly compatible with the Charter authority of these bodies. The United States should strengthen the hand of the Secretary-General to perform all of these functions.

Impartial fact-finding will often assist negotiations and the Security Council is authorized by the Charter to send commissions of investigation into the territory of member states. The authority of the General Assembly to do so, unless requested by the state in whose territory it will function, is controversial but can be supported by certain articles of the Charter. The reluctance of states to permit such fact-finding in their territory is illustrated by the long discussion over disarmament inspections. General recognition of the capacity of the General Assembly, perhaps through the proposed Peace Observation Commission, to send fact-finding commissions into the territory of a member state to report on emergency situations or allegations of treaty violation is desirable and should be supported by the United States.

If direct negotiation, mediation, and fact-finding fail, recommendations by the Security Council or the General Assembly, proposing procedures or solutions supported by world opinion, may be useful. In this regard the practice, regularly employed by the League of Nations, of appointing disinterested members to draft resolutions in consultation with both parties might be adopted. United Nations agencies can pass resolutions by majorities, differing in this respect from the League of Nations, which required unanimity of the members of the Council, except for the litigating states; consequently, their resolutions have often been drafted by interested states with the object of propaganda or political prestige. Such resolutions often tend to accentuate the cold war and other ideological differences and contribute little or nothing to peace or the settlement of the dispute. Reduction of international tensions and a general inclination of states to put peace ahead of particular views of what justice requires would increase the capacity of the United Nations, not only to prevent or stop hostilities but also to facilitate settlement of political disputes. The United Nations Charter puts peace ahead of justice. It must be recognized that while justice is the ultimate aim, it cannot be achieved if resort to military force is available to the parties. Under such conditions, the weak can never get justice against the strong. An American policy which regarded the realization of the purposes of the United Nations as the primary national interest, and which was reflected not only in the utterances but also in the actions of statesmen and diplomats, both within and without the United Nations, could do much to strengthen the political capability of the United Nations.

(d) To maintain the rule of law in domestic affairs has been a major objective of the American Constitution and liberals have always expressed their objective as "liberty under law." Statesmen have long recognized that while autocracies can govern through force, democracies can govern only through law. A wide consensus in policy-making, which is the essence of democracy, requires time to achieve, and this time will usually be lacking unless deliberate and peaceful procedures are maintained by law. Within the state, freedom from oppression is a function of judicial procedure, assuring equal protection of the laws and due process of law in controversies between individuals and groups.

In international relations, democracies have survived in the past when protected by geographical barriers or a stable balance of power. But in the shrinking world, making all nations immediately vulnerable to weapons of intolerable destructiveness launched from anywhere in the world, these protections are no longer available. Under present technological conditions, in a jungle world, all states tend to become "garrison states," in which regimentation, necessary for defense, supersedes democratic deliberation and personal freedom. Democracy becomes dependent upon maintenance of the rule of law in international relations.

The United States has theoretically recognized this situation and has, in principle, supported the development of international law and the arbitration of international disputes since the Declaration of Independence. But proposals to accept the compulsory jurisdiction of international tribunals to settle legal claims, uniformly supported by Presidents since 1896, have always been rejected by the Senate.

When the United States joined the United Nations, it automatically became a party to the statute of the International Court of Justice. But the statute gives the court no jurisdiction in litigated cases. Its jurisdiction depends on the consent of the litigants, which may be manifested by agreement in the particular dispute, by a treaty conferring jurisdiction in classes of future disputes, or by declarations under the optional clause of the statute establishing jurisdiction in all legal disputes between states bound by such declarations. Over thirty states, including the United States, have made declarations under the optional clause, but most of the important states have attached reservations, and those attached by the United States permit the United States to veto the jurisdiction in disputes which it considers domestic or which concern the interpretation of a multilateral treaty to which it is a party. The United States, therefore, in effect says, we accept the jurisdiction of the court in legal disputes, except those in which, at the moment, we do not want to accept it. Since the statute of the court expressly confers on the court the authority to decide on pleas to the jurisdiction, this reservation of self-judgment was contrary to the statute and thus seems to nullify the United States declaration altogether. In any case it is subject to reciprocal application and, therefore, while it gives the United States a veto on being sued, it gives the other state a veto on any suit initiated by the United States. Repeal of this Connally reservation and manifestation by the United States of confidence in the court would do a great deal to promote the rule of law in international relations. Many states which followed the United States in making such reservations would doubtless follow it in repealing them. Other states which have not made declarations at all would be more inclined to do so. The process of building up the compulsory jurisdiction of the court would, therefore, be advanced.

The rule of law, however, depends not only on compulsory third-party adjudication of legal disputes but also on the development of international law so that all states are convinced that its application will promote justice in the changing world. While the principle that no state is bound by a new rule of international law without its consent will doubtless for a long time preclude international legislation by majority vote, international law can be developed by the express consent of states manifested in treaties, by their tacit consent manifested through the growth of custom, and by their presumed consent manifested through ascertainment of the general principles of law accepted by all civilized nations. To this end the work of the International Law Commission of the United Nations should be strengthened by larger appropriations permitting the members to give full time to the work and by a more active participation by the United States in conferences for drafting general conventions codifying international law and bringing it up to date. The Geneva Conference of 1958 on the law of the sea did much in this field.

The United States declared in 1953 that it would not participate in the efforts of the United Nations to draft Covenants of Human Rights because of the fear that such covenants might encroach upon the normal domain of the states in the United States. This position has frustrated the United Nations' effort to implement the human-rights provisions of the Charter. Liberals should take a special interest in extending conventional international law into this field. The negative attitude of the government toward multilateral treaties should be reversed, and the United States should assume leadership in the development of international law, not only in the field of human rights but in other fields in which the rapidly changing world has made the traditional rules obsolete.

(e) A major part of the activity of the United Nations has been devoted to facilitating international co-operation for economic and social advancement, but this work, no less than the political activity, has been hampered by the cold war. The United States gave lend-lease aid to Communist, as well as free-enterprise countries during the Second World War and it participated in the United Nations Relief and Rehabilitation Administration (UNRRA) which, after the war, gave such aid for the rehabilitation of all countries. This participation was ended, however, after the cold war developed and the United States gave aid to non-Communist countries in Europe through the Marshall Plan, (originally opened to, but rejected by, the Communist states), and to underdeveloped countries in Asia and Africa through the Point Four plan. It has given aid directly to only a few Communist countries, such as Poland and Yugoslavia, although it has actively aided in the rehabilitation of its late enemies, Germany and Japan. Aid has increasingly tended to be given to allies and to be of military character.

The United Nations Expanded Technical Assistance Program (UNETAP) and the Children's Fund (UNICEF) give to all United Nations members according to need, regardless of political ideology, and the United States contributes to these programs, but the amounts are small in comparison with the total amount of economic assistance from the United States. The Atoms for Peace Program initiated by the United States in 1953 resulted in an International Atomic Energy Agency within the United Nations intended to distribute atomic isotopes for peaceful purposes and to maintain standards and inspections to protect health and to prevent diversion to military uses. The cold war, however, has resulted in the United States and other countries, which produce atomic energy, operating largely through bilateral agreements, thus seriously hampering the International Atomic Energy Agency.

This linkage of economic development to political opinion has had serious consequences. Some countries refuse aid from the United States because they think the United States is attempting to control their foreign policy, and all of the non-aligned underdeveloped countries, far from being grateful to the United States for the aid they receive, fear they may lose their independence because of their necessities.

Since the Soviet Union has developed its economy sufficiently to give economic aid to underdeveloped countries in addition to what it gives to its own satellites, it has done so without any apparent strings attached and with considerable more expedition than has the United States, bound by time-consuming procedures of congressional debate and appropriation. The Soviet Union has therefore gained more good will by its contributions than has the United States, although the contributions by the latter have up to date been much greater.

In certain areas, especially in the Middle East, competition between the United States and the Soviet Union in giving economic aid has developed, permitting the underdeveloped countries to play one side against the other. In this competition the Communist countries have had a considerable advantage for the reason stated above, and thus competition tends to draw the underdeveloped country into the Communist orbit. The situation of Afghanistan and Egypt are illustrations of this, although both of these countries have maintained their position of non-alignment. The Marshall Plan and rehabilitation loans in Western Europe, and United States aid to Germany and Japan have been successful in rehabilitating these countries from war losses, but in underdeveloped countries economic-assistance programs have been less successful. In spite of the considerable technical aid, economic assistance, and loans to these countries since the Second World War, the gap in levels of living between them and the developed countries has increased. The poor have been getting poorer and the rich richer. This dangerous gap is unlikely to be eliminated unless the underdeveloped countries reduce their rate of population growth, and either submit themselves to regimentation, reducing for a time even their present low levels of living through Communist discipline, as in China and earlier in Russia, building capital resources out of the suffering of the people, or receive much larger contributions from the richer countries whether by technical assistance, economic aid, or long-term loans at low rates of interest. Much of the needed capital goods can be purchased through exports in the ordinary channels of trade, and private capital may, in some cases, contribute loans, but in the main the projects needed are not of a character to attract such capital.

It is believed that a politically secure world requires the reduction of this gap, and that a world moving toward democracy and freedom requires the reduction of poverty and an increase in the level of living among the peoples of the underdeveloped countries of Asia, Africa, and Latin America without abandonment of individual freedom. Liberals certainly believe that increase in the welfare of people is a good in itself. The interest of the United States in this field is not "cold war" victory but the economic and social advancement of the poverty-stricken areas of the world under democratic conditions. Action toward this goal will contribute in the long run to peace, justice, and welfare throughout the world, and to American security and prosperity. On the other hand, efforts to use economic contributions for cold-war purposes will result in a competition in which the Communist world is likely to gain, and freedom is likely to be sacrificed in the underdeveloped countries.

For these reasons, economic-aid programs should be greatly increased, military-aid programs, especially to the underdeveloped countries, should be greatly reduced, and economic assistance should be given in the main through the United Nations without discrimination as to political ideology. The Soviet Union should be challenged to cooperate in contributing to such programs. It may not do so, because it has such advantages in competition, but the United States and the Western countries should urge its co-operation and utilize the United Nations, the International Atomic Energy Agency, and the specialized agencies for this purpose.

Various programs for economic development by loans less rigidly secured than those available through the World Bank, such as through the International Development Association and the United Nations Special Fund, have been established. These activities might well be co-ordinated with the Expanded Technical Assistance Program of the United Nations in a World Development Agency, with resources extending to billions of dollars in order to help the underdeveloped countries reach a condition in which their economies can develop through internal resources without the regimentations of communism. If military expenditures can be reduced, the wealthier states might well contribute a total of ten billion dollars a year for this purpose. In such programs, education, not only in methods of production but also in methods of population control should play a major part. In Egypt, India, and other underdeveloped countries the rate of population growth absorbs the increased productivity resulting from economic-assistance programs, with the result that there is no diminution of the poverty of the people. With well-planned programs of this magnitude it has been estimated that the underdeveloped countries could achieve self-sustaining progress in their economies within a decade.

It seems clear that the interest of the United States in the economic development of the poverty-stricken people of the world and the closing of the gap between the rich and the poor countries cannot be accomplished unless aid programs are wholly dissociated from cold-war considerations, a condition unlikely unless these programs are conducted mainly through international institutions. Only if aid is given on an international basis will the emerging nations of Asia and Africa be convinced that these programs are not designed to make them political satellites of one of the great powers or great power blocs.

Apart from the development of underdeveloped peoples, the United States has an interest in freeing trade. While the reciprocal trade programs and the General Administration for Tariffs and Trade (GATT) have assisted toward this goal, it is believed that a specialized agency under the United Nations to study, recommend, and facilitate negotiations in this field is desirable. The International Trade Organization, designed for this purpose after the war, was

killed by American protectionism, and the Trade Cooperation Agency (TCA) designed as a substitute, but with less
powers, was before the Senate for several years with presidential endorsement but no action. Ratification of the Organization for Economic Cooperation, with even less power,
was finally effected in the spring of 1961. This agreement
may convince the world that the United States is genuinely
interested in breaking down nationalistic and ideological
barriers to trade and facilitating the development of the
world through the pacifying influence of international
commerce.

Cultural exchanges by promoting understanding, stimulating fruitful borrowing from one culture to another, and
emphasizing the unity of mankind through common appreciation of the artistic achievements of all cultures have
been supported by the United States. The United States
has functioned in the United Nations Educational, Scientific and Cultural Organization (UNESCO). The great interest in this field developed immediately after the Second
World War through the United States National Commission for UNESCO should be reinvigorated.

This review indicates that the United States can do
much to strengthen the United Nations, but it will do so
only if the administration, the Congress, and people recognize that such strengthening is a major interest of the
United States for the security of its territory and its democratic institutions and for the further advance of its high
economic level. Liberals should seek to cultivate this recognition, subordinating lesser goals to the establishment of the
peaceful, stable, and just world order to which the United
States and most other states have committed themselves
by the United Nations Charter.

TWELVE

New Population Trends

BY KINGSLEY DAVIS

Chairman of Department of Sociology and of International Population and Urban Research in the Institute of International Studies, University of California

I

On March 5, 1957, the Chinese Communist party newspaper, *People's Daily,* carried its first editorial on birth control. Asserting that China's population is increasing by more than thirteen million per year and that economic development cannot yet catch up with this rapid multiplication, the editorial urged the government to spread the use of birth control and to encourage youths to postpone marriage until age twenty-five. This authoritative statement of policy was not the first indication of Red China's concern with population. In 1953 the State Council had instructed the health department to give public instruction in birth control, and efforts were made in 1954–56 to strengthen this program; abortions were permitted as early as 1954 under certain restrictions, and the restrictions were subsequently eased; party journals and the press carried articles on birth control. In 1957 intensive propaganda for family limitation began throughout the country, and a birth-control exhibition was opened in Peiping on March 8 of that year, three days after the editorial in *People's Daily.*

Although not sudden, the emergence of Red China's population policy represents a dramatic shift in Communist strategy. Russia's early liberality with reference to abortion and birth control ceased in 1935, and the official Communist line has always been that socialist economics alone can benefit people, that overpopulation is a myth designed to conceal the true cause of misery—capitalism. Russia still clings to this view. If, therefore, Red China is in practice deviating from the Soviet line, it is not out of caprice but because of her own severe problems. The census taken in 1953 reported a population of 583 million in mainland China, over a hundred million more than the United Nations had been estimating. The Red officials, faced with more hungry people than they had expected, with a rate of increase that taxed their ingenuity, doubtless found the mental gymnastics of reconciling birth control with Marxism easier than taking the awesome risk of doing nothing about the frightening accumulation of people in an already crowded country.

Since 1958 China has apparently canceled her national campaign to lower the birth rate. The motives for this are hard to specify, but it has not meant that policies indirectly unfavorable to reproduction have been abandoned. Contraceptives have continued to be available, early marriage has been discouraged while the entry of women into the labor force has been favored, and the absorption of the family in the communes has gone ahead.

China's population problems are by no means unique. The same demographic trends that force the Red government to adopt a population policy are affecting other areas of the world as well. In fact, in pursuing its policy, Red China is following, doubtless by conscious imitation, the examples already set by Japan, India, and Puerto Rico, where governments are encouraging the limitation of births. Other countries with analogous problems may adopt a similar policy in the future, regardless of whether they are Communist or non-Communist.

It is not easy for a nation to admit openly that it has too many people. It is hard to resist multiplying one's own kind indefinitely and hard to rise above the old elemental belief that numbers mean power, that multiplication and fruitfulness are identical. The forces leading to official anti-natalist policies must therefore be powerful ones; and if they are widespread as well, they must have international significance. Indeed, the population changes now occurring throughout the globe are so novel and so immense that they render obsolete much of the existing literature on political demography. Among other effects, they tend to widen or at least maintain the gap between the have and have-not nations, to exacerbate the political instability of the latter, and to give national population policies a new role, opposite in type to those of Hitler and Mussolini but greater in importance.

II

The most salient demographic change is the astonishing rise in the rate of growth of the world's total population. Observers have long called attention to the acceleration of the rate, but with the long secular decline of fertility in industrial countries many experts in the 1930s and early 1940s thought that population growth would soon slow down. Actually the jump in population since 1950 has far exceeded anything that has gone before, as the following figures show:

	World Population (Millions)	Average Annual Rate (%) in Prior Period	Years to Double at This Rate
1800	906		
1850	1,171	0.53	135
1900	1,608	0.64	110
1930	2,013	0.75	93
1950	2,476	1.04	67
1955	2,691	1.68	42

The world, with approximately 2.8 billion today, is gaining about fifty million each year.

One effect of this unexampled increase is to place an ever greater strain on the earth's resources and to intensify the international struggle for food and raw materials. The means of sustenance, the fuel and fibers and minerals for industry and armaments are becoming the ever dearer prizes and the talismen of international rivalry. The strain, however, is growing even faster than population, because human beings, with their inexhaustible wants, are constantly increasing their per capita demands. From 1900 to 1952 the population of the United States doubled itself, but the non-human energy used for work multiplied by three and a half times. Today the earth's billions, whether poor or rich, are aware of the possibility of wealth and are searching for opportunities to consume more goods. The greater strain on resources is therefore a product of the phenomenal population increase multiplied by the rise in per capita demand.

Yet the earth's resources are diminishing. No coal, oil, or natural gas is being added to the earth's crust. Fertile soil is being ruined faster than it can be made. The only hope of coping with the skyrocketing need for materials lies in technology, to use better the fossil fuels and soils that are left and to harness hitherto unused resources.

III

The rivalry for resources is complicated by the economic inequalities among nations, to which differences in population growth are contributing. Even an equal rate of population growth everywhere would be highly inequitous, because different countries start from radically different circumstances. The actual pattern is exacerbating the inequalities still more, for although population growth is universal, it is far greater in the poorer countries on the average than in the richer ones. This fact, which is relatively new, represents a recent demographic change of the greatest importance. Prior to 1914 the industrial countries showed a more rapid multiplication than the non-industrial. From 1914 to 1930 the rate was about equal as between the two types of country. Since then the natural increase in underdeveloped areas has risen so fast that it is approximately twice that of the industrial countries taken by and large, despite the postwar baby boom in the latter. The government of Red China, for example, believes that its population is growing at the rate of 2.2 per cent per year; that of the United States is currently moving at 1.8 per cent per year. The alleged Chinese rate, whether it is accurate or not, is actually below that of many underdeveloped countries today, while that of the United States is ahead of most of the industrial nations. Latin America's people, for example, are multiplying at the prodigious rate of 2.5 per cent per year, about five times as fast as those of Northwestern Europe.

The fact that the poorer countries are now contributing far more than their share to the inflated growth of the world's population has several implications. It means, for one thing, that the areas from which the industrial countries draw many of their raw materials are becoming glutted with people. It means that the greatest advances in science and technology are being made in those countries which have the least need of them in terms of population expansion. Above all, it means that the gap in wealth and power as between the rich and poor nations is becoming wider and wider.

Frequently the process of economic development in "retarded" areas is spoken of as if these areas were on the way to catching up with the industrial nations. This is not the case. Fifteen of the richest industrial countries in 1938 had an average per capita income roughly ten times that of twenty non-industrial countries. In 1952–54 the same industrial countries had an average per capita income about *eleven* times that of the same non-industrial nations. Over the period covered, the population of the fifteen industrial countries rose by 7.6 per cent, that of the twenty non-industrial countries by 10.7 per cent. If the rates of human multiplication had been reversed, national incomes remaining the same, the gap between the two groups in per capita income would have been narrowed rather than widened.

IV

Further evidence of the influence of population in widening the gap between industrial and non-industrial nations can be seen with reference to raw materials. Since 1929 the underdeveloped areas have substantially raised their share in the *production* of primary materials, but their share in the *consumption* of these has dropped. In other words, they are consuming less and less of what they produce in raw materials, despite the fact that they are adding more and more people.

The outstanding case of industrial raw-material consumption is that of the United States. On the basis of the Paley report, this country's role is usually stated in its most dramatic form: the United States now consumes over half the primary materials (excluding food) produced in the free world. The statement is true, but it omits the important fact, plainly shown but not emphasized in the Paley report, that the United States also produces far *more* than its share of primary goods. With 9.5 per cent of the free world's population in 1950, it contributed nineteen per cent of the bauxite, forty-nine per cent of the iron ore, twenty-eight per cent of the copper, forty-four per cent of the zinc, fifty-two per cent of the phosphate rock, ninety-one per cent of the sulfur, and fifty-seven per cent of the crude petroleum. If the United States consumes more than other countries, it is largely because she produces more. Nevertheless, it is true that this country is increasingly drawing upon imported materials to maintain its steady industrial progress. Of thirteen important minerals it was a net exporter of five in 1929 and of only two in 1950. Of the eleven in which it was a net importer at the latter date, its consumption above production was, on the average, twenty-nine per cent of what was produced in the rest of the free world.

Not only the United States but all industrial countries consume more primary materials than they produce, and vice versa. A French demographer, Frederic Tabah, writing in the French journal *Population,* has calculated that between 1929 and 1950 the underdeveloped areas increased their relative production but lost in relative consumption of seven out of ten important primary materials. "In the aggregate," he says, "two thirds of humanity consumes less than five per cent of the primary materials."

The continuing economic disparity between industrial and non-industrial nations comes from the technological advance of the one and the excessive population growth of the other. These two factors are interrelated. Unimpeded human multiplication is giving the non-industrial countries exactly what most of them do not need—more people. It is hindering their acquisition of what they do need—more capital, more skill, and greater productivity. The industrial countries are meeting the pinch on resources by a constantly greater use of scientific ingenuity to get more out of each kind of energy or material, to make substitutes, and to tap new resources. This is why the use of primary materials in the United States, and especially the importation of such materials, has not risen commensurately with national income. The poorer countries, on the other hand, find it difficult to acquire science, capital, and rational organization as fast as the industrial countries can add to their already overwhelming stock of these. The poorer areas have received generous aid, to be sure, but this help has had some dubious as well as beneficial results. It has enhanced population growth where it is not needed and has hastened the removal of resources under adverse terms of trade. At best the underdeveloped countries have achieved an absolute improvement; they have not achieved a relative economic gain vis-à-vis the developed nations.

As the struggle for resources intensifies, complex technology will play an ever greater role. Technological advances, however, will hardly be made by peasant populations living near the subsistence level and multiplying at a rate close to three per cent per year. Unless some *deus ex machina* intervenes, the gap between the industrial and non-industrial countries will not be narrowed.

v

The main factor in the explosive world population growth and in the faster increase of non-industrial peoples has *not* been a rise in birth rates. Fertility did rise in the industrial nations pursuant to the Second World War, and this rise has contributed its share to the accelerated global increase. But in most of the older industrial nations the baby boom has subsided. The primary cause of the earth's population upsurge has therefore been the spectacular decline of mortality in the underdeveloped areas, where drops of thirty to sixty per cent in the death rate in ten years have occurred.

These unparalleled achievements in death control are a tribute to the success of international co-operation, for they have come about with substantial aid from the industrial nations. Brand-new medical techniques and large-scale organization have proved effective in ridding massive populations of killing diseases at very low per capita cost and with minimum disturbance to the native way of life. Birth rates have remained high precisely because local customs have hardly been disturbed, and also because the embarrassments of larger families contingent on lowered mortality take time to be felt and understood. Furthermore, the international auspices that have helped to reduce death rates have done little or nothing to help reduce fertility.

Drastically lowered mortality with continuing high fertility has not only burdened the underdeveloped nations

348

with the greatest increase in human history but has also given them exceptionally young populations. Contrary to general belief, reduced mortality does not usually contribute to an aging of the population. The reason is that most of the reduction, especially when the death rate has been high, occurs in the younger ages. The advanced countries today, because of their secular decline in fertility, have about two and a half to three and a half people aged fifteen or over for each child under fifteen. The nonindustrial countries have between one and one fifth to one and four fifths. The latter countries accordingly have to struggle with a high proportion of child dependency, not fully compensated for by their lesser old-age dependency; and the high proportion of youth affords a fertile source of political instability. Unless jobs can be found for the swelling waves of young people coming into the labor market each year, their ebullient energy turns to agitation, revolution, and war. The recent Youth Festival in Moscow was a tremendous demonstration of the skill and sagacity of the Soviets in whipping up youthful enthusiasm. Colonel Nasser and Cheddi Jagan also understand what youth can do, as, to his chagrin, does Robert Lacoste. The dominance of students in the politics of many areas is one expression of the importance of youth when their number is disproportionately large and their opportunities disproportionately small.

VI

Much of the demographic and political future lies with the still underdeveloped majority of the world. Here, with the break-up of colonies, the number of sovereign nations has expanded. Here the squeeze of population growth and adverse economics, on the one hand, and rising aspirations and popular discontent, on the other, has become most intense. Under the circumstances, what are the leaders of these countries to do?

What the United States would like to see them do is to foster peaceful and democratic industrialization, a rising level of living, and adherence to our side. To this end we have given or lent money for agriculture, industry, transportation, public health, and arms. We have maintained that this is an effective way to head off communism because, as we say, chronic poverty breeds communism. This reasoning has much to commend it, but it ignores population trends and thus runs the danger of underestimating or misinterpreting the requirements for economic development. It also overlooks the fact that such economic progress as the underdeveloped countries are making is not lessening the gap between them and the richer ones, that the key of envy and revolt may not lie in absolute but in relative poverty.

The difficulties just cited are ones to which we have contributed. The United States, perhaps the most generous sponsor of public health programs around the world, has yet done nothing, at least officially, to aid the reduction of birth rates. At the same time we have enjoyed a continuing technological advance that enhances both our need for and our ability to command raw materials from abroad. Above all, we are encouraging by our example a very high level of aspiration which, if reached at all by the rest of the world, cannot be reached in the foreseeable future.

Let us look at it through the eyes of a leader in a nonindustrial country. Being in power, he is already committed either to communism or to some form of noncommunism. If Communist, his non-Communist opposition has little voice; but if he and his country are non-Communist, the Red opposition stands ready to profit from every weakness, every misfortune, of the regime in power. Communism promises a radical, if mythical, escape from poverty, and in a free political atmosphere this promise can receive constant reinforcement. The leader of a backward country with an illiterate peasantry and tight economic situation is hard-pressed to retain power against the promises and secret maneuvers of the Red opposition.

Suppose, for example, he is the head of a country of twenty million, sixty per cent of whom are engaged in agriculture, with an average of 500 farm people for each square mile of agricultural land. Suppose, further, that with the help of WHO, UNICEF, and the Rockefeller Foundation he has done an excellent job of reducing the death rate, so that the population is growing fast enough to double itself in twenty-five years. What can he do?

He can certainly *talk* about economic development to relieve the abject poverty of the people. But, with limited resources, he knows this will be a long pull. To double the national income might take twenty years, which would leave per capita income about the same. If he is smart, he will not rely solely on that long chance. If not a dictator already, he will crush opposition and become one. The less opposition he has to crush, however, the better. So he will find policies that yield the greatest effective support. He may, for example, scare the aristocracy into supporting him as a means of avoiding the Marxist evil and at the same time divert popular attention by a policy of aggressive nationalism, religious or cultural ethnocentrism, and international truculence—policies that may not appeal to the elite but do attract the expanding ranks of indigent youth. Blaming his country's economic ills on the machinations of outside nations, he may use threats and promises to obtain outside military and economic aid. If he is astute and lucky he will stay in power, but there is always the danger that his patchwork opportunism will not be equal to the real problems and that a Red dictatorship will supplant him. Once this happens, the country is seemingly lost to the free world, for it is easier to move into the Communist camp than to move back out again.

VII

Since most of the world's nations are small and many of these, especially the underdeveloped ones, are also poor, their international actions are born out of weakness rather than strength. If size is measured in terms of population, half of the independent countries have less than seven million people, although India has fifty-five times and the United States twenty-five times this many. If size is measured more realistically in terms of national income, the United States is the biggest nation, exceeding the United Kingdom by six times, France by ten times, India by seventeen times, and the average for fifty-five free-world countries by twenty-eight times. Curiously, among the fifty-five countries of the free world, the few large ones loom so far above the others that forty-six are below the average in national income and only nine above. Of the nine that exceed the average, only two (Brazil and India) are predominantly agrarian; whereas of the forty-six below average, twenty-nine are agrarian and only seventeen industrial. The hierarchy in the Communist world, though harder to document, is similarly skewed in the direction of small and poor countries.

In view of the sharply pyramidal distribution of size and wealth among countries, it is understandable why each of the two great political blocs is led by one or more giant countries that tower over the rest. A major problem in each bloc is that of solidarity—how to keep the members in line. The centrifugal pull of nationalism and sovereignty tends to weaken the solidarity; differential power tends to strengthen it. So far the Communists have seemingly achieved tighter solidarity, because they are more ruthless, more frankly revolutionary, and more willing to use foreign troops to support a local regime. They are not publicly impaled by what Sukarno has seen fit to call "chatterbox democracy." Whether in the long run their interstate solidarity can survive the strains that afflict both camps remains to be seen. The looser integration of the free world permits its members more easily to profess "neutrality," although Yugoslavia and Poland illustrate a similar tendency in the Communist group. The smaller countries strategically located with respect to natural resources or lying on the boundary between the Communist and free worlds are the bones of contention. The solidarity of the larger ones in each camp is the crucial question, determining how effectively the lesser ones can be handled.

In any case, the role of population as a guarantee of national strength is waning while its role as an economic and military liability is increasing. The ever larger dependence of industry and warfare on scientific technology enhances the value of trained as against untrained manpower; yet the unique rate of population growth now prevailing severely hinders an increase in the proportion of highly trained people, especially in the underdeveloped countries. It also hinders their employment when trained, because the capitalization of long-run industrial and developmental projects, which employ trained manpower, is difficult in the face of rising consumption demands on the part of indigent but increasing millions.

It is no accident, then, that similar policies aimed at halting runaway population growth are emerging in countries of opposite political persuasion and contrasting demographic doctrine. If today China is following Japan and India in this regard, other Communist as well as capitalist countries may do so in the future. As excessive population growth continues, they will feel the need of overcoming the effect of one government policy (mortality control) by another government policy (fertility control).

How effective the anti-natalist policies will be is hard to say. In Japan the government's encouragement of family limitation is certainly an important factor in the dramatic forty-one per cent drop in the birth rate from 1948 to 1955. In Puerto Rico the drop over the same period was thirteen per cent. In India a slight drop has probably occurred, but the government policy is too recent there to have had much effect. It is too much to expect that a sufficient number of underdeveloped countries will adopt anti-natalist policies, or that these if adopted will be sufficiently effective to reduce the rate of population growth soon. Many of the weaker countries feel too unsure of themselves, too lacking in sheer manpower, to follow yet the radical lead of more secure nations like Japan, India, and China.

It looks, then, as if the pace of human multiplication will rise still further before it reaches its peak and begins to decline. Even after the *rate* of increase starts declining, as it must eventually do, substantial growth can continue for many decades. The added strain upon resources and the exacerbation of existing inequalities is therefore likely to continue to complicate international relations. If the Communist nations are beginning to abandon the dogma that economic development alone is the panacea, independent of all else, it is time for the free nations, and particularly the United States in its foreign policy, to do the same.

ANCHOR BOOKS